THE LAND OF BOUDICA

BOUDICA

Prehistoric and Roman Norfolk

John A. Davies

Chief Curator and Keeper of Archaeology
Norfolk Museums and Archaeology Service

A Heritage Publication
published in association with

NORFOLK Museums
& Archaeology Service

THE LAND OF BOUDICA – PREHISTORIC AND ROMAN NORFOLK

© Oxbow Books and the author

'Heritage' is an imprint of

    Oxbow Books, 10 Hythe Bridge Street,
    Oxford OX1 2EW
    www.oxbowbooks.com

    published in association with 'The Norfolk Museums and Archaeology Service'

A CIP record of this book is available from The British Library

ISBN: 978-1-905223-33-6

This book is available direct from
Oxbow Books, 10 Hythe Bridge Street, Oxford OX1 2EW
(Phone: 01865-241249 Fax: 01865-794449)

and

The David Brown Book Company
PO Box 511, Oakville, CT 06779, USA
(Phone: 860-945-9329 Fax: 860-945-9468)

and

via www.oxbowbooks.com

Book design: Michael de Bootman
Cover design: Sue White

Contents

Figures

Preface

How did the Devil come? When first attack?
These Norfolk lanes recall lost innocence.
The years fall off and find me walking back
(John Betjeman, *Norfolk*)

This study evolved during my working years in Norfolk, which began in November 1984 and resumed, following a short period in the north of England, when I joined the Archaeology Department at Norwich Castle Museum in October 1991. Some sections originated as talks put together for societies and museum groups, mainly within Norfolk and Suffolk but also across East Anglia more widely. A major stimulus has been the relentless pace of archaeological discovery, which has served continually to enhance our understanding of Norfolk's past. Much of this new evidence has been in the form of individual archaeological artefacts, as well as aerial photography and fieldwork.

I have divided the study into four sections. The first will look at the distinctive nature of Norfolk as a region and will consider the way in which archaeology has developed in the county in modern times, which has encouraged a productive partnership between the local public and the professional workers.

In the second section I will provide a survey – a snapshot – of Norfolk from the Ice Age to the end of the Bronze Age. Many exciting new discoveries relating to this early prehistoric period have been made over the last fifteen years in the county. Some of these finds have proven to be of truly international significance and have served to turn the spotlight of attention onto the area from time to time. These discoveries will be outlined within a chronological framework, and against a background of developments in the area, which lead us though into the world of Boudica.

The third section will concentrate on Iron Age Norfolk, which was the period when Boudica lived. It will again focus on new discoveries and consider how these have changed our understanding of the land and society into which Boudica was born.

The final section will look at the world of Boudica's descendants. It will trace the development of Norfolk from the arrival of the Romans to their withdrawal from Britain in AD 410. We shall look at all aspects of the *Civitas Icenorum*, while once again focusing on the most recent discoveries.

Despite the many exciting new discoveries, the archaeology of prehistoric and Roman Norfolk has not been as well recognised nationally as it deserves to be. I hope that this book will help to communicate the importance during those periods of this distinctive part of Britain to a wider audience beyond the county's borders.

Acknowledgements

This work has made extensive use of otherwise unpublished source material, much of which comes from data supplied through the Norfolk Museums Service to the county Historic Environment Record (HER) and from records held at Norwich Castle Museum. I would like to express thanks and gratitude to many individuals who have contributed information and discussion during the years of my working life in the county, which has enabled me to undertake this study. In particular I would like to thank:

Steven Ashley, Trevor Ashwin; Sarah Bates; Jim Beckerleg; Oliver Bone, Michael de Bootman; Amanda Chadburn; Mike Chambers; Sue Clarke; Frances Collinson; Liz Cottam; Megan Dennis; Derek Edwards; Harriet Foster; Val Fryer; Julie Gardiner; Jenny Glazebrook; Barbara Green; David Gurney; J.D. Hill; Tony Irwin; Ralph Jackson; Robert Kenyon; Nigel Larkin; Alice Lyons; the late Sue Margeson; Adrian Marsden; Bill Milligan; Chris Pears; Kenneth Penn; Sarah Percival; Tim Pestell; Jan Pitman; Peter Rilings; Peter Robins; Andrew Rogerson; Chris Rudd; Barrie Sharrock; Fiona Sheales; Andy Shelley; Tony Stuart; Kate Sussams; John Talbot; Peter Wade-Martins; Heather Wallis; Alan West; Sue White; Mavis Whitmore; Tom Williamson; Derek Woollestone.

Illustration credits

The cover background photography was by Sue Clarke and design by Sue White. Figs 88, 89, 108, 110, 119, 143, 147, 165, 169, 171 and 183 were by Sue White.

The following images have been reproduced courtesy of Norfolk Museums and Archaeology Service: Figs 6, 12, 17, 21, 36-39, 45, 46, 48–50, 54, 63, 64, 67, 84, 106, 118, 123, 125, 127, 128, 134, 145, 146, 148, 155, 160 and 170. Adrian Marsden supplied Figs 93, 95, 97 and 101. Oliver Bone took Fig 4. Mary Davis took Fig 5 and Peter Silk took Fig 194. Fig 167 was supplied by Andy Shelley of NAU Archaeology. Fig 51 is courtesy of Andy Pritchett of Uglystudios.com. Fig 16 was by Philip Rye, 17 and 21 were by Nick Arber and 118 by Ivan Lapper ARCA. Figs 3, 164 and 171 were provided by Michael de Bootman. Fig

67 is reproduced courtesy of the Trustees of the British Museum. Fig 59 was taken by Sue Clarke, who also provided much assistance with the photography. Figs 81 and 82 were supplied by John Talbot. Figs 7, 114-117 were taken by David Wicks. Figs 143 and 147 are reproduced courtesy of the Norfolk Archaeological Trust. Specific artefacts were provided for illustration by Peter Rilings. Thanks are gratefully extended to all of these individuals and organisations. All remaining line drawings and photos are the work of the author.

This text was essentially completed in early 2006. Minor amendments have since been made for this final version.

John Davies
October 2008

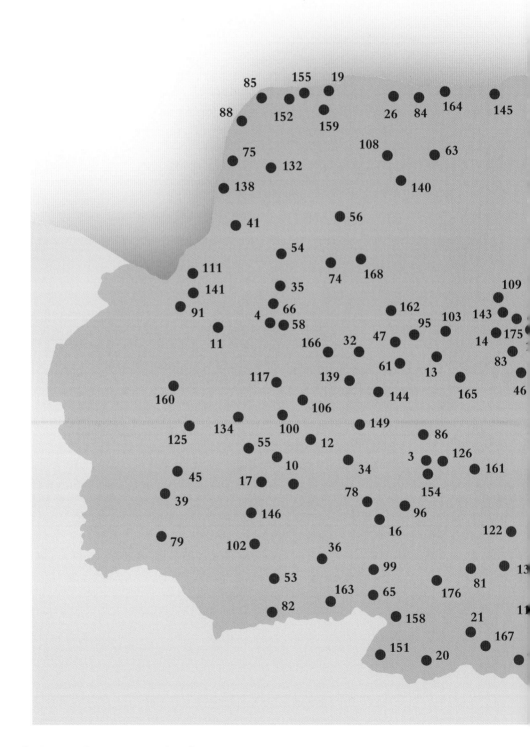

Fig 1: Map of sites mentioned in the text.

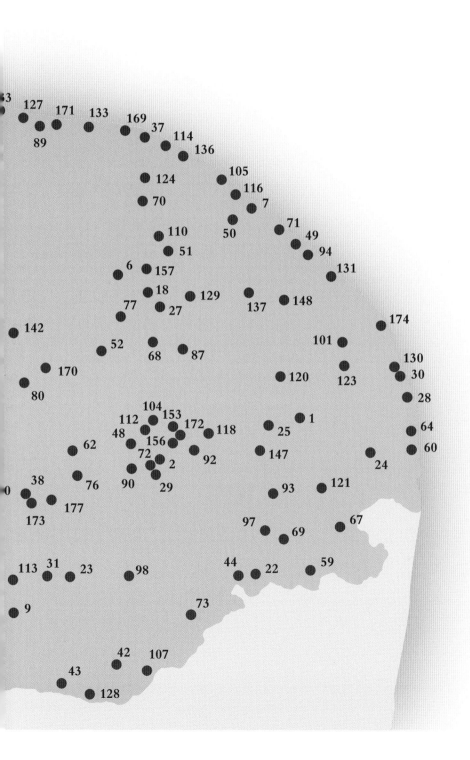

Main places cited in text

Chapter 1
Norfolk: the land of Boudica

In Norfolk we du different
(Old Norfolk saying)

NORFOLK'S IDENTITY

East Anglia is perceived to be an isolated, flat and exposed region of
eastern Britain, subject to an ever-increasing impact from the North
Sea and biting winds coming direct from Scandinavia. Norfolk sits in
the very north of this region (Fig 2). Its early past is not well integrated
into the national picture and there remains a perception that this area
must always have been a backwater, lagging behind other parts of the
country in terms of cultural development and, therefore, archaeological
interest. Such a superficial view could not be further from the truth.
An explosion of archaeological discoveries, particularly over the last
25 years, has emphasised how Norfolk was often at the very forefront of
development and innovation. At times, it has also been materially very
rich. These discoveries have come at a pace that has outstripped full
academic study and publication. Exciting new finds are still being made
there every single week of the year.

The modern county of Norfolk juts prominently into the North
Sea. As England's easternmost county, it is has often been characterised
as being cut off from the rest of the country. This exposed location has
indeed seen it bear the brunt of threats from the sea, including extreme
weather, flooding and incursions of people from abroad. It is perhaps
as a result of such conditions, combined with the element of isolation,
that this area has developed its distinct and strong regional identity.
The character of those who lived in this part of Britain seems to have
been moulded by the challenging location, and this isolation has bred
some strong local personalities, often characterised by a spirit of robust
independence.[1]

This book will follow the progress of the inhabitants of the area
now defined as the county of Norfolk, long before the modern county

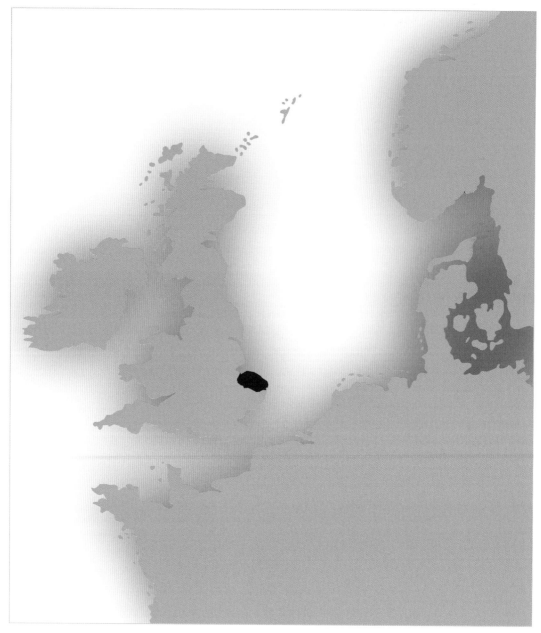

was formed. It will cover the period from the very earliest arrival of people to this area through to the end of the Roman occupation of Britain in AD 410. Archaeology is steadily revealing more information about these early people, our ancestors, and how they lived. Today, we are becoming more aware of the origins of modern populations and our own ancestry. There is an increasing fascination with our family roots, as new scientific genetic approaches allow us insights into our individual bloodlines.[2]

Fig 2: The location of Norfolk within the British Isles, and north-west Europe.

One of the first named persons who lived in the area we now call Norfolk also happens to be one of the most famous figures from the whole of world history. Queen Boudica lived here during the period known as the Late Iron Age, some 2000 years ago. In the following pages we shall trace the development of Boudica's homeland and follow the progress of her very earliest ancestors through to her descendents in the later Roman years. We shall return to Boudica herself in later pages.

As the subject of a regional study, the modern county conveniently presents a geographically discrete area. Throughout the centuries, the area now defined as Norfolk has been almost an island, surrounded by water on all sides to a greater and lesser extent. To the north and east is the sea, and on the other sides it has been cut off from the rest of Britain by rivers, once much broader than they are today, as well as by fenland, forests and heathlands. In earliest times, these factors sometimes made travel beyond the region to the south and west more difficult than trips by sea to the Low Countries and Scandinavia.

Norfolk's extensive coastline has long exerted a strong maritime influence. It is physically close to the Netherlands, Belgium and the Rhine mouth and has always been affected by influences from those parts of continental Europe. It also faces Norway and Denmark across the North Sea. Influences from that direction have often had more impact here than on most other parts of Britain. Norfolk's geographical isolation from the rest of the country has served to encourage its own distinctive cultural developments and strong regional identity. Archaeology is now beginning to reveal how people who inhabited this area many generations ago did things differently, in their own distinctive way. This local trait has been captured, in modern times, in the motto of the University of East Anglia, 'Do different', which is derived from an old Norfolk dialect saying.

Of course, there was no county of Norfolk during the period covered by this book. The modern-day county boundaries had not been established or defined in any way at that time. Towards the end of the period, this part of Britain comprised the heartland of the Iceni tribe, the people who are known to have inhabited the area during the Late Iron Age and Roman periods.

A SPECIAL PLACE

It is remarkable that so many artefacts, including superb treasures and objects of great beauty, were deposited in the soils of Norfolk and adjacent counties during antiquity. The reasons for the quantity of finds have long been debated, and there are clearly several different contributory factors. Firstly, Norfolk is an agricultural region, with large

Fig 3: A metal detectorist (Steve Brown) at work on a site in west Norfolk.

areas constantly under the plough. This action continually serves to reveal fresh evidence for earlier human activity. Secondly, archaeologists working in Norfolk have a long history, going back some thirty years, of recording finds made by users of metal detectors (Fig 3). So, as a result, we know more about what is actually being found in the county than is the case in some other places. But it is also the case that Norfolk was an important and special place at certain times in its development, which at least partly explains the richness of the artefacts. Other reasons for the deposition of this material will be considered throughout the following chapters.

Examples of some of Norfolk's more spectacular discoveries include numerous Bronze Age metalwork hoards, the world-famous Iron Age treasure found at Snettisham and a remarkable late Roman treasure from Thetford. Discoveries such as these, together with many more ordinary finds, make up a rich resource from which we can reconstruct the archaeology of this intriguing part of Britain.

ARCHAEOLOGICAL DISCOVERIES IN NORFOLK

Many of the most exciting archaeological discoveries in Norfolk have been made through the contribution of amateurs. Many have been merely chance finds, although local enthusiasts keep regular meticulous checks on specific parts of the local landscape and know when to look at an area; for example, after a storm, where coastlines are eroding, or where gravel quarrying is taking place. However, most discoveries are made by metal detecting, which has taken off as a hobby over the last three decades. Most new discoveries in Norfolk have been reported through the involvement of Norfolk Museums Service; the close relationship between the Museums Service, professionals and members of the public has stimulated an ever-increasing flood of information into the county records. The decision to promote the involvement of the public was taken as part of an 'open door' policy which can be traced back to the involvement of Roy Rainbird Clarke, who was Curator of Norwich Museums from 1951 until his death in 1963.

Clarke, who was also Keeper of Archaeology at Norwich Castle, was a believer in popularising his subject. He wrote for local newspapers and journals, and appeared on radio and television. In 1962 his Anglia Television series *Once A Kingdom* promoted archaeology to a wider audience. Clarke was also a believer in relating the Museum collection to the wider county landscape, and the Museum collecting policy was developed to represent evidence from archaeological sites. Clarke's legacy also included the foundation of the county Sites and Monuments Record (SMR), now known as the Historic Environment Record (HER), which continues today as a complete record of all archaeological finds and discoveries in the county.

It was the foundation work of Rainbird Clarke that eventually led to the positive liaison with metal detectorists, which was an extension of the 'open door' policy and involvement with local amateurs. The name of Tony Gregory, who joined the Archaeology Department at Norwich Castle in 1974, is also inextricably linked with the establishment of this liaison. At that time there was very little in the way of material discovered by metal detector in the county records, but the amounts of metalwork being brought in by the public for identification by Museum staff were increasing, and Tony realised that this was the result of deliberate searching by metal detectorists. He was quick to see that this approach offered significant benefits for archaeology and for the county records, if undertaken responsibly.

THE BIRTH OF THE METAL-DETECTOR LIAISON

In the early 1970s, advancing technology enabled metal detecting to develop into a practical hobby right across the country. Its popularity took off as the increasingly sensitive metal-detector machines also became readily affordable. It was at this time that a potential conflict began to arise between archaeologists and the growing numbers of hobbyists who were beginning to recover quantities of ancient metalwork artefacts from the ground; archaeologists across Britain became alarmed at the thought that 'their' sites would be looted and that important evidence would be removed and lost, and a strong anti-metal-detector lobby quickly grew within the profession. This was not the case, however, in Norfolk; archaeologists in this area acknowledged and openly endorsed the potential benefits of close liaison with detectorists. A climate of trust and cooperation was fostered at an early stage in the development of the hobby, and continues to the present day.

The first metal-detected finds actually appeared on the Sites and Monuments Record in 1973. In that year they comprised a mere 1% of new records. However, their contribution to the county records increased steadily year by year through the 1970s and 80s until, in the early 1990s, metal-detecting was accounting for 40% of new records in the county each year.

Today, some 20,000 individual objects are recorded in Norfolk every year, a total which is far higher than that for any other part of Britain. Today, the most important items are identified as Treasure, which is the legal term for material classified as archaeologically significant, replacing the previous name of Treasure Trove (Treasure Act 1996). Norfolk consistently deals with a quarter of all legal cases in Britain that involve Treasure. In 2004, no less than 80 Treasure cases were reported in the county, and the number continues to increase year by year.

The first detector clubs

In 1976–7, work on the construction of a bypass at Caister-on-Sea, to the north of Great Yarmouth, caused a flurry of interest among local archaeologists and the growing number of detectorists within this infant hobby. Professional fieldwalking was organised and a programme of systematic metal detecting was arranged to complement it. This local interest led to the formation of the region's first metal-detector club, which was established with the regular participation of archaeologists. Known as The Norfolk and Suffolk Metal Detecting Society, this club rotated between venues at Martham, Postwick and Haddiscoe. The club, now called East Norfolk Metal Detectors, is still thriving today, under the chairmanship of one of its founder members, Barrie Sharrock.

Tony Gregory enthusiastically promoted the establishment of other metal-detector clubs in the area. He continued to attend these clubs, together with his professional colleagues, until he eventually left the county in 1989. During his years in Norfolk Tony promoted the benefits of positive metal-detector liaison on the national stage, through television and radio appearances and through written articles, in spite of strong anti-detectorist feelings among other professional archaeologists at that time.

The Norfolk system

It was through the development of the liaison process that an unwritten 'Norfolk system', an informal rapport and trust between responsible hobbyists and professional archaeologists, was established. Although national interest at the time preferred to focus on the illegal looting of some sites by 'nighthawks' – people who undertook damage and theft from archaeological sites, often under the shadow of night – rather than on the positive benefits of liaison work, by the mid 1990s up to 20,000 individual objects were being reported to Norfolk Museums Service each year and were steadily transforming our knowledge of the county's past.

The climate of opinion within the archaeological profession changed during the 1990s. In 1996, the old law of Treasure Trove was replaced by a new Treasure Act, which was accompanied by its own Code of Practice. This code stated that discoveries should be reported to professional archaeologists, which in turn required a workable mechanism within which this could take place. This necessitated that a system of positive liaison, as had been undertaken in Norfolk, should proceed on a national basis. The current national Portable Antiquities Scheme followed. There are now 37 Finds Liaison Officers located across England and Wales who undertake positive liaison work with metal-detector users. In just ten years the climate of opinion across Britain transformed from one of open hostility to one of active cooperation, a new attitude which was based very largely on the model established in Norfolk and developed in close liaison with colleagues in Suffolk and north Lincolnshire.

Metal-detectorist liaison in Norfolk over a period of thirty years has amounted to a massive sampling exercise right across the county's

Fig 4: The statue of Boudica at Westminster, London.

plough-soil, accumulating information which has created a magnificent resource for understanding Norfolk's past. Discoveries have been made which revolutionise our understanding of the prehistoric and early historic periods in Norfolk. It is now time for this information to be analysed, and the potential for re-evaluating Norfolk's early archaeology has never been greater.

WHO WAS BOUDICA?

Fig 5: The statue of Boudica and her daughters in City Hall, Cardiff.

Boudica is one of the best-known historical figures of all time, associated with attributes such as victory against the odds, great courage, strength in the face of adversity and glory in defeat. She is recognised as a great British heroine and has been immortalised throughout history. Her statue on the London embankment (Fig 4), at the heart of Britain's capital, has stood as a symbol of British courage in adversity throughout the 20th century, and another magnificent statue of her and her daughters is given prominence in Wales, inside Cardiff City Hall (Fig 5). Boudica has become a figure of myth, and the fact that she was a real person is sometimes lost in the method of her portrayal, associated with folklore and legends. What do we know of Boudica and the land and times she came from?

The general public, when questioned, often associate the warrior queen with Colchester, although her links with that place were only relatively brief, during her destruction of the early Roman town. Boudica was in fact queen of the Iceni tribe, who inhabited northern East Anglia during the Late Iron Age. She lived during the very early years of the first millennium and was born just a few years before the death of Jesus Christ, who was crucified in an eastern province at the opposite end of the Roman Empire. This period was at the interface between what we describe as late prehistory and early history in Britain. History, which is defined by the use of written records, started in Britain with the arrival of the Romans, at about that time.

The Iceni lived within the area covered today by the county of Norfolk, and it appears that Icenian influence also extended at times into parts of north-east Cambridgeshire and northern Suffolk. However, it is possible that the watery boundaries of modern Norfolk – the River Waveney and the fenland – provided a substantial physical barrier to the land beyond for long periods. This study is concerned with Norfolk – the heartland of the Iceni. This was Boudica's land.

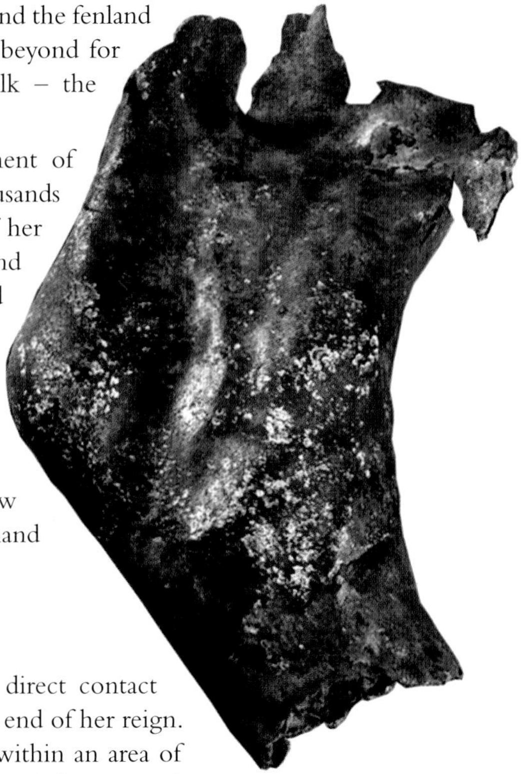

But first, this study will look at the development of Norfolk from the arrival of the first humans, many thousands of years before Boudica. It will trace the progress of her ancestors as they learned to use and exploit this fragile and unstable region, which has been continually moulded and changed by natural forces such as mighty glaciers and the relentless North Sea. Then the study will continue through the years of Boudica's own life, to look at the region in the aftermath of her rebellion against the Romans and through to the end of Roman occupation in the region. It is through the exciting new archaeological discoveries that the story of Boudica's land will be told.

IN TOUCH WITH THE PAST

A number of fascinating discoveries have provided direct contact with Boudica's lifetime and the dramatic events at the end of her reign. In 1979 a large chunk of ancient bronze was found within an area of known Iron Age and Romano-British occupation at Ashill in central Norfolk. Close examination showed that this was a fragment from a life-sized statue, and was cast in the shape of the knee of a horse (Fig 6). This fragment was described at the time as having been 'hacked and torn at both ends'. Another very famous statue fragment, a bronze head of the emperor Claudius, had previously been found some 60km away in the River Alde at Rendham (Suffolk) in 1907. This had come from the statue of the emperor on horseback that had stood at the Temple of Claudius at Colchester at the time when the town was sacked by Boudica's army. Both of these items are linked by their alloy, which has a distinctively rare low lead content, and appear to come from the same statue. It seems that they were looted from Colchester by members of Boudica's army, finding their way back to East Anglia in the packs of soldiers that had been present throughout the campaign and had survived the final battle against the Romans. Did these veteran warriors of Boudica consign these trophies to the rivers of the region as offerings to the gods in thanks for sparing their lives? Perhaps they were just afraid to be caught in possession of such 'souvenirs' by Roman soldiers following them back into Icenian land.

In 1982, the Norfolk Archaeological Unit undertook an archaeological survey of an important Roman site at Crownthorpe, to the west of Norwich. Use of metal detection was a routine component of

Fig 6: Fragment of the Roman equestrian statue, in the shape of a horse's knee, found at Ashill, central Norfolk. Length 356mm (copyright Norfolk Museums and Archaeology Service).

Fig 7: The Crownthorpe hoard of drinking vessels.

such surveys in Norfolk and the benefits were soon realised. The detector user, Derek Woollestone, received a loud signal. As he investigated its source, a large bowl-like vessel was revealed, which looked as if it might be Roman in date. The Archaeology Department at Norwich Castle Museum were informed and their conservator was able to ensure the careful extraction of the find. The first bowl was found to have another bowl above it, which was upside-down and formed a lid. When this was lifted, other vessels that had been packed inside were revealed (Fig 7). Close examination and subsequent study at the Museum showed that these vessels dated from about AD 60. Derek had revealed a hoard of metalwork items that had been hidden in the ground as the Iceni, under Boudica, rose in revolt against the Romans. We shall consider just who may have buried this hoard in Chapter 10.

In 1992 another metal-detector user was walking a field at Saham Toney, near Watton in central Norfolk, when he began to reveal a group of items that did not, at first, look out of place in a modern farm setting. They were all horse harness fittings, including harness rings and old worn horse bits. The finder regularly showed all his finds to staff at Norwich Castle Museum, and upon closer examination it was realised that these were in fact very early items of horse furniture (Fig 8). They included some very beautifully enamelled discs which would have been used as horse decorations during the early first century AD. These items came from what we now know to have been a major settlement at the time of Queen Boudica, one which she would certainly have visited.

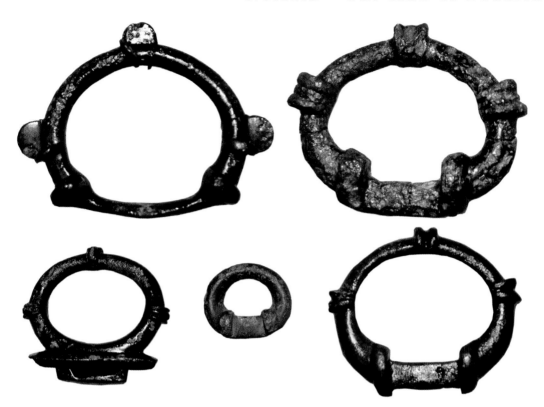

In 2000 a magnificent bridle bit came to light at a farm in Swanton Morley, in central Norfolk. It is curiously asymmetrical in its detail and unique in its design (Fig 9). Each of the rein-rings has different Celtic-style enamelled decoration. Decorated bridle bits of such high quality are exceptionally rare. It is thought that this example was made and used during the final decades of the Iron Age, and its quality suggests that it was owned by a high-status individual of the Iceni.

These exciting finds that have been made in recent times all belong to the age of Boudica; they are direct evidence from the period when she and her family lived in this area. They belonged to prominent individuals of the time and Boudica may have seen, or even handled, these same items.

Fig 8: Group of Iron Age terrets discovered at Saham Toney in 1992. Maximum diameter of top left terret 115mm.

THE THEMES TO BE FOLLOWED IN THIS BOOK

A series of themes can be seen to recur again and again throughout the millennia in relation to the study of Norfolk. They relate to the landscape and to the people who have inhabited it and who have been moulded by it. Even today it feels as if Norfolk is cut off from the rest of Britain. To the south, transport routes are still slow. As a result, travellers do not tend to casually visit or pass through Norfolk, requiring instead a significant reason to undertake the journey into the area.

Fig 9: The Iron Age bridle bit found at Swanton Morley in 2000. External diameter of rings 75mm.

As noted above, Norfolk's isolation within Britain has sometimes led to the superficial perception that it has been culturally backward. Archaeology is now showing the contrary; that it was not, in fact, a backwater. Norfolk has always received influences from continental Europe and from across the North Sea. Even in later historical times it has been considered closer to the continent than to distant parts of Britain. Indeed, this part of the country was often the first to be confronted with new peoples and new ideas from abroad. It was, in fact, often at the forefront of innovation as a result of its continental contacts.

This has been in spite of the fact that Norfolk's landscape is essentially unstable. It is low-lying and has been especially affected by changes in sea level and the coastline. This continues to be the case today, and there is an increasing feeling of unease as the east coast erodes away at an alarming rate. Could the east of the county soon be covered by the sea once again, as it was in the distant past?

So, Norfolk has always had its own distinct character. We shall trace the development of the inhabitants as they responded to a series of changes in this distinctive regional landscape. Today, the importance of *regional* studies in archaeology is increasingly being recognised. As we look further into all parts of Great Britain we appreciate how misleading it can be to generalise about archaeological periods and to base assumptions on the study of 'type sites' in disparate areas. The more we look, the more distinctive Norfolk's archaeology is seen to be.

Chapter 2
The Norfolk landscape

> We are the children of our landscape; it dictates behaviour and even thought in the measure to which we are responsive to it.
> (Lawrence Durrell, *Justine*)

THE LOCATION – THE 'ISLAND' OF NORFOLK

Water has always dominated the land that falls within the modern county boundary of Norfolk. Sea and rivers have steered the development of its communications, transport and economy. Water, in the form of ice sheets, has also left its physical mark on the landscape. The Norfolk landmass juts prominently into the North Sea, with a long and diverse coastline that stretches some 150km from Kings Lynn in the west to Great Yarmouth in the east. All parts of the county are within just 65km of the sea and still closer to its many rivers (Fig 10). Even today, the only way to enter Norfolk without crossing over water is to pass through a narrow corridor of land, which separates the headwaters of the Rivers Little Ouse and Waveney, between Thetford and Diss.

Norfolk is cut off from the midlands to the west by the Fenland basin, which has always formed a barrier to good communication in that direction. The main land connection is therefore southward through what is now Suffolk. However, there have long been deep-seated rivalries between the inhabitants of Norfolk and those of that area, forming a barrier of a different kind. The main natural entrance to the county has always been Breckland, through which an ancient trackway known as the Icknield Way and an important Roman road called the Peddars Way pass.

The county is part of Britain's Lowland Zone. Today, the terrain is largely gentle and flat, with much of the land lying below 60m OD. It is at the meeting point of varied geologies and is characterised by comparatively soft young rocks which were rubbed smooth by glacial erosion and then covered by glacial and periglacial deposition.[1] The soils are varied but are generally deep and fertile.[2]

The inhabitants have long been affected by the strong maritime influence, which has provided many with a way of life for thousands of

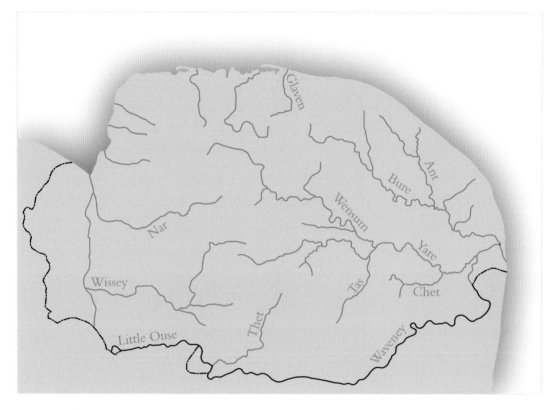

years; they have wrested a hard living from the sea, creek and fen, as well as from the fertile land in the interior.

Fig 10: Norfolk's main rivers.

THE DEVELOPMENT OF THE LANDSCAPE

Norfolk was severely affected by the Ice Age. It lay beneath ice sheets which covered Britain as far south as Essex and north London. The fluctuation between the cold stages and the interglacials were associated with a constantly changing environment, and have left their mark on the landscape. Melting ice deposited a thick blanket of till, or boulder clay. Streams at the ice front deposited extensive sands and gravels. Permafrost, or permanently frozen ground, is found in arctic regions today but few realise that this was once a feature of Norfolk. Its former presence is evidenced today by fossil ice wedge casts, which are found in gravel pits and seen in cliff exposures. Broadland's landscape at the end of the last glaciation would be almost unrecognisable from that of today. Its river valleys were once deep and had steeply sloping sides.[3]

Norfolk was not always bounded by sea. Britain was once joined to the continent of Europe and the sea lay far to the north of its current position. The coast was far away, forming a line running from the present Yorkshire coast to the northern tip of Denmark.[4] The area that is now the North Sea was a fertile plain. It was populated by vast herds of animals, in the way that the Serengeti plain is in modern times. Today, as fishing boats cast their nets, alongside the catches of cod, sole and turbot they regularly find the bones and teeth of creatures that once roamed this great plain. Dick Mol, a palaeontologist from Holland, has recovered many tons of bones of giant extinct animals from the sea bed. Employing a fishing trawler in the most dangerous of seas, he has made the most exciting discoveries. At depths in excess of 20m, Mol has recovered bones of woolly mammoth, woolly rhinoceros, wild horse and bison in very large quantities, reflecting the sheer numbers of creatures that once roamed this expanse.[5] This was once a very rich terrestrial environment.

After the glacial period the ice melted and the sea level rose, steadily encroaching upon the land. However, it was not until around 8000 years ago that the coastline reached approximately its present-day position. From about 3000 years ago until about 1600 years ago, sea levels rose once again and coastal estuaries and marshes were extensively flooded. Today's rivers were broader and deeper, forming more formidable boundaries. After the Roman period, the water level dropped. This recurring cycle has continued, with sea levels rising again before the 13th century.

The process of coastal change is still going on. During the 17th century the sea eventually overwhelmed the village of Eccles on the east coast, 12.5km to the north of Great Yarmouth. Eccles has become a lost village beneath the sea,[6] its buildings being occasionally exposed in ghostly fashion at low tides today. On the same coast, in the vicinity of Happisburgh, sea defences are being washed away and coastal erosion is proceeding at an alarming rate. While recent constructions are being destroyed in this way, causing alarm among today's coastal population, evidence of former landscapes is being exposed. These often delicate traces of former times and environments are deserving of urgent study by archaeologists before they are lost once again.

THE REGIONS OF NORFOLK

Norfolk comprises a number of regions which are very different in character and appearance (Fig 11).[7] A combination of natural processes and human interventions have combined to create a part of Britain that exhibits remarkable diversity. In the first instance, the long and varied coastline itself can be considered to form a region of its own. Along the north coast, there are stretches of saltmarsh, calcareous dunes, shingle banks and brackish marshes. To the east of these are cliffs, extending between Weybourne and Mundesley, and, further east, another stretch of dunes begins which continues around the east coast. A further area of saltmarsh occurs in the vicinity of Breydon Water, just inland from Great Yarmouth.

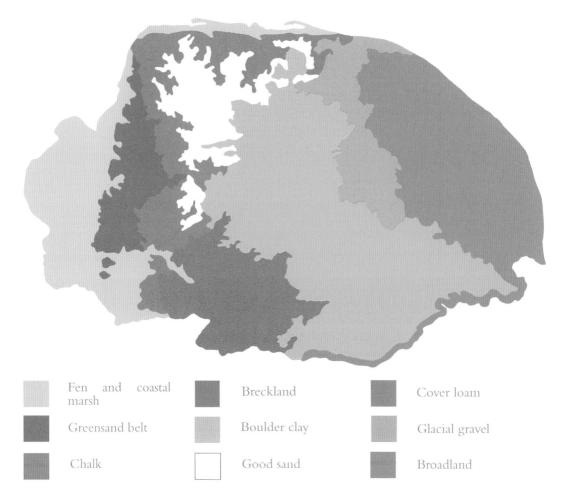

Fen and coastal marsh	Breckland	Cover loam
Greensand belt	Boulder clay	Glacial gravel
Chalk	Good sand	Broadland

Ports have been situated at key locations around the coastline for many centuries. They have been foci for prolific activity and trade which has, in turn, been the source of great wealth. In historical times, major trade routes linked the area with Scandinavia, Russia, the mainland of northern Europe and the Mediterranean. Commerce was also generated from coastal fishing. The influence of the coast and waterways was equally significant in earlier times, way back into prehistory.

The Goodsands of north-west Norfolk consist of an area of rolling upland. They extend from the coast between Hunstanton and Salthouse and are bounded by Breckland in the south. Settlements in the region have long been situated in relation to the availability of water sources, in the lower parts of valleys. Rainfall is higher than in the Breckland or Fenland. This is an area of fertile soils, good for growing cereals (especially barley) and grass. It also contains stretches of acid heathland.

In the west of the county is the Greensand belt. Adjoining the Fenland in the west, it stretches to the Wash, meeting the Goodsands

Fig 11: The regions of Norfolk.

16

at Hunstanton. These deposits are acidic, free draining, and associated with heathland. This area contains iron-rich strata and produces a form of local stone, used for building, known as carrstone.

A thick layer of boulder clay covers the centre of the county and a band running through to the south-east.[8] This glacial deposit is bordered by the Goodsands and Breckland in the west and Broadland in the east, and has been cut by streams and river valleys. It is acidic in the north and becomes more limey as it merges into chalky boulder clay to the south-east. The clay becomes easily waterlogged and has often been avoided for arable farming, especially in the less fertile parts, where the greatest concentration of ancient woodland can still be found. However, this region is particularly good for cereal production. The central watershed runs in an arc through the clayland and divides the rivers which flow towards the east coast from those which flow to the Wash.

To the west of the claylands lies the Breckland, which is a region of undulating heathland spanning the Norfolk–Suffolk border. It is centred on the town of Thetford and extends north past Swaffham to Castle Acre, while adjoining the Fenland in the west. The Breckland has low rainfall and suffers extremes of temperature, including warm summers and late frosts. It has light soils which are marginally productive but freely draining. These sandy soils were favoured by Neolithic people, who found the area easier to exploit than the thickly wooded claylands or the areas of wetland. The ancient trackway known as the Icknield Way passes through this region.

The Broads are a wetland zone which lies between Norwich and the east coast. They were formed by the digging of peat in the medieval period, diggings which have since flooded with water.[9] The peat extraction ceased in the nineteenth century and today the Broads are a National Park visited by thousands of holidaymakers each year. In earlier times the Broadland contained watery and boggy areas which gradually merged into the coastal marshes and a large estuary. The estuary was fed by rivers from the north and west, which were important for water transport for long distances inland; the area was always important for water-borne trade. The activities of fishing, catching eels and waterfowl and growing reeds have always been associated with Broadland.

On the opposite side of the county are the Fens, which, within Norfolk, consist of 200 square miles of wetland. Man's use of the Fenland has always been dependent on changing sea levels. The northern part, adjacent to the Wash, is covered by marine silt which was laid down just before the Roman conquest. In the south are the black peat fens. The Fens were formed as an extensive area of reed swamp and marshland vegetation by the rivers of eastern England flowing towards the Wash. As the waters became increasingly stagnant, dead plant material was unable to rot down and peat began to form. Greater areas then became flooded. The lime-rich fen peat provided perfect conditions for the establishment of trees: initially alder, then birch, oak and elm. The landscape became a wetland with nascent forest, which was largely impenetrable except by water.

Some small islands which projected above the peat and around the fen-edge became rich landscapes in prehistoric times. As the peat growth continued, later prehistoric peoples were forced back towards the surrounding chalk slopes. The first people were attracted by the rich natural resources of fish, fowl and game. They were initially restricted to the higher parts but forest clearance later revealed the benefits of the rich peaty soils. Specialist lifestyles developed and the inhabitants became boat builders, thatchers and basket weavers. They learned to exploit the wildfowl, fish and eels.

NATURAL MATERIALS

Norfolk suffers from a lack of good building stone. The people who have lived in this part of the country have needed to either adapt other local materials for construction or bring in stone from further afield, and as a result there are a number of building materials that characterise the region. The absence of building stone is a feature of archaeological excavations within the county.

The chalk bedrock has provided an abundance of flint for a variety of uses, in addition to that of building, including tool production. It is found right across the county from King's Lynn in the west to Great Yarmouth in the east. The flint of Breckland is exceptional in quality and has always been exploited. The nationally famous flint mines at Grimes Graves, just north of Thetford, are an example of its importance at an early prehistoric date.

West Norfolk has a form of brown sandstone called carrstone, mentioned above, which has been used for building in that part of the county. Ironstone is also found in the west. In Breckland, a yellow-grey form of chalk rubble, known as 'clunch', has been used for construction in historical times. Chalk has also been used for construction right across the county. However, the most ubiquitous building material in this rural county has always been timber.

CLIMATE

Despite its description as a watery place, Norfolk is in fact the driest county in England in terms of rainfall. Nowhere in the county receives more than 27 inches of rain each year. The climate of the area is particularly suited to the production of arable crops, as has been the case from the very earliest times.

This area is also characterised by cold winters. Biting easterly winds speed in across the North Sea, unchecked by any physical barrier, direct from the Urals. Eastern parts, notably the coastal strip and the flatter inland Broadland area, are particularly exposed to these inclement conditions.

FAUNA

Today, the British Isles are not rich in types of mammal. Just forty native terrestrial species are listed. There was much greater diversity in the period covered by this book. In prehistoric times large beasts inhabited Britain and were exploited by the inhabitants. Some of the exotic species that roamed what is now Norfolk have included mammoth, elephant, hippopotamus, rhinoceros, bear, hyaena and types of monkey. As recently as ten thousand years ago there were aurochs (a form of early cattle), red and roe deer, reindeer, elk, wolves, otter, beaver, wild pig and crane. Numbers of different plant and animal species have steadily declined as habitats have been altered and removed over the centuries.[10] Very few larger species survive today, although red and roe deer are still present in Norfolk.

The sands, gravels, clays and peats laid down by Norfolk's rivers contain the fossil bones and teeth of a wide variety of these mammals and other vertebrates. The world-famous Cromer Forest Bed is exposed in the cliffs of north-east Norfolk and the largely marine Weybourne Crag deposits at the base of the sequence have an age in excess of 1.5 million years. These deposits have long revealed fossil mammal remains of great importance. It is with the discovery of one of the world's most famous giant mammals on the coast of north Norfolk near Cromer that our study of Norfolk's past will continue in the next chapter.

Chapter 3
The age of ice
750,000 – 8000 BC

This sea was once a lake of ice. High mountains
overlooked a glacial plain frosted with snow and
scoured by the freezing wind.
In ages still to come, boulder waste and till will speak
of the ice pack's tortuous inching over buried rock.
The sea-floor here was prepared long before there was
a sea to cover it. In the interim came the governance
of ice.

(Lawrence Norfolk, *The Pope's Rhinoceros*)

When we view the Norfolk countryside it is hard to believe that this
same landscape was once covered by hills and valleys, and was similar
in appearance to parts of northern Britain today. This was the Ice Age,
which lasted between 700,000 and 10,000 years ago. During that time,
the world's climate changed dramatically many times. Not only was the
land of Norfolk very different in appearance, but it also suffered extreme
climatic conditions, often much colder and drier than today, when it
became covered with grasses and sedges. The prevailing cold conditions
were occasionally interrupted by warmer periods called interglacials,
followed by more extreme phases of intense cold and glaciation. It was
the glacial ice which steadily scoured the land, leaving it as flat as we
find it today. For relatively short phases of a few thousand years each,
the thick sheets of ice and glaciers covered large parts of the entire
northern hemisphere. Sea level fell hugely on occasions, by as much as
100m during the times when water became ice. Between these cold
phases, forest trees became re-established and the climate was much
more similar to that of today.

Ice Age Norfolk was the home of huge and exotic creatures.
Giant elephants taller than double-decker buses roamed the landscape.
They were preyed on by huge cats and, eventually, their carcases were
dismembered by scavengers, such as hyaenas, in a scenario we would
consider more characteristic of today's African savannah. Less than
ten miles east of Norwich, astonishing evidence has been collected

for some very large exotic mammals. A site at Norton Subcourse has revealed fossil skeletons belonging to creatures who lived during a warm period between 750,000 and 500,000 years ago.[1] Fossil bones include those of a giant form of hippopotamus weighing between six and seven tonnes (compared with the mere four tonnes of a modern hippo). Although sounding like a work of fiction, this picture continues to be consolidated and enriched each year by exciting new discoveries in parts of the county.

Today, the accelerating rate of erosion along the north and east coast of Norfolk is dramatically exposing ancient geological deposits which are revealing finds of great significance relating to the early fauna as well as to the very first human colonisation of the British Isles. This is another field of study where amateur fieldworkers have made a significant contribution. Some of the most important discoveries have been made by those who frequent sites of potential importance on a regular basis, looking to record new evidence from the ground. One such discovery was made in 1990 on the north coast, near Cromer, adjacent to the village of West Runton.

THE WEST RUNTON ELEPHANT

At the base of the cliff on the East Anglian coast, beneath the sands and gravels deposited by the glaciations, lies a dark geological deposit known as the Cromer Forest Bed. It is exposed at intervals right round the east coast between Weybourne, in central north Norfolk, and the vicinity of Kessingland, in Suffolk. The deposit was laid down between 1.5 million and 500,000 years ago, during the Lower and Middle Palaeolithic (see below). This pre-glacial deposit has been famous since the nineteenth century for the important fossil remains that it contains.

West Runton in north Norfolk is the best place to see the Cromer Forest Bed. Within this deposit is the Freshwater Bed, which is extremely rich in fossils, and provides evidence for a fauna very different to that found in Europe today.[2] Bones of large mammals, such as bears, bison, giant moose and even rhinoceros, are found in layers whose age has been calculated at between 600,000 and 700,000 years. The astonishing size of these creatures has led us to use the term *megafauna* to describe them.

In the aftermath of a storm, during the winter of 1990, Harold and Margaret Hems took a walk on the beach at West Runton to see if any fossils from the Cromer Forest Bed had been uncovered by the sea.[3] What they found was indeed spectacular. An enormous bone – far larger than that belonging to anything alive today – had been exposed in the cliff face. Dr Tony Stuart of Norwich Castle Museum was called in and his investigation showed this to be the pelvic bone of a huge male elephant. Fieldwork then revealed yet more bones from the same creature. Further erosion of the Freshwater Bed occurred during the winter of 1991, when heavy seas exposed even more bones. In 1992 a major rescue excavation was carried out by Norfolk Museums Service staff, together with a team of volunteers.

Study of the bones showed that the West Runton Elephant, as it had become known, belonged to the species called *Mammuthus trogontherii*, which is known as the Steppe Mammoth (Fig 12). This had become the dominant species of mammoth in Europe about 750,000 years ago. Despite having a diet based on types of grass, Steppe Mammoths were probably the largest species of elephant that has ever lived. The creature originally stood 4.5m at the shoulder and weighed no less than ten tons, which is double the weight of the largest elephants living today.

Fig 12: A reconstruction of the West Runton Elephant by Sam Brown *(copyright Norfolk Museums and Archaeology Service).*

Norfolk is in fact one of the best places in the world to discover mammoth fossils. Three of the four known species of mammoth have been found within the county's soils and gravels. Remains of the woolly mammoth, *Mammuthus primigenius*, evolved from *trogontherii* during the colder periods of the Ice Age, have also been found in Norfolk, as have those of the earlier *Mammuthus meridionalis*.

Further excavation at West Runton followed in 1995 in order to recover the rest of the elephant. Dr Stuart's second excavation was a much larger project, employing a wealth of specialist support from right across Europe. This international team removed the remainder of the skeleton, culminating in the lifting of the skull from the beach in a specially constructed steel cage.

The preservation of the West Runton Elephant is truly remarkable. Only a few of the very smallest bones are now missing from the skeleton, including those of the feet, which had been chewed away by spotted hyaenas. The hyaenas have, in turn, left their own mark at the site in the form of their coprolites, which were dropped after eating parts of the elephant. So, we can perhaps consider the elephant's entire skeletal remains to survive in this way! Scientific study of the elephant's teeth shows that it was forty years old at its death, over half a million years ago.

The Cromer Forest Bed has been a focus of study for at least a century and a half. The absence of human artefacts associated with this early pre-glacial geology suggested to archaeologists that man's appearance in this area was not of the greatest antiquity. However, some very recent discoveries from northern East Anglia's rapidly eroding coastline are now showing that there was indeed a very early human presence here – much earlier than was previously thought possible.

THE EARLIEST HUMAN INHABITANTS

The first appearance of early man in Norfolk, and indeed in Britain as a whole, is now being significantly redated. Evidence currently being revealed is suggesting that people may have been around even as early as the time of the West Runton Elephant and it is now seen as just possible that early humans could have been present in the area to witness the death of that very creature. New discoveries from our coast are providing some of the earliest evidence for human occupation in the whole of north-west Europe.

The very earliest humans evolved in Africa over 2 million years ago. Their descendants spread out from that continent, reaching the temperate parts of northern Europe over half a million years ago. The period from the very first presence of humans until approximately 8000 BC is called the Palaeolithic, or 'old stone age'.

The Palaeolithic can be separated into three phases: Lower, Middle and Upper. The Lower coincides approximately with the time that the earliest humans, who we call *Homo erectus*, moved out of Africa and into Europe, some 750,000 years ago. *Homo erectus* appears to have evolved into the pre-modern form of *Homo* which we call *Homo heidelbergensis*. Perhaps the best-known species of pre-modern *Homo* is *Homo neanderthalis*, or Neanderthal man, who first appeared over 200,000 years ago and became extinct only about 30,000 years ago. The Upper Palaeolithic in Europe begins with the appearance of the first *Homo sapiens*, or anatomically modern humans.

It should perhaps be noted at this stage that the human occupation of this country was not a single continuous process. Archaeology can trace a series of separate occupations throughout the Palaeolithic. The earliest bands of hunters to reach Britain had to contend with extreme climate conditions and there were long episodes, during the harshest periods, in which people were completely absent from Britain. Extinctions were followed by recolonisations. The final extinction of humans came at the end of the last glaciation and it was only after this, towards the end of the Palaeolithic period, that our direct ancestors entered Britain.

Excavations in the early 1980s at Boxgrove in Sussex produced evidence for a very early human presence in Britain, between 524,000 and 478,000 years ago, in the form of *Homo heidelbergensis*. In 1993 the same site produced a single human *tibia* and two teeth, which remain the earliest human skeletal remains in the whole of north-west Europe.[4] However, the discoveries now coming to light along the coast of northern East Anglia indicate an even earlier date for the arrival of the first humans.

From the mid 19th century, very early flint handaxes have been discovered along the beaches of Norfolk, from the vicinity of West Runton in the north round to Gorleston and Hopton, below Great Yarmouth, in the east. These tools are often rounded from having been rolled in the sea and it has not been possible to associate them with dated archaeological deposits. The more northerly examples, from Trimingham through to Weybourne, are cliff-derived and come from gravels that have been eroded from the adjacent cliff tops, where several examples have been found *in situ*. Others come from sites that are now submerged beneath the North Sea. Dr Peter Robins has suggested that those examples in the east were dispersed by a coastal drift, having

Fig 13: The site at Happisburgh.

possibly originated in the vicinity of Happisburgh.[5] This material has now been supplemented by new finds of even greater significance.

Fig 14: The peaty sediment at Happisburgh.

Since 1957, when major coastal flooding hit the east coast, tidal defences of timber and steel have been erected for the protection of local communities against the North Sea. Despite these constructions, erosion continues to accelerate along the stretch of coast between Great Yarmouth and Cromer, making this the fastest retreating stretch of coastline in Europe today. One of the worst affected beaches is at Happisburgh, where the cliffs have been eroded into an embayment (Fig 13). As recently as the year 2000 evidence came to light for the presence of very early human activity within the pre-glacial deposits of the Cromer Forest Bed. Simon Parfitt of the Natural History Museum in London first discovered 'cut marks' made by a flint tool on an animal bone which had been discovered in the deposit at Happisburgh by the local geologist A Savin. This showed that humans had been present at that location at least half a million years ago. Shortly after this stunning discovery a local beachcomber, Mike Chambers, was walking his dog at Happisburgh when he saw the flat edge of an object poking up from the surface of a peaty sediment on the wave-line (Fig 14).[6] This turned out to be an almost complete and perfect ovate handaxe (Fig 15). Not only was it in fresher condition than other handaxes found on the same coast but it had also been found within a dateable geological deposit, *in situ*.

In the summer of 2005 Jonathan Draper and Ruth Burwood interviewed Mike Chambers about the circumstances of his discovery.

> It was just a normal day. I wasn't expecting to find anything specific. It happened to be a very low tide. And it was damn cold – I remember that! The previous tide had eroded quite a layer of the beach itself. Walking along, the eye was drawn to this straight line. Straight lines don't occur very often in nature. This (object) was sitting upright in the clay. You could see it was a handaxe or an axe.
>
> Until I spoke to the museum I didn't realise how important it was. They sent me a chart which showed the cliff and said please tell us where you found the axe in the cliff. I said I didn't find it IN the cliff – it was another 10, maybe 15, feet down. That's when the interest really started.[7]

In May 2000 Professor Jim Rose of Holloway College, University of London, undertook an excavation at Happisburgh to determine the age of the peaty deposit. He was able to prove that the deposit was part of the Cromer Forest Bed and dated earlier than the Anglian glaciation. Moreover, he determined that this location had been part of the floodplain of the ancient Ancaster River (a tributary of the prehistoric Bytham River) and dated to around 680,000 years ago. This was proof that there had been humans present at Happisburgh at an even earlier time than at Boxgrove.[8] Simon Parfitt and Mike Chambers had found direct evidence for the earliest presence of human occupation anywhere in north-west Europe.

Fig 15: The Happisburgh handaxe. Length 122mm.

Finds from the Happisburgh site now include over thirty pieces of worked flint and animal bones, several of which also have cut-marks on them. This evidence shows that roe deer and an ancient species of cattle were being butchered and eaten by the early humans. At that time, Britain was still joined to continental Europe and the climate was similar to ours today, although perhaps a little cooler and more like the north of England. The early people who stopped beside the Ancaster River were passing through what was a gentle marshy valley. It contained a slow-moving river in which ducks and frogs lived; the plants included sedges, common spike rush and curled pondweed. There were trees nearby, including silver birch and Norway spruce (Fig 16).

These early humans were *Homo heidelbergensis*, an ancestor of both the Neanderthals and modern humans. They were the earliest people to migrate across what is now the English Channel, probably on a seasonal basis, to colonise the colder climatic parts of northern Europe.

In 2004, fieldwork just 20 miles further south, at Pakefield in Suffolk, investigated southern Cromer Forest Bed deposits. Some 32 worked flints have subsequently been discovered there.[9] The Pakefield sediments appear to have a similar date to the Happisburgh site but are probably slightly older. Happisburgh and Pakefield together now provide evidence for a much earlier – by over 200,000 years – presence of humans in this part of Europe.

THE LONGEST-LASTING TOOL

Most of our evidence for the earliest people in Norfolk comes in the form of their flint tools, which we find today on farmland, on beaches and in gravel quarries. The main tool of the Palaeolithic was the flint handaxe, which was one of mankind's most significant creations and which, in a variety of forms, remained in use for about a million years.[10] We find these early handaxes in Norfolk in a variety of different shapes and sizes, all of which were carefully crafted to fit comfortably into the hand and had a range of uses. Despite their name, the main purpose of these axes was not the cutting down of trees (in fact, there was no deliberate deforestation, or tree removal, during the Palaeolithic). These

Fig 16: A reconstruction of the prehistoric site at Happisburgh by Philip Rye.

people were hunters, and the axes were for cutting, chopping, skinning and dismembering animal carcasses. When the cutting edges of their tools became blunted through use, they could be resharpened by blows from a hammerstone or piece of antler.

The handaxes were accompanied by other tools, such as scrapers, burins, flakes and points. Other non-flint tools were used but they do not survive so well. Bone was employed to make harpoons, multi-purpose points and needles. Wooden tools and implements would also have been used.

There are huge differences between some of the crude handaxes that were made at the start of the Palaeolithic and the more delicately worked flint tools that belong to the end of the period. The Lower Palaeolithic economy had been a very specialised one, specially geared towards the exploitation of reindeer. Later, modern man was to develop a more diverse toolkit, employing a range of tools.

Fig 17: A Norfolk landscape during the Cromerian interglacial stage, between 470,000 and 500,000 years ago by Nick Arber *(copyright Norfolk Museums and Archaeology Service)*.

A JOURNEY THROUGH THE ICE AGE

The landscape of Ice Age Norfolk would have been completely unrecognisable to us. In particular, this part of Britain was still physically joined to mainland Europe and the drainage system of major rivers across East Anglia was very different to that which exists today. The landscape was to develop and change significantly over a period of half a million years.[11]

The Ice Age was not a single event but a series of successive glaciations, known as the Anglian, Wolstonian and Devensian. Before the Anglian and between the glaciations were warm periods known as interglacials.

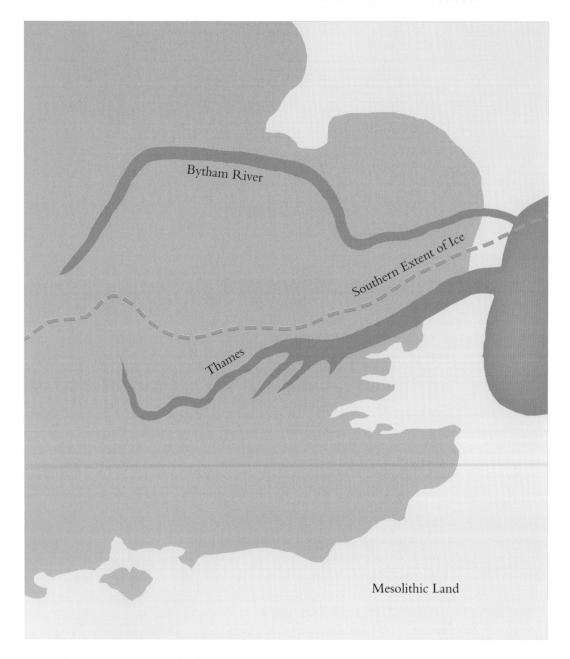

The Cromerian interglacial

The period from 500,000–470,000 years BC covered the geological warm stage known as the Cromerian.[12] During this interglacial (named after the type-site of Cromer, on the north Norfolk coast), Norfolk was covered by temperate forest, which stretched all the way across what is now the North Sea to the European mainland (Fig 17). There were regular mass migrations of herd animals across this whole area.

Fig 18: The ancestral Thames and Bytham rivers.

Evidence collected from the Freshwater Bed deposits near Cromer shows that there was a rich and diverse fauna that would be familiar to us today, although larger and more exotic species were also present, including rhinoceros, elephant, wild boar, lion, spotted hyaena and macaque monkey.

This landscape embraced a system of major rivers which drained the mainland of Europe and flowed into the North Sea, which lay far to the north of its present position. An ancestral River Thames flowed from south-west to north-east across the areas now known as Essex, Suffolk and Norfolk. It was joined near modern Bury St Edmunds by another river flowing eastwards from the Midlands, north of modern Leicester, which we call the Bytham River.[13] This river flowed right across the landscape now covered by the Fens (which did not exist at that time). The Bytham River entered Norfolk in the vicinity of Kings Lynn and flowed south through Feltwell. It then passed through the area of modern Suffolk at High Lodge. Turning eastward, it flowed near Bury St Edmunds and through Lowestoft (Fig 18).

Our evidence for human activity at that time is steadily increasing. Flint flakes and a scraper were found at Briton's Lane Gravel Pit in Sheringham. Worked flints have also been found at South Acre. There is also increasing evidence for early man in Suffolk. Unfortunately, no human skeletal remains have been found for this very early period in Norfolk. We also have no evidence for houses or structures from this early time; people would probably have lived in simple hide-covered shelters, perhaps made from wood or even from the bones of large mammals.

Fig 19: A Lower Palaeolithic handaxe from Brettenham. Length 190mm.

The Anglian glaciation

The onset of the Anglian Cold Stage (470,000–400,000 years BC) saw major glaciation affect the whole of East Anglia. Norfolk was covered in a thick sheet of ice, which extended south almost as far as Clacton and Thurrock in Essex. This was to have a major effect on the earlier river systems. It destroyed the Bytham River and forced the Thames further south, to its present position.

There were some ice-free intervals during the Anglian period, during which the vegetation consisted mainly of grasses and sedges. Gravel deposits beside the River Waveney, such as those at Homersfield (just over the border into Suffolk) show a diverse megafauna, which included woolly mammoth, woolly rhinoceros, reindeer and bison. Finds from across Britain show that there were regular visits by humans to Britain during some warmer phases, but evidence for hunters in Norfolk becomes more common during the Late Anglian stage. Their flint tools have been found at sites including Weybourne, Runton,

Sidestrand, Mundesley, Bacton and Lessingham. Coastal locations have also produced Palaeolithic flints in the vicinity of Anglian glacial deposits at Cley-next-the-Sea, Overstrand, Paston, Sea Palling and Happisburgh.

The Hoxnian interglacial

The Hoxnian interglacial (400,000–367,000 years BC) was characterised by a mild oceanic climate and saw the reappearance of temperate vegetation and animals. Lake sediments from Hoxne in Suffolk, which gives its name to this interglacial, contain pollen records which clearly show a changing vegetation. There, a temperate mammal fauna, which includes beaver, horse, red and fallow deer, rhinoceros and macaque monkey, was found in association with handaxes left by early humans. Indeed, by the middle of this period there was an expansion of hunter-gatherer presence across East Anglia and Britain in general.

The Wolstonian glaciation

In comparison with previous periods, there is only sparse evidence from the Wolstonian Cold Stage (367,000–128,000 years BC) in Norfolk. An ice sheet covered the whole of west Norfolk for part of this phase. River Waveney terrace gravels and the site of Broome Heath contain fossils of mammoth and bison. Some handaxes have come from west Norfolk, from South Wootton, Feltwell, Hockwold cum Wilton, Brettenham and Weeting (Fig 19). There are also sites with rich flint assemblages at Southacre, Keswick and Kirby Bedon, on the outskirts of Norwich.

Fig 20: A flint scraper and knife from Whitlingham. Length 97mm and 62mm.

Whitlingham (Kirby Bedon) and Keswick are two of the richest Palaeolithic sites in the whole of East Anglia. The site at Whitlingham was discovered in 1926, when a gravel pit was opened up, and subsequent excavation revealed flintmaking activity (Fig 20). Handaxes and flint flakes littered what had originally been the gravelly water's edge of a river channel. A similar handaxe industry was discovered in gravel workings at Keswick, just south of the River Yare.

At Snare Hill, Brettenham, a mile from Thetford, flint axes and picks were recovered from a low-lying site adjacent to the bank of the River Thet. Another important site was found at Bartholomew's Hills, Southacre, in 1934. Flints included handaxes, flaked cores and thick stone-struck flakes. Further west, at Shrub Hill, Feltwell, lies a low gravel-covered rise in the fens, just 1.2m above sea level, where fragments of deer antler and horses' teeth were recovered in association with flint tools. This is one of the richest handaxe sites in Norfolk, alongside Whitlingham and Keswick.

The Ipswichian interglacial

The last of the interglacial periods, the Ipswichian (128,000–75,000 years BC), has left prolific evidence for its wildlife at gravel pits in the county's main river valleys. At Swanton Morley, Shropham and Beetley, fossils include large mammals such as hippopotamus, an extinct straight-tusked elephant and aurochs. Pollen records indicate that the land was covered by temperate forest. The combination of species indicates that summer temperatures were at least two degrees Celcius warmer than those of today.

The Devensian glaciation

The final cold stage, the Devensian, occurred between 75,000 and 13,000 years ago. The period from c 20,000 to 15,000 BC saw the last advance of the ice sheets. This glaciation only just reached the now-coastal area of north-west Norfolk. Some sparse flora survived in unglaciated parts but there were no humans left anywhere in Britain at this time (Fig 21). Then the climate began to improve and our ancestors followed herds of game northwards and repopulated Britain as the land thawed, crossing the land bridge that joined Britain to Europe. East Anglia thus became the main passageway from Europe and genetic studies are showing very early cultural links between peoples of Frisia, the North Sea Plain and Norfolk at this time.[14]

Fig 21: A Norfolk landscape during the Devensian cold stage, about 30,000 years ago by Nick Arber *(copyright Norfolk Museums and Archaeology Service).*

Mammoths and woolly rhinos returned towards the end of the Devensian but they became extinct everywhere in Europe by c 12,000 years ago. It is still uncertain to what extent the climatic changes and

over-hunting by our own species *Homo sapiens* each contributed to the extinction of these species. Cold conditions continued for a further 2000 years, during which time reindeer remained present.

Further south, at Shropham in south-central Norfolk, abundant bones of bison and reindeer have been found, showing that vast herds crossed the ancestral River Thet on seasonal migrations. The concentration of bones is evidence for a high mortality at this crossing place. This scenario is reminiscent of the African Serengeti today, where predators congregate at river crossings to pick off migrating wildebeest.[15]

It was during the Devensian period that modern man first reached Britain. The 'moderns' are thought to have reached the British Isles about 33,000 years ago. Initially, they shared the landscape with Neanderthals, whom they eventually replaced. However, the Neanderthals also managed to leave a significant mark in Norfolk's archaeological record.

NEANDERTHALS IN NORFOLK

More than 1200 handaxes of the Lower and Middle Palaeolithic have been reported from over 200 sites in Norfolk. Very few sites have yet produced the bout coupé form of handaxe, which is associated with the former presence of *Homo neanderthalis*. However, an increasing body of evidence is showing how these hardy early humans were able to survive in this area

Fig 22: John Lord and Nigel Larkin with a newly discovered mammoth bone, at Lynford in 2002.

during periods dominated by particularly harsh climatic conditions.

Although similar to modern man in many ways, Neanderthals were a distinct species.[16] They possessed physical characteristics which enabled them to survive in the colder climate, being thickset in appearance, with stronger bones, powerful muscles and strong hands. They were shorter and stockier than the earlier *Homo heidelbergensis* had been. Their brain was also larger than that of modern humans.

Evidence for Neanderthals in Britain as a whole is still slight and no single bone from one of their skeletons has yet been found anywhere in the country. Evidence is restricted to just a few of their teeth and their tools.[17] Even their flint implements are quite scarce. Very few of their sites have been excavated in modern times, employing modern scientific methods and techniques.

Neanderthals were efficient hunters and lived in small social groups of eight to ten individuals. They behaved similarly to modern man in a number of ways. We know that they cooked on hearths, wore clothes and made flint tools, tipped their spears with stone blades and used flint tools to prepare their food. Pertinently for archaeologists, their 'toolkit' was a characteristically distinctive one.

The bout coupé is an elegant form of handaxe: thin and with a characteristic flat butt end. A single bout coupé handaxe was recovered

from a bank of the Blackwater stream at Little Cressingham, in the Breckland.[18] Others have been found in a small gravel pit at Mousehold, Norwich, and from the surface at North Wootton, near King's Lynn in west Norfolk. In early 2002 a most spectacular addition to this small corpus of bout coupé handaxes was made at another site in the Breckland.

Fig 24: A freshly discovered handaxe during the preliminary investigation at Lynford, prior to the excavation.

Neanderthals in Thetford Forest

At Lynford in Thetford Forest is a group of gravel pits located on a flood plain terrace on the south bank of the River Wissey. These gravels were deposited tens of thousands of years ago, during the Ice Age. Part of a mammoth tusk and bones were reported during gravel working there in the 1980s. Handaxes have also been recorded from the vicinity but their relationship to the gravels had not been clear.

In March 2002 local archaeologist John Lord was undertaking a watching brief at the site, following initial discussions and encouragement from the late John Wymer, and was present when one of the gravel diggers unearthed an unusual find about 3.5m below normal ground level.[19] John recognised this as a woolly mammoth tooth. The most significant part of the discovery was that the tooth was within a channel of black peaty sediment. Further investigation revealed other mammoth teeth within the same archaeological deposit. John contacted Norfolk

Museums & Archaeology Service, who sent their mammoth specialist Nigel Larkin to look at the site. Whilst collecting further bones, John and Nigel discovered another significant find; a beautiful black flint handaxe, in perfect condition, within the same layer of sediment, where it had lain undisturbed for tens of thousands of years. Significantly, it was a handaxe of the bout coupé form. The association of mammoth bones (Figs 22 and 23) together with flint tools (Fig 24) within an archaeological deposit was a unique opportunity to investigate how Neanderthals had lived in Britain during the Ice Age.

An excavation was subsequently mounted during the summer of 2002 by the Norfolk Archaeological Unit, revealing what has since been considered to be the best Neanderthal site ever found in Britain.[20] Optical Stimulated Luminescence dating (OSL) was used on samples of sand, dating the

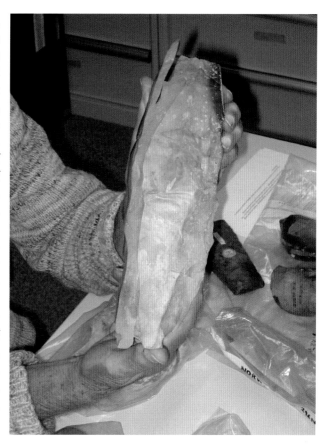

Fig 25: Peter Robins with a reconstructed blade core from Carrow Road.

Neanderthal presence to between 64,000 and 67,000 years ago. This was approximately 30,000 years before modern humans arrived in the British Isles. The site had been located beside a river, where both large mammals and predators had come to drink. Their faunal remains show that these included reindeer, bison and horse, together with larger and more exotic creatures including woolly rhinoceros, brown bear and spotted hyaena. Study of the 150 species of insects recovered confirms that this was an area of stagnant water surrounded by marshes, probably a side channel beside a larger river.[21] Even dung beetles were found, showing that mammoths regularly visited the spot to drink. No less than 45 handaxes were recovered during 2002, all with a fresh appearance and in exceptional condition. The complete toolkit was that of the Mousterian stone tool culture and included specialist flake implements in addition to the handaxes. These included burins, points, knives and scrapers.

We now have an unparalleled insight into the environment inhabited by the Lynford Neanderthals. The animal and plant species were adapted for cold conditions and show us that they were living during a cold climate phase. The plant and insect remains indicate that it was too cold for any trees to grow there. Instead, the landscape was one of grasses, mosses, reeds and sedges. The Neanderthals would have lived in temporary shelters within a hostile, cold and open landscape. There was no wood for them to use and they may have constructed the shelters from some of the larger mammoth bones. They may have returned to the site at different times of the year.

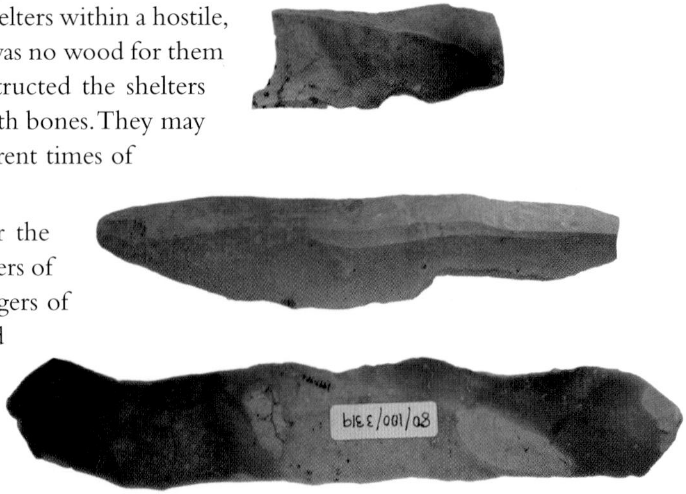

We cannot be sure whether the Lynford Neanderthals were hunters of the large game or merely scavengers of dead meat from animals that had died of other causes. However, this is the only butchery site known in the British Isles and we can see how they had used their flint tools to cut meat from the mammoth carcasses. Altogether, the remains of at least nine Woolly Mammoths (*Mammuthus primigenius*) were found at the site, including one juvenile animal. The absence of big mammoth limb bones suggests that they were being intentionally removed from the site. The Neanderthals used their handaxes to cut away these meat-bearing bones, which were then being taken to a safe distance to eat, away from other predators that were visiting the site to drink.

Fig 26: Flint long blades from the Upper Palaeolithic site at Carrow Road. Length of bottom blade 234mm.

Mammoths died out just 10,000 years ago. In fact, many types of large mammal became extinct in Europe between 40,000 and 10,000 years ago. The extinction of the mammoths was probably due to a combination of global climatic changes and the increasingly successful hunting techniques of modern humans. The excavation at Lynford provides a fascinating insight into the exploitation of these massive creatures by early humans during the Ice Age.

The Neanderthals dominated Europe for over 200,000 years. Then, within just 10,000 years of the arrival of modern humans, they disappeared.

'CAVEMEN AT CARROW ROAD'

Flintworking technology underwent significant development during the middle Devensian period. The range of items within man's toolkit was expanded beyond the basic handaxe, with the addition of a series of tools designed for specific tasks. Among these was a new blade-based technology: long narrow flint flakes made from elongated cores. There are many sites with long blade industries in the south-west of the county, along the courses of the Rivers Wissey and Little Ouse. There is also a focus of sites on the River Wensum.[22] One significant concentration of long blades comes from Lynford Quarry, where over 100 pieces have been found.

Another site yielding a long blade industry was discovered in the Carrow area in the heart of Norwich in 2003, during excavations at the Norwich City football ground in advance of construction of a new stand. This gave rise to an excited headline in the local newspaper, drawing attention to what was seen as a fascinating new discovery of 'cavemen'.[23] This excavation at Carrow Road revealed two distinct undisturbed deposits of worked flint of Upper Palaeolithic date on a sand island, where people had stopped while tracking migrating herds of reindeer probably around 11,500 BC.

There were some 300 pieces of flint including waste material: by refitting many of the blades onto cores from the site, Peter Robins has shown how people were knapping flint here (Fig 25). The long blades may have been used somewhat like hunting knives today (Fig 26). This hunting camp was probably one of a number of similar sites situated on sand bars along the River Wensum. This site provides what is currently the earliest evidence for human occupation within the heart of the modern city of Norwich.

THE END OF THE ICE

The final effects of the ice, at the end of the Devensian Cold Stage, were coming to an end around 13,000 BC. The climate and environment of Britain had begun to change. As conditions became milder, populations moved north into the area of Norfolk in increasing numbers, following herds of game. These people were presented with new opportunities for subsistence as they adapted to new, post-glacial, conditions. The period following the final retreat of the glacial ice is known as the Mesolithic, and the way that our ancestors rose to the new challenge during that period will be related in the next chapter.

Chapter 4
The age of wood
8000 – 4300 BC

People quickly began to adapt to the rapidly changing post-glacial environment. This period, from about 8000 BC, is known as the Mesolithic, or 'middle stone age'. As the climate became warmer, the land became covered with natural forest, which today we call 'wildwood'. People and animals steadily returned from further south to the improving conditions in the area which is now the landmass of Britain, which soon became occupied by small groups of mobile hunters and gatherers who exploited the increasingly abundant wildlife that was all around them in the woodlands, marshes, sea and rivers.

The temporary homes of these hunter-gatherer people were constructed from trees, branches and wooden stakes. People also made good use of organic material resources such as wood and reeds to make tools and utensils for everyday use. Evidence for Mesolithic settlements is rare and very fragile, and survives well only in waterlogged environments, which are only rarely encountered by archaeologists. This period can most appropriately be referred to as 'the age of wood'.

Where the delicate evidence does survive, we can see a society of skilled craftsmen; people who worked wood and flint to a very high standard. They consructed logboats, which were paddled along Norfolk's rivers and streams. They made bows, spears and harpoons for hunting. Fishing was assisted by the use of nets and fish traps. However, most of our surviving evidence comes in the form of their flint tools.

A FIND FROM THE SEA BED

At the start of the period, when Britain was still part of the European landmass, the North Sea was still far away and small freshwater streams flowed across the great plain of Doggerland that joined Norfolk to the mainland of Europe. Archaeological evidence has been found to show that people were living on the plain and moving across it (Fig 27).

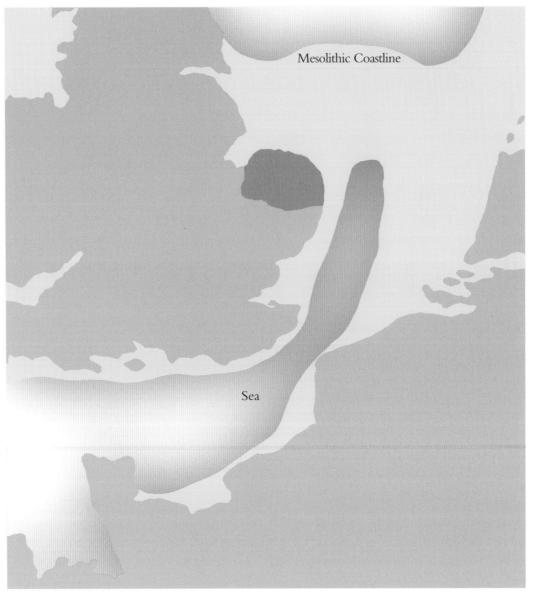

Mesolithic Coastline

Sea

In 1931 a most remarkable find was made, some 40km beyond the north coast of Norfolk, in the North Sea. A trawler fishing north-east of Cromer dredged up a block of freshwater peat from the sea bed.[1] It contained a beautiful polished barbed spearhead made from red deer antler. This magnificent weapon had been either dropped or fired by a prehistoric hunter. Radiocarbon dating subsequently showed that this area of peat had been formed around 9800 BC, confirming that the spearhead had been used during the very early post-glacial period. This impressive object is now in the possession of Norwich Castle Museum. Its fresh appearance looks newly crafted and belies its great age.

Fig 27: The approximate position of the coastline at the start of the Mesolithic. Shown against a background of the modern coastline.

AN ISLAND IS FORMED

As the northern ice sheets continued to melt, sea level rose and the plain of what we now call Doggerland steadily became covered by the North Sea. Sea level was rising by between 23mm and 33mm each year, and as the diminishing land bridge became wet and marshy it became more hazardous for people to cross. The relatively large population which had been drawn to the plain by its abundant natural resources now needed to move inland, in both directions, as Britain became cut off from mainland Europe.

By about 6500 BC, Doggerland had been fully submerged beneath the North Sea. Britain had become an island and the coastline of Norfolk was broadly in the position that it is today.[2] A coast of beaches, marshes and mud flats formed, and this became a rich area for hunting, fishing and gaming. The coast extended slightly further east than today, and water separated the higher areas of Flegg and Lothingland from the mainland. The place where the town of Great Yarmouth now stands was under water. Lakes formed further inland. From this point onwards, cultural development took divergent paths on either side of the North Sea.

The increase in air temperature at this time meant that areas which had previously been tundra could now be colonised by plants. Forest spread right across our landscape. The open steppe-tundra of the Ice Age gave way to a woodland of first birch, then pine-dominated and finally broadleaf forest in which the predominant trees were oak, elm, hazel, lime, ash and maple. There was also hornbeam, yew and pine. Animal species were also changing with the developing climatic conditions.

We know that today's flat Broadland landscape in east Norfolk would have been unrecognisable. River valleys were deep, with steady sloping sides. Pollen analysis of deposits from Ranworth Fen showed that between 7000 and 5000 BC the Broadland region was dominated by pine and birch woodland.[3] The presence of alder by 4000 BC shows that trees and shrubs tolerant of damper soils were invading the valley floors by that time.[4]

WHAT PEOPLE ATE

The Mesolithic population were no longer just hunters but were now 'hunter-gatherers', and their way of life was much broader-based than that of people living in the Upper Palaeolithic. The changing climate meant there was an increased availability of plants that could be used for food, as well as a greater variety of game for hunting, than in the previous period.

There was a notable trend towards a decrease in hunting and an increasing dependence on gathering over this period. Milder conditions contributed towards a greater exploitation of plant foods. It is still the case today that there is a greater use of plants for food in warmer places, while people depend more on meat-based diets for providing warmth where conditions are colder. Despite these developments, the population still led a seasonal, mobile, lifestyle and not a sedentary one.

The hunter-gatherers were drawn particularly to Norfolk's coast and river systems. The coastline allowed people to exploit sea fish, sea mammals and marine shellfish. The resources provided by other wet landscapes, such as those of the Broadland and Fens, were also of sufficient importance to attract people from a considerable distance for specialised or seasonal exploitation, notably for the abundant fish, waterfowl and shellfish. Fish were caught with hooks made from barbed slivers of antler.

Red and roe deer and wild pig bones are prominent on sites. People also hunted aurochs and elk. Our evidence shows that the killing of these animals was selective. We can detect a form of management of specific species, as opposed to random hunting. Surplus males were culled, together with females above breeding age, but the young were not taken.

Not only was the landscape changing naturally, but man now began to make changes through forest clearance; trees were cut down and clearings opened up by burning vegetation. This was initially undertaken to encourage the growth of grasses and succulent plants that would attract game. It was in this way that people began to manage and maintain their supply of food, and to facilitate passage through wooded areas.

All in all, the improved nutrition base was a major reason for a significant increase in the population after about 5000 BC.

THE CHANGING TOOLKIT

A more diverse and specialised range of flint tools was developed with the onset of the Mesolithic, after about 8000 BC.[5] This toolkit included long flint blades but is characterised by small flints, known as microliths. They were delicately fitted into wooden shafts and bone handles to make a range of tools and weapons, such as barbed spearheads.

A new form of tool, known as the tranchet axe, was gradually adopted at this time right across southern Britain. These were made from an elongated flint core, with an edge sharpened by the removal of flakes from one end. It could then be resharpened by the removal of further flakes. Another significant innovation during this period was the progression from the handaxe to the use of the hafted flint axe. Together with the use of fire, hafted axes made a very significant contribution to the rate of forest clearance. This form of axe was more effective for woodworking generally, enabling a quicker and easier method of construction for boats.

Other materials were used alongside flint to make tools. Some examples have survived and have been found in excavations, including deer antlers, which were used as mattocks and picks. Wood was also worked with stone adzes made from hafted flints and saws made of notched flints. Clothing and some other everyday items were made from leather and grass.

THE LAND OF MOBILE HUNTERS

Both modern scientific excavation and the collection of flints from fieldwalking have provided evidence for the activities of the Mesolithic population at many locations right across Norfolk. There is little direct evidence for their settlements but the county is rich in Mesolithic flintwork. This material tends to be found on sandy soils, next to rivers, and thus there are notable concentrations in central east Norfolk, associated with the main river systems, and in the south-west, along the fen-edge.

A site at Kelling Heath, west of Sheringham, is one of the richest deposits known to us from the Early Mesolithic.[6] The location is just 2km inland from the north coast, occupying a naturally high position on the top of the Cromer Ridge, where it provided hunters with a magnificent view for miles across the great plain of birch and pine forest. From here they could view migrating herds of deer and other animals, as well as passing groups of people, for many miles distant. The site has yielded prolific scatters of Mesolithic flint artefacts, spread over a large area. Unfortunately, the acidic soil conditions have destroyed all evidence other than flint. Hundreds of tiny flint microlith points, which would have been used to repair hunting tools such as spears and arrows, have survived (Figs 28 and 29). The location was used by the hunters on a seasonal basis.

Another rich Mesolithic site is at Titchwell, which is now on the north-west coast, 9km north-east of Hunstanton.[7] This location is more famous today as an RSPB nature reserve, and is visited by many thousands of 'twitchers' every year, most of whom are totally unaware that this beautiful natural landscape was a focus of human and not just

Fig 28: A group of flint microliths from Kelling Heath. Length of longest flint 72mm.

avian activity some 9000 years ago. Settlement here spanned the Late Glacial and Early Mesolithic periods, following the recession of the last ice sheet from this area. At that time, Titchwell was another open inland site, possibly situated close to a river, the presence of which could have attracted people to this specific location. They may also have been attracted by the availability of good-quality flint, which was exposed in the glacial till.

Fieldwork at Titchwell revealed a flint industry based on blade production, with scrapers, burins and some retouched pieces. There were no microliths, projectile heads or heavy axe-type tools. This combination is a very distinctive form of Mesolithic industry belonging to a Late Upper Palaeolithic tradition. Similar flint tool types have been found along the present beach, nearby, between Thornham and Brancaster, but in smaller numbers. It is possible that they are evidence of other similar sites of the same period which lie within inter-tidal deposits. Other similar sites may also exist to the south-west, beneath the southern Fens.

Fig 29: Flint scrapers from Kelling Heath. Length of far right flint 70mm.

Mesolithic settlements in general were often located beside lakes and rivers. Such sites are known further inland, at Two Mile Bottom near Thetford,[8] at Hockham Mere and at Wretham Mere. The light, sandy, soils of Breckland were favoured during the Later Mesolithic and contain numerous scatters of flint tools, including a large concentration at Banham.[9] More tranchet axes have been found there than anywhere else in East Anglia; direct evidence for an intensive process of forest clearance by man. Other flints, including a possible arrowhead, have been recovered from Cranwich, on the western edge of Breckland. Finds of Mesolithic flint tools have also been made at sites within the Wensum valley, at Hellesdon, Sparham and Lyng. In addition, communities were attracted by the rich resources of the Fens; there are numerous scatters of Mesolithic flint around the edge of the chalk next to the peat Fen. Other sites have been identified along the valleys of the Little Ouse, Lark and Wissey. At Ken Hill, Snettisham, in the north-west, flint axes, cores, blades and flakes have all been collected.

Mesolithic sites are less common on the poorly drained till plain of central Norfolk, which is some distance from rivers. However, one site was discovered at Great Melton, situated 10km to the west of Norwich, which is some 300m distant from the nearest water source and also on higher land.[10] Great Melton was initially identified by a concentration of flintwork which shows similarities to the assemblage from Kelling Heath. The site contained large numbers of microliths and convex-edged scrapers, and appears to have been a short-lived seasonal hunters' camp (Fig 30).

Evidence for Mesolithic activity was found at Spong Hill, near North Elmham in central Norfolk.[11] Environmental samples showed that the immediate area was covered with pine-dominated woodland, which was, judging by the quantities of pine charcoal and evidence of burning recovered, being cleared by the population. The assemblage of flint tools at Spong Hill was small, comprising microliths and some associated debitage, and it does not appear to have been a major occupation site. Hunters may have used the site as a base to stop and repair their hunting weapons as they moved across the area.

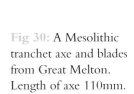

Fig 30: A Mesolithic tranchet axe and blades from Great Melton. Length of axe 110mm.

THE ACCELERATION OF CHANGE

Although Mesolithic people were increasingly making temporary clearings for settlement, the population was then so low that it had little real impact on the landscape. However, the density of population increased after Britain became an island.

We have no burials or even certain skeletal remains for Mesolithic people in Norfolk. A single human skull found in the bank of the River Yare at Strumpshaw in 1954 was considered at the time, and for many years after, to be that of a male of Mesolithic date.[12] However, this attribution remains to be confirmed by scientific dating methods.

As the period continued, populations on either side of the North Sea began to develop independently. However, contact between them did not cease. Major changes were taking place across mainland Europe and these found their way into Britain through the existing cultural links. The distinctive Mesolithic flint toolkit died out around 4300 BC and it was replaced by a new material assemblage, which signalled the arrival of a new way of life.

Chapter 5
The first farmers
4300 — 3200 BC

The onset of the Neolithic, or 'new stone age', was a time of radical new developments covering all aspects of daily life, making this perhaps the most fascinating episode in the whole of British prehistory. This was the period in which large ceremonial monuments were introduced to Britain. We are also able to identify ritual behaviour in relation to the formal treatment of the dead. A further important development was one that helps archaeologists to locate Neolithic settlements – it was at this time that people first began to make and use pottery.

Norfolk had retained sea-borne links with the continent. It was through that connection that it became one of the first parts of Britain to adopt perhaps the most significant of the new developments: agriculture.[1]

THE ORIGINS OF FARMING

The Neolithic saw a whole package of crops and animals introduced to Britain, which provided the resources through which communities were able to gradually develop a more settled way of life. This meant that people would eventually no longer need to migrate across the countryside in the way that their hunter-gatherer predecessors had done. Populations would be able to come together and live in larger groups.

The cultivation of crops and the domestication of animals first occurred in the Near East around 12,000 years ago, within the context of a rapidly changing environment at the end of the last Ice Age. Farming spread throughout the Near East and then to adjacent countries. It had reached the plains of central Europe by 6000 BC. From there, this way of life travelled westwards through the light soils of Germany and into the Low Countries and northern France.

The adoption of the new lifestyle in Britain involved a transfer of the innovative ideas. Until very recently, the new agriculturalists were characterised as 'pioneers' moving steadily westwards to new areas, carrying the 'package' of domesticated animals and plant seeds with them. There may indeed have been some influx of population to accompany such a major innovation, but we no longer envisage the widespread displacement of local peoples. This theory is supported by current research into genetic origins, which confirms that there was some element of Neolithic population spread across Europe. Studies show evidence for a 'gene flow' into eastern England from the Low Countries of northern Europe at this time.[2] These would have been experienced farmers from the continent who relocated to Britain and helped the local population establish and develop farming here.

The introduction and mastery of the new ideas was a process which took many generations. There was certainly no sudden changeover to a sedentary way of life. The Norfolk evidence shows that Neolithic sites within the county were still used only on a seasonal and not a permanent basis. Modern archaeology is increasingly showing that there was no rapid changeover to full-scale farming.

An immediate benefit of the first domesticated crops may have been one of prestige, demonstrated by feasting, which was an important feature within prehistoric societies. The new crops would have initially added an exotic and impressive element to feasting and eating, rather than being a purely practical improvement to the diet. The earliest growing of wheat and barley might also have been used more for the production of beer than for bread.[3] This, too, may have had an association with communal feasting. So, the initial introduction of farming might be seen to have developed more for purposes of status within social groups through the provision of luxury consumables.

THE INTRODUCTION OF FARMING TO EASTERN BRITAIN

As we have seen, the people living around the east coast of Britain had existing social and cultural links with the population of the near continent, remaining in regular contact with their counterparts living in the Low Countries and northern France. As new ideas reached those parts of northern Europe there would have been little delay in their reaching eastern Britain. As a result, communities living in the area of Norfolk were some of the first people in Britain to encounter and adopt the new farming methods.

Domestic wheat and barley, together with the first domesticated animals, must have both been introduced to Britain through existing channels of contact. They would have been carried across the North

Sea by boat. The vessels used may have been similar in form to the elaborate Bronze Age boat discovered at Dover in 1992.[4] This was made from sculpted planks that were held together with cleats, wooden wedges and stitches. It had been constructed to withstand the stresses of sea travel and clearly shows that its makers had an advanced knowledge of sea travel by that date. Similar technology may have been available at this earlier time.

The most significant change in the post-glacial mammal fauna of the British Isles was the introduction of domestic livestock. Four species were initially involved. These were sheep, goats, cattle and pigs. Sheep and goats were originally natives of the Middle East and had no wild ancestors in Britain. There had been wild ancestors of both cattle and pigs: the wild auroch and the wild boar. However, there is no evidence for domestication of wild aurochs nor any signs of their interbreeding with domestic cattle.

Neolithic settlements in East Anglia are recognised as far back as the 5th and 4th millennia BC, at the sites of Shippea Hill in Cambridgeshire and Broome Heath in Norfolk. There was certainly no sudden break with the Mesolithic lifestyle. A gradual shift towards the new way of life is suggested by evidence from sites right across the county and in particular from the Fenland Project in south-west Norfolk. At Two Mile Bottom, near Thetford, flint microliths, which are characteristic tools of the Mesolithic, were found together with Neolithic scrapers, flakes and their associated debitage, reflecting continuity, rather than a revolution, within society.

THE LANDSCAPE AND NATURAL ENVIROMENT

By the time man was actively cultivating the soil, the coastline of eastern England had reached its approximate present position. The land surface had been completely covered by plants and most was tree-covered, although this woodland was not uniform across the whole area.[5] The degree of cover depended on the local moisture content, acidity and alkalinity of the soils. Around 4000 BC the woodland cover suffered a setback which is traced in the archaeological record. A decline in elm pollen is detected, not only in Norfolk but right across Britain. This 'elm decline' has been associated with the spread of farming and is also accompanied by an increase in the pollen of weedy herbs and cereals.

The Neolithic community was also responsible for widespread woodland clearance across much of the area, although permanent large-scale deforestation was a process that stretched over centuries. It is at this stage that we begin to get evidence of burning, which is rare in the archaeological record before the introduction of agriculture. Pollen studies have shown that substantial woodland clearance did not reach many parts until the Late Bronze Age/Early Iron Age. However, some areas had already become more open by the onset of the Neolithic, on the dry and infertile soils of the Breckland in south Norfolk, for example, where there was grassland. Much of the Broadland flood plain was wooded at this time but there were also open areas that would have produced reed, sedge and rush.[6]

Fig 31: A polished stone axe from Pulham St Mary. Length 157mm.

The native fauna at this time included red deer, roe deer, badger, wildcat, weasel, polecat and marten. There were also species now lost from the British countryside, including wild boar (present until the 17th century), aurochs (until the Bronze Age or possibly later), wolf (until the 17th century), brown bear (until the 10th century) and beaver (until the 12th century).

The population exploited local materials for the construction and maintenance of dwellings and for stock feeding. Wetland plants would have been used for thatching. In the Fenland, as farming was embraced, there was more dependence on livestock than arable.[7] New types of tool and equipment associated with these early farmers are found all over Norfolk.

NEOLITHIC TECHNOLOGY

The changes in the types of artefact found from the Neolithic reflect the change from a hunter-gatherer lifestyle to a farming and ground-clearing existence. The main material which survives is, once again, flint, and some specific items characteristic of the Mesolithic were replaced by new types of tool.[8] Most noticeably, the composite microlithic projectile points were replaced by leaf-shaped arrowheads and flaked adzes by larger axes made from flint and also from other types of stone (Fig 31). In Norfolk these stone axes include items of continental jadeite, Cornish greenstone, Welsh stones and Irish porcellanite. Some of these were ground and polished to a smooth and beautiful appearance, with very strong cutting edges. Other specialist tool types were knives and sickles (Fig 32).

Fig 32: A Neolithic flint dagger from Bowthorpe. Length 157mm.

The first use of pottery has left a strong legacy in the archaeological record. The use of fired-clay technology added new forms of containers to the leather and wood repertoire of the hunter-gatherers. This enhanced the development of a more sedentary lifestyle, allowing farmers to build up their resources in a more permanent fashion. Plain, round-based, usually carinated bowls are found from this initial period, as discovered at Sparham and Brettenham. The two main local traditions of bowls are Grimston Ware and Mildenhall Ware.[9]

SETTLEMENTS

Unlike in some other regions of Britain, such as south-west and northern England, there is relatively little evidence of Neolithic activity within Norfolk's present-day landscape. This is partly because the same fertile soils have been reused and ploughed over many thousands of years, and partly because houses were merely light shelters and have left little evidence behind. As people were still mobile, they used only structures that could be easily dismantled. Thus the fragile evidence of our early agricultural settlements has largely been removed.

Where Neolithic settlements do survive, they are found as scatters of domestic rubbish, pits and postholes. They favoured the lighter soils and Norfolk's rivers provided the focus for good fertile farming locations. A significant concentration of finds is found at the confluence of and to the south of the Rivers Yare and Wensum. Another grouping comes from the southern fen-edge. There was also a considerable Neolithic population in Breckland, where the remaining wildwood had been cleared, never to recover. We have records of several individual settlements in the county.

Eaton Heath

Aerial photography provided initial evidence for a settlement at Eaton Heath, Norwich, showing a circular enclosure to the east of a barrow group.[10] Excavation revealed a cluster of pits and post-holes; the latter formed two groups which may represent individual roofed structures. Radiocarbon dates, together with pottery of Mildenhall style, place the date of the site towards the end of the 4th millennium BC. The most interesting features were twenty-one shafts which formed a circle around the posts and pits. These produced sherds of plain Neolithic bowls and an East Anglian Beaker, and it is possible that they had an early ritual significance, not dissimilar to the shafts which are found next to *oppida* sites across Iron Age Europe.

Broome Heath

Occupation had begun on a small scale at Broome Heath, Ditchingham, by 3474 BC.[11] This settlement was positioned on a terrace just north of the River Waveney. Large numbers of storage pits were found right across the site, producing clear evidence for the production of cereal crops. Just over 100m to the north lay an earthen long barrow and also

a round barrow. A total of 8000 pottery sherds was recovered during excavation, 750 of which showed imprints of plant remains (Fig 33). Seventy-five of these revealed identifiable cereals, including emmer and einkorn wheat and barley. Saddle querns and rubbing stones, which had been used in the grinding of grain, were also found.

Fig 33: Neolithic pottery from Broome Heath. Scale 1:2.

The archaeological evidence shows that settlement persisted at Broome Heath for some 1500 years, although use of the site may have been intermittent, perhaps on a seasonal basis, possibly as part of an agricultural cycle or in connection with funerary rites associated with the nearby long barrow.

Spong Hill

Another settlement of the earlier Neolithic was revealed during excavations at the early Saxon cemetery at Spong Hill in mid Norfolk.[12] Once again, this settlement was situated in a commanding position in the landscape, on a south-facing knoll adjacent to the confluence of small streams flowing into the River Wensum. Post-holes which represent a possible rectangular building were located. Another row of post-holes represent either the side of another building or a possible fence line. Finds included lithic material and prolific amounts of pottery, with both Mildenhall Ware and Grimston Ware prominent.

The Neolithic occupation at Spong Hill was spread over a wide area but appears to have been formed by a number of separate and relatively brief episodes at the same location. As was the case at Broome Heath, these may have been seasonal occupations.

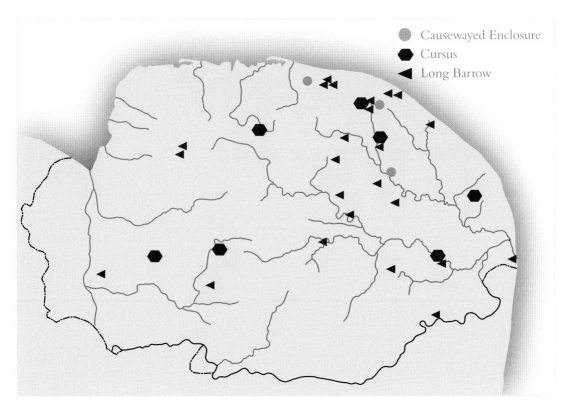

Causewayed Enclosure
Cursus
Long Barrow

The accumulated evidence from Norfolk suggests that Neolithic people continued to move around the landscape in much the same way that they had done in earlier times. Sites used at this time were still exploited on a seasonal basis and the transition to a sedentary lifestyle, as noted above, appears to have been a much longer process than has often been assumed.

Fig 34: The locations of Early Neolithic field monuments in Norfolk.

FIELD MONUMENTS

The Neolithic was the time when communal field monuments appeared in Britain (Fig 34). The east and south-east of England are not as rich in these monuments as the west, but they are more common in Norfolk than is often recognised and new examples are still being discovered in the county on a regular basis, as our scrutiny of the landscape increases. Like the settlements, they are concentrated in the west, the south-west and central river valleys. There is also prolific evidence inland from the headwaters of the Great Estuary in east Norfolk.

All of these constructions required organised labour, which shows that significant new developments were occurring within society. The increasingly static farming groups were coming together and sharing these feats of engineering. The Neolithic population of eastern England was relatively small, so these constructions must have required the involvement of much of the regional population at any one time. The construction of these monuments can, however, be seen against the background of a growing population. This was the first real pressure on the use of the landscape and people were beginning to spread into previously unoccupied areas. As the farming groups became established they began to identify themselves by marking the landscape through their highly visible monuments. These earthworks were to remain significant features in the landscape for many generations to come.

Causewayed enclosures

These large enclosures take their name from the interrupted ditch circuit that surrounds them. They are one of the earliest types of monument associated with divisions in the landscape. Three causewayed enclosures have been identified in Norfolk. They are all in the north-east, at Hainford, Roughton and Buxton. All are relatively small examples, and are surrounded by single ditch circuits. It has been suggested that these monuments may have been used as meeting places for surrounding communities.[13] An alternative theory is that they may have been constructed at the centres of territories belonging to individual farming groups.[14]

Long barrows

The development of ritual behaviour is apparent in the lives of the early farming groups through their treatment of the dead and their formal arrangements for burial. Numerous examples of the large burial mounds called long barrows are known in Norfolk. These were placed at highly visible locations within the landscape. An example at Broome Heath was part of a larger group of monuments, which also included several round barrows and an earthwork enclosure. Another at West Rudham was a highly impressive monument, measuring approximately 46m long. Other examples have been identified at Harpley and Felthorpe. Most recorded examples are found in east and north-east Norfolk.

Cursus monuments

Seven cursus monuments have been recorded in the county. A cursus is a very long rectangular earthwork which shows as a pair of banks and ditches. It is thought that they were also associated with ritual and may have been ceremonial avenues along which the dead were carried on their way to interment. Examples are widely distributed within Norfolk, being found, for instance, at Langley with Hardley in south Norfolk; Hanworth and Fulmodeston, both in north Norfolk; Beachamwell and Holme Hale, in Breckland; and Tuttington and Rollesby, in Broadland.

SHAPING THE LANDSCAPE

The communications linking the early farming communities included both rivers and a network of trackways. Evidence for wooden tracks built over wet ground has been found in the west of England in the Somerset Levels, where they could stretch for several kilometres. Such evidence remains to be found in Norfolk.

So, man was beginning to shape the landscape around him. As the population grew, the process of finding, settling and exploiting the best land available became more and more important. Pressure was growing on the natural environment and the landscape was undergoing an accelerating process of irreversible change.

Chapter 6
Henge land
3200 — 1800 BC

Then felt I like some watcher of the skies
(John Keats, *On First Looking Into Chapman's Homer*)

New field monuments appeared in the later Neolithic, after 3200 BC, acting as focal points in the landscape and possibly taking over from causewayed enclosures in this respect. These new monuments, known individually as 'henges', were carefully located in the most visible positions. Studies have also shown that their orientations appear to have been constructed in alignment with the heavenly cycles. The understanding of and ability to predict the seasons, as reflected in these monuments, was of great importance to Neolithic farmers for the growing and harvesting of crops. People at this time had already developed a deep understanding of their natural environment but were now learning to control it.

The term 'henge' is an evocative one for British prehistory, recalling our most famous monument: Stonehenge, in Wiltshire. Norfolk had its own henge, located at Arminghall, south of Norwich. Another more recently discovered site at Holme-next-the-Sea, on the north-west coast, has also mistakenly been given this classification. Both of these Norfolk 'henges' will be considered separately in this chapter.

This period also witnessed the earliest signs of the agricultural exhaustion of less resilient soils, which resulted in some of the earliest farmland being returned to grass and scrub.[1] It also saw the abandonment of earlier forms of field monument. The old communal tombs were being sealed up and replaced by a new form of burial construction known as round barrows; these were built on the lightest soils, which were no longer used for cultivation.

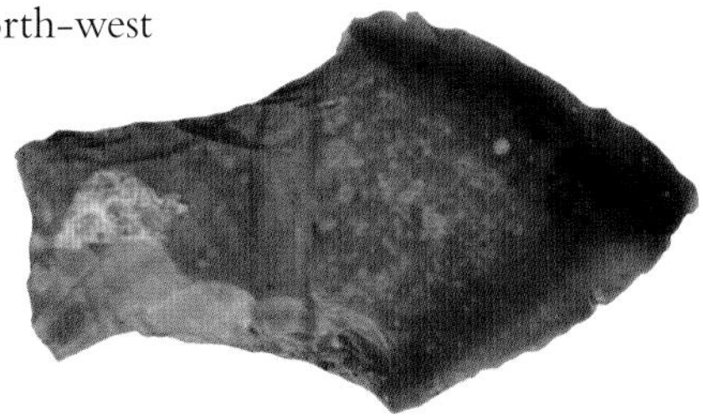

Fig 35: A Bronze Age flint projectile head from Norfolk. Length 83mm.

Another development at this time appears to be indicated by the appearance of flint arrowheads, large numbers of which are found in

Breckland (Fig 35). These finds, predominantly made in south Norfolk, may be some of the earliest evidence we have for warfare.

THE LANDSCAPE AND THE ENVIRONMENT

This chapter covers the period of the later Neolithic and the Early Bronze Age, which saw a rise in sea level. Part of the east coast was covered by the sea, while wide river valleys flowed into the great eastern estuary and marine waters penetrated far inland. Sea levels remained high for a time, before eventually falling again later in the Bronze Age. This was also a period of favourable climate, with conditions warmer and drier than today, and the Norfolk landscape was widely exploited by the developing farming community.

   The abundant rivers provided the quickest and safest method of transport across the area. It is perhaps surprising that boats and canoes of this period have not yet been discovered in Norfolk. Such evidence undoubtedly remains buried beneath the peat, awaiting discovery by future generations.

MONUMENTS IN THE LANDSCAPE

Norfolk is not rich in the major field monuments associated with this period. Although there were many round barrows, they do not appear to have been accompanied by a prolific or widespread building of other large monuments, which are more common further west. Constructions were built from earth, wood and stone. However, sources of stone were scarce in northern East Anglia and so timber was predominantly used here. The construction process continued to provide a focus for communal activity within society.

Henges

Henges clearly played a special role in society. They can be defined as a form of round enclosure consisting of a bank which normally lay beyond an internal ditch. They are generally found in low-lying and non-defensible locations, but are also located in special places of longstanding importance, which may be indicated by the presence of earlier constructions such as long barrows. It has been shown that henges were associated with natural phenomena such as sunrise and sunset at key points in the year. They thus appear to have had a function associated with the tracking of the stars which may have been both practical and ceremonial, possibly being tied in with religious beliefs.

Arminghall henge

The wooden monument at Arminghall in south Norfolk was one of the earliest henges in Britain, dating from about 3200 BC.[2] It was originally discovered by aerial photography and would have been a site of regional significance. In form it was circular, the central area being recorded as 90 feet (27.5m) in diameter, and was entered by a causeway. A ring-ditch 28 feet (8.5m) across surrounded it. The ditch was originally 8 feet (2.5m) deep and was itself surrounded by a bank, beyond which was a shallower outer ditch. In the centre were eight massive oak posts forming a horseshoe shape; each post was two and a half feet (0.8m) in diameter and probably stood over eight feet (2.5m) high.

This monument, itself a highly impressive feature, was part of an extensive ritual and funerary landscape on the edge of the boulder clay plateau. It was constructed at a major river confluence, where the River Tas joins the River Yare, at the headwaters of the system that flowed into the Great Estuary. This was also a focus for one of the largest concentrations of round barrows in the county. The henge was ringed by burial mounds positioned on slopes right across the landscape and clearly visible from the site. This was clearly a special location and was to remain so through the Iron Age and into the Roman era, with successive settlements being constructed at Caistor St Edmund close by.

With regard to the monument's alignment and function, modern computer visualisation shows that Arminghall did have a crucial series of alignments in relation to the local topography. Virtual reconstruction shows that at the midwinter sunset 4000 years ago, the sight-line from the henge would follow the setting sun 'rolling down' the side of the most prominent nearby hill. In addition, the axis of symmetry of the central wooden structure points towards the top of the same hill.[3]

Another half-dozen Norfolk henge monuments have been suggested through analysis of aerial photographs. All are in the east and north-east of the county. Unfortunately, none has yet been investigated through excavation. They include a smaller example at Foxford, Great Witchingham, which has been flattened, and a possible example at Costessey, 4km west of Norwich, at the confluence of the Rivers Wensum and Tud.[4]

Broome Heath

A smaller monumental complex developed around the settlement at Broome Heath. This C-shaped earthwork enclosure was constructed adjacent to the long barrow (Chapter 5) sometime after 2217 BC.[5] The enclosure measured 150m by 105m and consisted of two closely spaced banks with external ditches, which were open to the east. Stake holes indicated that there had been an internal timber revetment. There had also been an inner tower or platform. The precise role of this enclosure remains far from clear.

Fig 36: The Little Cressingham grave group. Length of dagger 204mm *(copyright Norfolk Museums and Archaeology Service)*.

Round barrows

Very few round barrows have been excavated in modern times. The greatest volume of new evidence in recent years has come from aerial photography. Around 1200 examples, or their flattened remains in the form of ring-ditches, are now known from Norfolk. These monuments frequently occur in cemetery groups, such as those at Little Cressingham, Salthouse and Weasenham All Saints, and they are not distributed uniformly across the county.[6] Their distribution shows that they avoided the heavier clay soils of central Norfolk and also the wetter soils. Major concentrations occur in the Breckland and in the north-west. They were frequently sited near to water, especially rivers.

The locations of round barrows within the landscape were carefully chosen. Healy has suggested that many were built within occupied and cultivated landscapes, rather than on the periphery of settlements.[7] Their dates span from 2880–2490 BC (Norwich Southern Bypass) to 1860–1510 BC (Weasenham Lyngs).

Unlike in Wessex, Early Bronze Age burials in Norfolk were only sparsely accompanied by grave goods, although these could include pots, jewellery (jet, amber and gold) and weapons. Wessex-type burials, though rare, are known from Norfolk. One spectacular Wessex-type barrow burial was found at Little Cressingham, near the Icknield Way. This is the most important grave group of this date in East Anglia[8] – indeed, it is the best example from the whole of eastern England (Fig 36). The finds include an amber necklace (Fig 37), a gold plate, three small cylindrical gold boxes and two daggers. Evidence in the form of the snails found during excavation shows that Little Cressingham stood in an open landscape. Some charred barley grains indicate that cultivation was also taking place nearby.

SETTLEMENTS

Settlements of the later Neolithic and Early Bronze Age are, once again, very scarce in Norfolk, as were

Fig 37: Group of Early Bronze Age amber beads from Sustead *(copyright Norfolk Museums and Archaeology Service).*

those of Early Neolithic date. One reason for this is that they are very difficult to identify owing to subsequent occupation and agricultural land use. However, where evidence for occupation has been found, it still points towards more of a seasonal rather than a fully sedentary use of sites at this time. In general, settlements were concentrated in the river valleys and on better-drained soils. The distribution of Late Neolithic pottery differs from that of the earlier Neolithic, extending towards the north coast, with finds coming from Brancaster, Hunstanton, Warham and Runton.[9] There is also an absence of finds from the fen-edge, although material comes from the uplands to the east of it.

Burial monuments tended to be positioned away from settlements and so they are not of significant help in indicating where people lived. Neither do barrows directly indicate the size of the population, the known examples only accounting for the burial of a small proportion of the overall population.

Ceramic assemblages from occupation sites tend to be dominated by Peterborough Ware, Grooved Ware or Beaker ceramics, as at Spong Hill,[10] where evidence for occupation during this period consisted

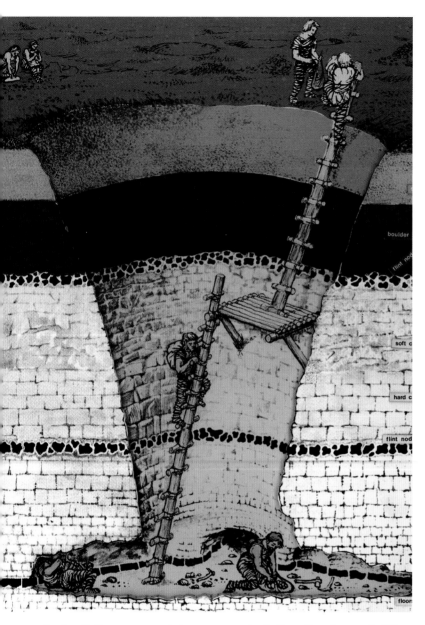

Fig 38: Reconstruction of a flint mine at Grimes Graves *(copyright Norfolk Museums and Archaeology Service)*.

of subsoil features containing pottery, including Peterborough Ware, Grooved Ware, Beaker, Food Vessel, Urn and Collared Urn, together with struck flint. No structures were identified. Burials took place nearby. A round barrow and two ring-ditches are located to the north of the excavated area.

In 1970 road-building at Redgate Hill,[11] to the south of Hunstanton on the north-west coast and adjacent to the Wash, revealed a number of pits. Subsequent excavation uncovered evidence of a Neolithic and Early Bronze Age settlement. A number of the pits contained rich assemblages of Grooved Ware, Collared Urn, Peterborough Ware and Beaker pottery. There were also numerous post-holes, together with a large trapezoidal enclosure and a circular hut of Early Bronze Age date.

A site of the Neolithic and Early Bronze Age period is known at Edingthorpe in north-east Norfolk, approximately a mile north-east of North Walsham. Finds have been discovered from there over many years and discoveries of Bronze Age urns were noted as long ago as the early 19th century. In 1948 large numbers of hearths were disturbed by ploughing and quantities of Neolithic, Beaker and Bronze Age pottery were found. A significant assemblage of over 600 worked flints, which included a polished flint axe, was also recovered. Trial excavation in 1948 revealed pits, but post-hole structures were not located. Other finds of the same date range have continued to come from the site.

GRIMES GRAVES

This period saw the working of flint mines in East Anglia. Grimes Graves, located in the Breckland at Weeting, south-west Norfolk, is the largest Neolithic flint mine in Europe. The site covers 37ha and some 360 shafts were sunk up to 15m deep into the ground.[12] Today, individual shafts still show as shallow depressions across the heathland, creating a pock-marked landscape which can best be appreciated via aerial photography. Nearly 100 radiocarbon dates show that the deep galleries were worked for around 500 years, from 2675 BC until about 2200 BC.[13] It has been calculated that, from a single excavated shaft, 45 tonnes of flint would have been removed by up to 20 miners, a task taking up to 100 days. Some of the shallower open-cast quarries were worked until about 1975 BC. It is possible that there was a specialist mining community living and working at Grimes Graves.

The miners used ladders to climb down to dig the flint. Their shallow galleries, which followed the flint seams, were dug outwards from the central shafts (Fig 38). Their tools included rakes, which were made from antler, while other tools were made of wood and basketry. Picks, also made from red deer antler, were used to excavate the flint blocks, which were carried to the surface and then taken away for finishing. The working floors have been located on the surface right across the area. The use of naturally shed antlers implies a careful management of the red deer herds in the vicinity; the excavators calculated that it would have needed approximately 120 red deer to supply enough antlers to excavate one or two pits each year.

A particularly special discovery was made at the base of one of the shafts. A pedestal of chalk blocks had been constructed, upon which a small chalk figurine of a large female figure, which may be associated with a 'mother goddess', was located. On the floor next to the figure was a chalk carving of a phallus. Opposite the figurine was a chalk cup, set upon a pile of flint and next to seven antler picks. This carefully structured arrangement may be some of our earliest evidence for religious behaviour in Neolithic Britain.

Other flint mining sites are known in Norfolk but are much smaller in scale. Individual sites are located in two areas: the chalk ridge of west Norfolk and the river valleys of east Norfolk.[14]

BEAKERS AND THE FIRST USE OF METAL

Around 2700 BC new ideas and materials, including the first use of metal, began to appear in Britain. A range of gold, copper and bronze objects were introduced, together with the knowledge of how to work these metals. The introduction of metalworking technology was accompanied by the appearance of a new elaborate style of pottery, known as Beakers (Fig 39). These were highly decorated fine earthenware drinking vessels. Distinctively orangey in colour, they were tall and open-mouthed, with narrowed necks, and were inscribed with lines and geometric motifs. Beakers are found in burials and on domestic settlements.

The arrival of Beakers is no longer associated with a wholesale invasion of people from the continent. However, it does appear that some people did enter Britain from mainland Europe at that time, bringing with them another new introduction, an additional and important domesticated species. It was at the time of the Beaker phenomenon that horses were introduced to this country.

Beaker settlements

Many sites associated with the Beaker period survive in Norfolk as spreads of artefacts and rubbish, although they lack archaeological features cut into the ground.[15] Such sites occur at Forncett, Heacham, Weasenham and Reffley Wood, King's Lynn. The last two mentioned sites survived as spreads of rubbish beneath round barrows. A concentration of Beaker period sites is known on the fen-edge;[16] Frances Healy describes this area as a focus of population and wealth.[17] Most of the sites are again known from rubbish scatters and the nature of occupation appears to have been seasonal. In general, the evidence suggests that groups tended to use and reoccupy the same sites at this time. However, the population was still steadily increasing.

The new technology

Metalworking was a considerable development over flint technology. It involved a process of smelting and casting metal in preshaped moulds. Objects of copper and bronze (an alloy of copper and tin) were first introduced to Norfolk around 2700 BC. The sources of the

metal ores used were outside Norfolk. Early Bronze Age metalwork is well represented in general terms in Norfolk. Of the early forms of implement, a riveted dagger was found at Barton Bendish and a spiral-headed pin was found at East Dereham. Metal objects, including daggers, flat axes, pins and awls, were all made using relatively simple casting techniques. Given the relatively low level of settlement and burial evidence, this provides the best evidence we have for Bronze Age life in Norfolk. The findspots appear to confirm that the eastern edge of the Fens was a major regional concentration of settlement and metalworking.

Fig 39: Beakers found in Norfolk. Scale 1:4 *(copyright Norfolk Museums and Archaeology Service).*

SEAHENGE

Early in 1998 Mr John Lorimer was walking on the beach at Holme dunes when he made the startling discovery of a large inverted tree trunk sticking up above the sand.[18] As he scanned the area more closely he came upon a bronze axehead nearby, which he recognised as being Bronze Age in date. Mr Lorimer took the axehead to Norwich Castle Museum Archaeology Department, where a date of c 1600–1400 BC was assigned to the object.[19] He returned to the beach and drew attention to other timbers which formed an oval enclosure around the central tree trunk.

As knowledge of this intriguing site became more widely disseminated, it quickly acquired the popular name of 'Seahenge'.[20] However, it was soon appreciated that it was not a henge monument but was in fact something much more unusual. Excavation by the Norfolk Archaeological Unit showed that the site comprised an oval arrangement of oak posts surrounding the upside-down central oak. There were 56 posts in the oval enclosure; these had been split in half and their split surfaces faced inwards, creating a flat inner wall. The central oak was dated by dendrochronology and was shown to have been felled in 2050 BC, with other sampled timbers yielding dates in 2049 BC.

It has been calculated that no fewer than 51 axes were used during the felling and dressing of the timbers.[21] As is seen elsewhere in Bronze Age Britain, the construction of this site would have been a significant communal undertaking. Francis Pryor suggests that perhaps 200 people might have been involved.

Although discovered on what is now the north Norfolk beach, 'Seahenge' was originally constructed at a low-lying inland location. It had a single entrance which faced south-west, aligned towards the midwinter sunset, and may have been a mortuary structure, where a dead body would have been exposed. Alternatively, it could have served as a shrine. Pryor has associated it with a symbolic significance of trees and woodland and suggests that the construction points to a belief in another dimension – a world located below the ground.[22] Perhaps this construction was considered a way of connecting with the underworld.

The Norfolk 'Seahenge' is certainly an unusual monument in national terms and appears to be a regional form of Bronze Age monument. It is difficult to interpret this construction in isolation and originally it may have been strategically situated within a wider ritual landscape. Future discoveries in the area may provide more clues towards its original function.

THE DEVELOPMENT OF A SACRED LANDSCAPE

The period considered in this chapter shows a developing relationship between man and his natural surroundings, whereby monuments were constructed at special places in the landscape and specific places were venerated. Today, archaeologists are finding that artefacts were also being placed as offerings at such locations. This process becomes particularly evident with the first use of metals, and continues through later periods. Deposits of Bronze Age weapons and metalwork hoards have long been associated with watery places, indicating a ritual nature to the deposition. Some special forms of object were being produced specifically for the purpose of ritual deposition. In this way, people were returning selected precious materials, in the form of manufactured tools and weapons, back to nature – from where the raw materials had originally come.

The significance of water in this process has a particular resonance for Norfolk, where the landscape was dominated by sea and rivers. Special places can be detected across the landscape through the location of special objects, buried hoards and the locations of field monuments. The headwaters of the Great Estuary in the east of the area is one such special place, the significance of which was to continue for many years to come.

Chapter 7
An empty land
1800 – 700 BC

WHERE WERE THE PEOPLE?

Perhaps the greatest puzzle of prehistoric Norfolk is the question: just where were the people during the Middle–Late Bronze Age?[1] So far, archaeologists have been able to identify very few settlement sites for the period between 1800 and 700 BC.[2] The decline in identified sites is a national trend but it is more pronounced in Norfolk than elsewhere. Not only does evidence for occupation virtually cease but, even more problematically, pottery of this date is not found either;   it was still being manufactured but is relatively indistinct in appearance and tends to be friable, meaning that it is seldom intact and not well recognised and datable even when it does survive. Neither have we been able to locate enclosures or land divisions that definitely belong to this period. So far we have not been able to recognise this society's mark on the landscape of Norfolk to any significant extent.

Could it really be the case that Norfolk was depopulated at this time, perhaps resulting from an event such as a great plague? The answer to this question seems to be no: another form of evidence, in the form of metalwork, indicates that this was not the case. Indeed, the great quantity and general distribution of bronze objects that have been recovered from the plough zone across the county serve to show that people definitely must have been present – and in large numbers. In fact, the quantity, quality and variety of Bronze Age metal objects from Norfolk is unsurpassed elsewhere in Britain. This body of evidence alone shows not only that there must have been a sizeable population, but also that they were wealthy in material terms. The overall distribution of bronze objects is concentrated very largely towards the west of the county and, specifically, towards the fen-edge. It is likely that this pattern also reflects, to a large extent, the distribution of population at the time. However, if not for this metalwork, it would appear to us today that there may have been a mass migration from the Norfolk area.

RECONSTRUCTING LATE BRONZE AGE LIFE IN NORFOLK

Evidence from elsewhere in Britain, particularly from Wessex and the Thames valley, helps to compensate for the paucity of Norfolk's archaeology and provides a fuller context for local discoveries. Once again, this period saw major changes across Britain.

The construction of the great ritual monuments ceased and there is very little evidence for burials. However, there is increasing evidence in many places for the exploitation of the agricultural landscape and the creation of divisions within the countryside. Considerable areas of woodland were now being cleared. This process accelerated in the later Bronze Age as food production became more important in the light of an expanding population and began to be controlled.

This was also a period of major environmental change. The climate once again deteriorated somewhat towards the end of the Bronze Age, with an overall trend towards colder and wetter conditions.

LATE BRONZE AGE SOCIETY

There were some clear developments in society at this time which are demonstrated through the types of artefact made. Elaborate body armour, long slashing swords and spears appear, indicating that warfare was taking place. In general, there was a more diverse and specialised material culture, which can be associated with the growing importance of show and prestige in society. Individual finds indicate that society's elite demonstrated their status and power through their rich and distinctive appearance. At the same time it must be remembered that the basis for everyday life was still agriculture. This was basically still a simple and industrious farming community.

TRANSPORT

People in this period moved freely about the landscape, developing long-distance transport routes. This was also the time when animals began to be used for traction and transport. In Norfolk, river transport was still of major importance. It is perhaps surprising that no boats of this date have yet been recovered from archaeological deposits in the county. Later Bronze Age boats of quite sophisticated construction have been discovered on the banks of the River Humber at North Ferriby and, more recently, in 1992, at Dover. The discovery of similar vessels in the riverine deposits of east Norfolk must surely be just a matter of time.

SETTLEMENT EVIDENCE

Despite the fragile nature of the material evidence for this period, glimpses of settlements are now beginning to occur, although the absence of firm dating is often an additional problem. Some good evidence comes from the upper fillings at Grimes Graves, where signs of settlement were preserved in secondary contexts in the flint mine shafts.[3] Other settlement evidence comes from the fen-edge, within a landscape that has shown continuity of use through from earlier prehistoric periods. One of our best-known examples is a site at Methwold.

Methwold

During the Middle Bronze Age conditions changed. The sea level, which had risen in the later Neolithic and Early Bronze Age, did not fall again until later in the Bronze Age. The southern Fenland was generally less favoured for settlement at this time, but some populations did visit the area. A remarkable collection of Middle Bronze Age metalwork items have been recovered from a site at Methwold, in the south-eastern Fenland. In 1996, following a deep ploughing of the area, Derek Woollestone undertook a metal-detector survey of the southern extent of the parish. An initial discovery of diagnostic metalwork items indicated that a significant site had been disturbed by the agricultural activity. Derek organised an excavation of the area, in collaboration with the Norfolk Archaeological Unit, later that year.

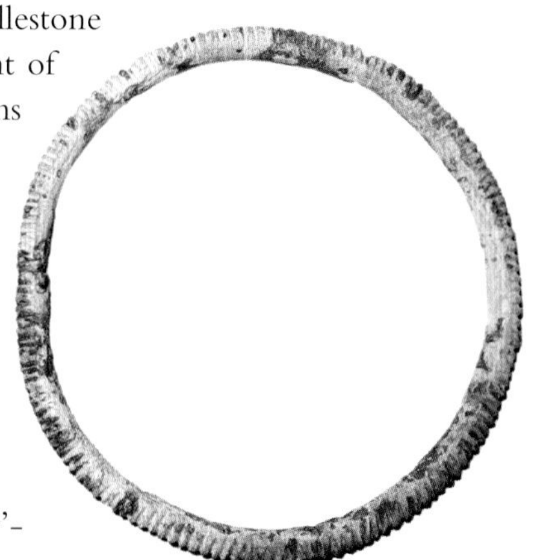

The metalwork from Methwold belongs to the earlier part of the Middle Bronze Age, between c 1500–1300 BC. The finds include a range of dress items, ceremonial pieces, weapons and functional tools. Bronze bracelets and a very rare amber-headed decorated 'Picardy'-type dress pin were present (Figs 40 and 41). There was also an unusual bronze ceremonial dirk. The weapons included a beautiful slender bronze rapier. Numerous sherds of Bronze Age pottery were also recovered during the excavation.

Fig 40: Bronze bracelets from Methwold. Diameter of bottom example 62mm.

Other non-metalwork finds from Methwold included fragments of human bone, with skull, femur and rib fragments all present. Faunal remains included red and roe deer and beaver; domesticated species included cow, sheep and an early occurrence of horse. The excavation did not identify any archaeological features, although patches of burnt flint were recorded. The Middle Bronze Age material was found to be associated with a woody peat layer, which may indicate that the site was within a wooded environment. It was situated at the interface between the wetland and upland zones, a location that would have been covered with trees.

The concentration of metalwork at this wetland-edge location is consistent with the more general correlation between the deposition of weapons in wet places, such as rivers and bogs. The collection of Middle Bronze Age dirks and rapiers from the whole of the south-eastern Fenland is substantial and is exceeded only by the number recorded from the Thames.

Moving further east, a radiocarbon-dated pollen sequence from Scole provides evidence for significant woodland clearance in the area. This previously wooded region was transformed into an open landscape at that time.

It can be seen that our archaeological evidence for the period is far from being balanced. One possible reason why the occupation sites are so difficult to identify might be that the settlements were largely seasonal and temporary in use and were still flimsily constructed. The evidence for any obvious shift to static settlements is still lacking at this time. It would appear likely that the population of the area still contained a significantly nomadic element.

RITUAL BEHAVIOUR

Many Bronze Age objects are found in isolation, without any archaeological association or context. However, this period also saw a growing practice of special deposition of material for ritual purposes, in special places. Some of these places were associated with boundary ditches or storage pits. However, an important location for depositing such material was in watery places such as rivers, lakes and bogs.[4]

Ritual deposits account for the findspots of many individual Bronze items. Hoards of bronze items are also found in such contexts. It may be considered that the vast majority of Bronze Age artefact finds from Norfolk are the result of deliberate deposition, where there was no intention of recovery.[5]

Fig 41: Head of an amber-headed 'Picardy'-type dress pin from Methwold. Length 96mm.

BURIALS

A rare Wessex-type barrow burial was discovered at Harford Farm, to the south of Norwich. This burial contained faience beads, which indicate a date of no earlier than c 1300 BC.[6] A group of 30 small round barrows in the midst of the larger Salthouse Heath barrow cemetery may also date to this period.[7]

However, it was during the later Bronze Age that earthen barrows ceased to be built. Most evidence for burial at this time from Norfolk has been in the form of pottery urns in unmarked cemeteries. Bucket urns of this date have been found inserted into earlier round barrows at Salthouse and on the Norwich Southern Bypass.[8]

THE METALWORK

It is the metalwork, as indicated above, that provides the most profitable source of information for this period in Norfolk.[9] New forms of metalwork appear in the Middle Bronze Age. These include palstaves, rapiers and socketed and looped spearheads. This was a period of experimentation and innovation in metalworking. The palstave was the most common form of axe in southern England. It carried a loop on one side, which secured the axe to its haft. The repertoire of the metalworkers and the complexity of the objects increased as the practice of adding lead to the bronze was introduced and the casting quality of the bronze was improved.

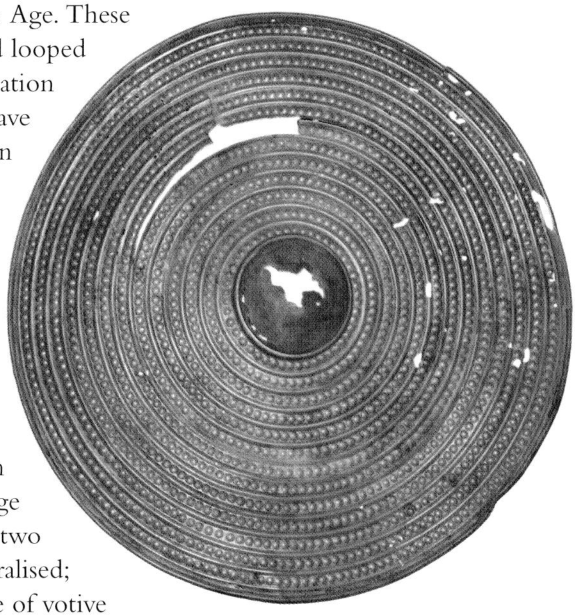

Bronzes are most commonly found in the west of Norfolk.[10] The concentration of bronze objects on the eastern fen-edge in the south-west of the county suggests two things: firstly, that production was centralised; and, secondly, that there was a high degree of votive activity in this watery area. Finds show that nearly two-thirds of products made in this centre were tools and the rest were mainly weapons. There was also a very small number of ornaments.[11]

Fig 42: The bronze shield from Sutton, decorated with 13 concentric ribs and circles of small bosses. Diameter 547mm.

In 1990 an item from a well-known class of Middle Bronze Age weapon known as dirks was discovered in peat at Oxborough in west Norfolk. Dirks were stabbing weapons, made of bronze and fitted with handles which were secured in place by metal rivets. The difference in the Oxborough dirk was its massive size. Neither did it have rivet holes nor sharpened edges. This item had not been made for practical use; it was intended for ceremonial use and had been deposited in water for this purpose. The Oxborough example matches a small number of examples known from Holland and France, similarly thought to have been ceremonial weapons and known as the Plougrescant-Ommerschans type. They can be dated to about 1500–1300 BC.

More elaborate items of the Late Bronze Age include a magnificent decorated shield from Sutton, which was made of beaten sheet bronze (Fig 42). There were also leaf-shaped swords. Other weapon finds include daggers and rapiers, which are commonly found in the Fenland. An example of the latter, an elegant and well-preserved bronze rapier 27cm in length, was discovered in 1994, on the beach at Sea Palling, between Winterton and Eccles on the north-east coast. It was buried just below the surface within a part of the beach only visible at low tide, and was embedded within layers of peat and clay. Swords are less common in Norfolk. They tend to be found as fragments and most commonly in hoards, as at Weston Longville and South Creake (see the Waterden hoard, below).

Contact with the continent

There were clearly close links between East Anglia and the European mainland during the Bronze Age. In particular, there was a connection with the Rhineland.[12] Evidence for this once again comes in the form of the metalwork finds. Some of the very earliest Bronze Age metalworking styles betray continental influences,[13] while some East Anglian forms of palstaves are known to have been exported, having been found in north German hoards.[14] A recent find in Norfolk has provided important new evidence. A group of four bronze axes were discovered by metal detector in Deopham, near Wymondham, in April 1997 (Fig 43). All are 'flanged' axes dating from around 1600 BC. The fourth example was unusually large. At 240mm, it measured twice the length of the other, typically British, examples and had a strange notch in its blade. This very unusual find was identified at Norwich Castle Museum as a continental form of axe, and was found to come from Langquaid in Germany.[15] Its presence confirms the presence of links between Norfolk and that region of Europe at this time.

Metalwork hoards

Around the 8th century BC there was a rise in the level of metalwork production. The range of metalwork types expanded once more. Hoards are associated with the Middle and Late periods, and over 50 were buried in Norfolk. Late Bronze Age hoards are found right across Norfolk, distributed from the fen-edge in the west to the shores of the

Fig 43: The Hackford (Deopham) hoard, comprising four bronze axes. Length of bottom axe 240mm.

Fig 44: A group of socketed axes from the Gorleston founder's hoard.

Great Estuary in the east. They are spread evenly across the countryside but tend to have been buried close to rivers (although not actually in them). They appear to have been deposited at a regular frequency across the landscape, at locations where we might expect settlements to have been located. In the absence of settlement evidence for the period, these hoards may be a pointer to where the settlements were. The contents of the Late Bronze Age examples indicate that the area was closely linked with south-east England at the time. Some of the more important hoards will be considered below.

Waterden

The Waterden hoard found at South Creake is one of the largest of its kind from the county. A small deposit was originally located there in 1952. Forty years later, between 1992 and 1994, a combination of metal-detector survey and excavation at a location close by recovered a further 180 pieces. All were fragments from leaf-shaped swords and socketed spearheads. Subsequent study has produced several cross-joins of these fragments, linking the separately buried deposits.

Gorleston

One of the largest hoards of Late Bronze Age weapons and axes found in the region was discovered in the grounds of Peterhouse Junior School

Fig 45: The bronze cauldron from Feltwell Fen. Rim diameter 590mm *(copyright Norfolk Museums and Archaeology Service).*

at Gorleston in 1952,[16] when a sewer trench was dug next to the school. The new hole clipped the edge of an ancient pit, which contained 111 bronze objects. As well as axes, the hoard contained spearheads, swords, a single chisel and a rare looped guide-ring. It is known as a 'founder's hoard' and had been buried in about 800 BC (Fig 44). So-called 'founder's hoards' are commonly discovered across Britain and all contain broken objects which could be used for melting down and reworking into new items by itinerant metal smiths.

Excavation showed that the Gorleston hoard had been intentionally buried: it had been contained within a leather bag and buried in a wet place. This may have been a ritual offering. Other founder's hoards across Britain sometimes show signs of having been deposited in a ritual way. No settlement has been located in the vicinity of the hoard.

Eaton, Norwich

At Eaton in south-west Norwich, a concentration of Late Bronze Age founder's hoards that were buried within a restricted area have revealed a place which clearly had great significance at that time. Two hoards were initially recorded at Eaton, while a third was subsequently discovered barely one mile further east, on the city's Unthank Road.[17] In April 2005, Dr Tim Pestell of Norwich Castle Museum was called out to participate in the recovery of a fourth deposit from the vicinity, which turned out to be the largest Bronze Age hoard yet recovered from the county, comprising almost 150 individual pieces. This third Eaton hoard had been buried in a pit lying just above the flood plain of the River Yare.

Feasting

Another form of metalwork provides a very different insight into social behaviour. Cauldrons and flesh-hooks, which represent material evidence for feasting, are found at a number of places across northern Europe as well as in Britain. The ritualised preparation of meat and drink appears to have remained an important social activity. In particular, feasts can be associated with religious ceremonies and other significant events, such as funerals.

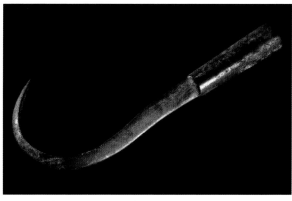

Fig 46: The Feltwell flesh hook. Length 180mm *(copyright Norfolk Museums and Archaeology Service).*

A Late Bronze Age cauldron, which dates from the 12th or 11th century BC, was discovered in Norfolk at Feltwell Fen (Fig 45). It is one of only two such vessels, which are known as the Colchester type, and was made from three sheets of metal fastened together by metal rivets. It has distinctive handle fittings and forms three quarters of a sphere. It could have originally carried an amazing 60 or 70 litres of liquid. The method of construction suggests a continental influence, again reflecting the wide-scale contacts linking distant parts of Europe at this time. This form of manufacture was not used after the start of the

Fig 47: The Carleton Rode hoard. Scale 1:4.

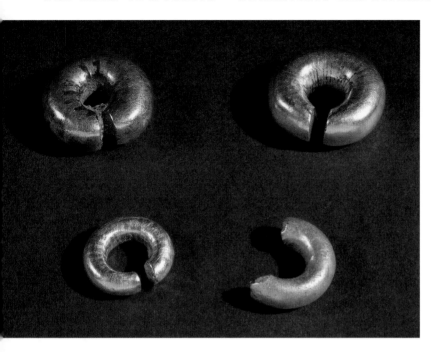

Fig 48: Examples of 'ring money' in the collection at Norwich Castle Museum. Scale 1:2 also see Fig 51 *(copyright Norfolk Museums and Archaeology Service).*

first millennium BC. A flesh-hook, which was used to pull meat from the cauldron, was also found at Feltwell (Fig 46). It had a single prong and wooden haft. Flesh-hooks are rare finds but another was present in the first Eaton hoard (see above).

Evidence for bronze tool production

The discovery of bronze moulds that were used for the production of metalwork items is a rare occurrence. One such example, a particularly unusual axe mould, was found within a small Late Bronze Age hoard from Hevingham. This mould is distinctive through having ribbed decoration on one half of the mould only. Only one other such asymmetrical mould has been recorded, from Southall in Middlesex.[18] Two axes are known which have decoration on one side only; one is from Croydon in Surrey and the other from Carleton Rode in Norfolk (Fig 47).

Late Bronze Age gold rings from Norfolk and personal adornment in the Late Bronze Age

Our modern-day taste for personal adornment goes back thousands of years. Evidence for the wearing of personal decoration can be found from as early as the Bronze Age in Norfolk. Status in Bronze Age society can be linked with the possession of rare, beautiful and valuable items of jewellery. This trait might have also been the case in earlier societies, through the wearing of non-metal items that have not survived or been recognised. Even in these early societies, individuals achieved standing within groups, receiving respect, deference and privileged treatment from others. Such status could be identified through the possession and showing-off of material items. The value and variety of prestige goods increased in relation to the complexity of social ranking.

A small gold ring was discovered by the Norfolk Archaeological Unit at Scratby, north of Caister-on-Sea and close to the coast of north-east Norfolk, during the construction of the Bacton–Yarmouth pipeline in 1999. It is just 1.45cm in diameter and is penannular, with a gap between the plain flat terminals. Despite its tiny size, it has been beautifully fashioned, with whitish, silver-rich, gold wire spiralling around a gold ring, forming a banded appearance. Small penannular gold rings of this type used to be extremely rare but in recent years they have become much better known as a result of metal-detector use. Some examples are banded, like the Scratby example, while others are plain gold. A broadly Late Bronze Age date is now generally agreed for them. Just six others have been recorded from Norfolk, with most coming from the south and west of the county: three come from Breckland, two from west Norfolk and one from near Aylsham in the east. Of these, five have been found since 1995.

These small rings used to be referred to as 'ring money' because it used to be thought that they were an early form of currency (Fig 48).[19] Today, they are seen more as a form of personal adornment, although

Fig 49: Group of seven Bronze Age gold bracelets discovered at Foxley in 2006. Diameters 57 to 68mm, also see Fig 51 *(copyright Norfolk Museums and Archaeology Service).*

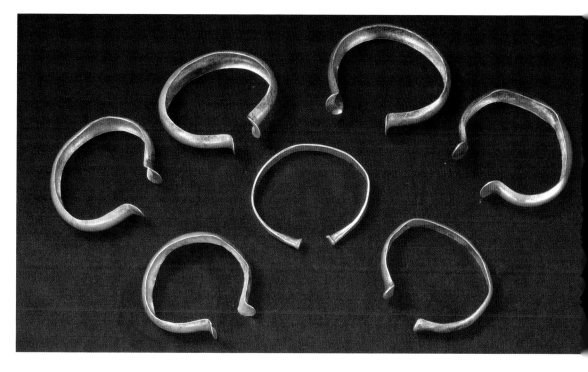

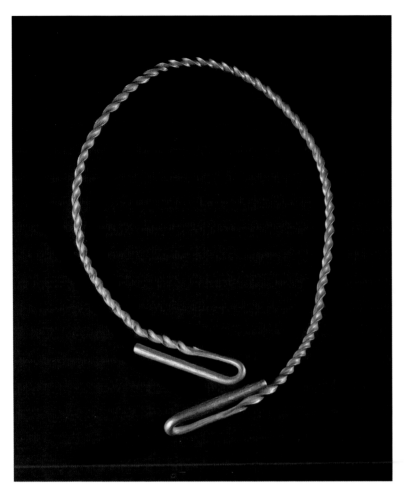

Fig 50: Gold torc with left–handed twist and elaborate recurved terminals from Foulsham. Maximun diameter 350mm *(copyright Norfolk Museums and Archaeology Service).*

it is not clear how they would have been worn to adorn their owners. Suggestions perhaps reflect contemporary trends and fashions.[20] Could they have been worn as nose rings? The gap could have served to allow the ring to be pushed over the septum of the nose. They could also have been worn on other parts of the body, such as the ears. Another possibility is that they were strung onto braided hair as tress rings. These items would have belonged to important individuals. It may be no coincidence that the banded form resembles the shape and appearance of the later Iron Age torcs, which were also a form of dress associated with status.

Other types of gold jewellery were used in the Late Bronze Age and examples have been found elsewhere in Norfolk. A hoard of four plain penannular gold bracelets was found near to Scratby, at Caister-on-Sea. Although much larger and not banded, these were of similar shape to the smaller rings. Other bracelets have come from Methwold and Sporle. Most recently, in 2006, a spectacular new discovery was made by metal-

Fig 51: Bronze Age persons wearing gold jewellery by Andy Pritchett for Uglystudios.com.

detector when a magnificent group of seven gold penannular bracelets was found at Foxley (Fig 49); this has been acquired by Norwich Castle Museum through the Treasure process. A superb Bronze Age gold torc was found at Foulsham (Fig 50), while other early examples of torcs have been found at Stoke Ferry and Sporle. Amber beads were recovered in a burial at Little Cressingham and decorative pins of quoit-headed form were found at Boughton Fen and Pentney.

All together, this jewellery shows that there was great wealth in Norfolk during the Late Bronze Age. In this period gold was worked and traded separately from bronze; gold objects are not found in bronze hoards and it is thought that much of the gold found in East Anglia is of Irish origin. The items in question, therefore, would have belonged to exceptional individuals within society (Fig 51). These people may have been those who owed their status to the control of the trade in metal between Norfolk and other parts of Britain and Europe at that time.

Chapter 8

The rise of chiefdoms
700 – 80 BC

It is difficult to give a precise date for the start of the age of iron. The transition from the world of bronze into the period known as the Iron Age was a gradual one (Figs 52 and 53). Indeed, it is difficult to detect a clear separation from the preceding Bronze Age anywhere in the archaeological record. However, some significant developments can be detected within society from the time when iron was first adopted.

The Iron Age in Norfolk is considered to have lasted longer than elsewhere in Britain. The conventional date for the end of the period is normally taken to be when the Romans invaded the country in AD 43. However, in Norfolk, the date is extended for a further eighteen years, until the defeat and death of Boudica in AD 61. The next two chapters will concentrate on the Iron Age in Norfolk. In this chapter we shall set the scene, charting developments in society from the first use of iron to the period when the Roman world began to have a significant influence on this country.

Fig 52: A Bronze Age socketed axe from Norfolk. Length 69mm.

THE TRANSITION FROM THE BRONZE AGE

A complex social structure had become established during the Bronze Age. Power had grown through the control of long-distance trade networks which had ensured the provision of the raw materials used to make bronze. Then, as ironworking was adopted, this system fragmented. As the supply and production of metalwork became easier, the basis for the organisation of society changed.

As the Iron Age progressed, society became organised into chiefdoms and tribes. These groupings fluctuated in size and composition over time

and were associated with territories. At the
same time we can also detect an increase
in warfare, which was to play a significant
role in social relations. Fighting seems to
have been common practice within and
between tribal societies.

Settlements went on to become
more self-sufficient. In the preceding
period, specialist activities like textile
production had not been widespread, but
had been confined to specific places. Then,
as more settlements adopted the use of iron
and produced their own metalwork, they also began to develop other
subsistence activities. A more uniform subsistence lifestyle developed
across the countryside which depended on an agricultural regime based
on intensive mixed farming.

Fig 53: A later socketed
axe of Bronze Age form
from Norfolk, made of
iron. Length 105mm.

Then, around 400 BC, the previously close relations with the
continent appear to have lapsed and European artefacts were no longer
being brought into Britain. It was at this stage that developed hillforts
dominated the landscape in parts of the country. There was also an
appreciable growth in the number of settlements and population
pressure began to develop on the better agricultural land.

By about the 2nd century BC increased economic specialisation can
clearly be seen in the archaeological record once again. Special items,
such as glass and beads, were made at some places and not others. Salt
was produced at coastal sites. Some chalkland sites specialised in different
types of cereals. A system of weights was developed and artefacts were
produced for exchange. It is at this stage that we have evidence for
increasing conflict within society.

CLIMATE AND THE LANDSCAPE

Substantial woodland clearance was underway in most places by the
beginning of the Iron Age. By the end of the period, the landscape
had become intensively farmed and management of the land became
more important. Tree species that had not coped with the practice of
coppicing, such as pine, disappeared. As the area of remaining woodland
became smaller, woods became islands within a sea of farmland.
Investigation of the area around Scole has shown that the landscape in
the south of Norfolk had been cleared of most of its woodland by the
Early Iron Age. Herb-rich grassland steadily took its place.

Heath vegetation spread as the period progressed, notably on the
sandy soils of west Norfolk but especially in the Breckland. These
southern heathlands would have provided grazing for sheep and horses.

The extensive central claylands became more fully exploited during the Middle Iron Age but were not fully occupied until the Late Iron Age.

There was a major marine transgression from c 250 BC, which lasted through to the end of the Roman period. Sea level rose to 1.5m above that of the present day. By the time of the Roman invasion, rivers had swelled and a wide estuary dominated the eastern approach to Norfolk. The network of rivers provided natural routeways, sources of food and a greater range of natural resources to exploit. Watery places, together with the extensive coastline, gave this region a distinct identity. Special places, often associated with water, which acted as a focus for the ritual deposition of artefacts continue to be identified in the Norfolk landscape. The rivers and estuaries also facilitated contact with peoples further afield, both in Britain and across the North Sea.

The Fenland became much wetter at this time. The maritime incursion reached into the central Fenland and the coastline lay south of its current position, running approximately from Wisbech (Cambridgeshire) to Downham Market. The southern Fens comprised freshwater wetland, which contained some dry land on islands and promontories. Sea level dropped during the 1st century AD and the northern part of the Fens began to dry out.

The watery features of the Fens and River Waveney which today form the boundaries of Norfolk might indeed have formed more imposing physical barriers at this time. It is possible that the peoples who inhabited the region respected these features as tribal boundaries, for at least part of this period.

By the Late Iron Age much of Britain had an organised landscape of farmsteads, ditched field systems and managed woodland which was able to support the steadily increasing population. Agricultural divisions of this date have been recognised in parts of the Norfolk landscape.[1] For example, co-axial field systems have been identified in the south in the Scole–Dickleborough region of the central Waveney valley, where the principal features have been seen to pre-date the Roman Pye Road. Several other areas on the clayland are thought to carry similar systems, including the areas around the Hales and Loddon parishes of south-east Norfolk[2] and around Wells on the north coast. These field systems belong to the period of settlement expansion and are largely restricted to the heavier soils, which were in the main devoid of settlement before the Late Iron Age.

DAILY LIFE

The Iron Age agricultural system in Britain was a culmination of 3500 years of experience and development. By this time people had developed a well-balanced relationship with their environment which

involved an intensive agricultural regime alongside the exploitation of all natural resources within the landscape. However, people did not over-exploit the resources available to them.

The population lived in small basic farmsteads which were spread across the landscape possibly as frequently as every kilometre. Ditches, field systems and stock enclosures associated with the farmsteads can all be detected from aerial photography. Proximity to water sources was important in order to maintain herds. Agricultural technology was simple. The ground was broken with an ox-drawn plough, an implement that was improved during the Iron Age by the addition of an iron shoe or point to the plough, known as an ard, which enabled farmers to work the heavier soils. Crops were sown and also reaped, using a sickle, by hand.

Crops were stored both in sealed pits in the ground and in above-ground granaries. The most popular crops grown were spelt wheat and six-row barley. The animal species that were exploited are evidenced on sites by their bones. A wide range of domestic and wild animals is encountered, including cattle, horse, sheep, goat, pig, dog, cat, red and roe deer.

Other natural resources were exploited for daily needs. Wood was the most important raw material, being the basic building material for houses, fences, storage structures and tools. Reed and straw were needed for thatch and basket making. Animal hides were used for

Fig 54: Two Late Iron Age dress toggles from Cranwich. Length 17mm and 28mm *(copyright Norfolk Museums and Archaeology Service)*

leather working. Of course, these materials very seldom survive on archaeological sites.

DRESS

We know rather more about the dress from this period than we do about that from earlier times.[3] Men of the Iron Age generally wore long-sleeved shirts and tunics with long trousers. The women would wear long skirts. Ancient descriptions tell that their dress was colourful. Clothes, some of which were embroidered, were made from wool and linen. Cloaks were also worn, especially during winter.

Buttons were unknown at this time (Fig 54). People used belts and pins to hold their clothes together (Fig 55). Brooches were first used in the 5th century BC. Examples made of iron or bronze were used to fasten the cloak at the shoulder. A number of brooches of Middle Iron Age date have been found in Norfolk. Although not common, these La Tène-style forms have been found at Caistor St Edmund, Wicklewood, Gayton, Beachamwell, Hockering and Narborough.

TECHNOLOGY IN THE IRON AGE

The production of bronze was not completely replaced by that of iron. Although iron had the advantage of providing stronger edges for bladed weapons and tools, bronze working continued for the production of fine items. In particular, a large number of ornately decorated fittings and items of personal adornment continued to be made in bronze. Craftsmen of the period were capable of producing metalwork of great beauty, comparable to anything produced today.

It was not just bronze technology that continued into the world of iron. More surprisingly, the use of flint has also now been recognised as lasting well into the Iron Age at some sites. Flintworking was discovered at London Road, Thetford, in association with Middle Iron Age pottery,[4] and was subsequently recognised at the Middle Iron Age site at Park Farm, Wymondham.[5] This phenomenon has now been noted elsewhere in the area, as at Warborough Hill, Stiffkey[6] and Micklemoor Hill, West Harling.[7] It has also been found further south, in Essex.[8] Iron Age flintworking has not, as yet, been recognised generally across Britain and could have been a feature of the Iron Age in East Anglia.

EARLY IRON AGE SITES

It is only by the Iron Age that the first convincing evidence for widespread sedentary settlement is at last found across Norfolk. This lifestyle steadily took hold during the Early and Middle Iron Age and the population became less nomadic as the period progressed. Other

Fig 55: A ring-headed-type pin, from Norfolk. Scale 3:1

manifestations of stability eventually appeared, in the form of land boundaries and field systems, which belong to the Late Iron Age.

Iron Age populations thrived in the far east and far west of the county. Andrew Rogerson has revealed an intensity of settlement and land use in the parish of Barton Bendish, near the northern edge of Breckland in the south-west.[9] Broadland, in the far east, provided a rich watery environment. Iron Age communities made extensive use of wetlands for fishing, wildfowling, seasonal grazing and the exploitation of various plant materials. Although they exploited these landscapes they left them essentially unmodified.

Evidence for an Early Iron Age settlement comes from Cauldron Field, Feltwell, where in 1962 F Curtis found evidence of a roundhouse 20 feet (6m) in diameter which had a packed-chalk floor.[10] Surface debris indicated that a second roundhouse of similar construction, and perhaps others, had originally stood close by. Spinning and weaving was evidenced through the discovery of spindle whorls and a weaving comb (Fig 56).

The sandier and lighter soils of Breckland to the east of Thetford appear to have favoured settlement of the Late Bronze Age and Early Iron Age transition. That area in the south of the county has revealed a cluster of settlements, the best-known of which is a small farmstead which was excavated at Micklemoor Hill, West Harling.[11] This was situated on a gravel hillock next to the River Thet. The east end of the site was defined by a circular turf bank and shallow ditch. To the south was an oval enclosure. Roundhouses were situated within both enclosures. There was also a rectangular structure inside the southern area.

Fig 56: An Iron Age comb, made from bone, from Norfolk. Length 128mm.

Another enclosure was located just one km to the east of Micklemoor Hill. This settlement was again defined by a circular-shaped bank. Pottery of similar type to that from Micklemoor Hill was found, which suggested that both sites were in use at about the same time. Close by, at Bridgham, a pot of the West Harling style was dredged from the river. This isolated find may be just a stray find from the West Harling site but it might also suggest a greater spread of settlement in the vicinity at the same time.

At Snarehill in the parish of Brettenham, between Harling and Thetford, yet another site of this period was discovered. Just 4km south-east of Thetford, on the banks of the Little Ouse River, an Early Iron Age farm with some slightly earlier Late Bronze Age pottery was revealed in a gravel pit in 1959. Two phases of occupation were recognised at the site, each of which had three roundhouses, three or four rectangular structures and pits of various sizes. Unlike the nearby West Harling sites, this one was unenclosed.

In the north-west of the county two Early Iron Age sites are known. A complex of interconnecting pits containing pottery of this period was discovered at Redgate Hill, Hunstanton.[12] The pits also contained domestic rubbish, flint and animal bones, and were described as 'working hollows'. The site also produced shellfish, a loomweight and a rare bronze swan-neck pin. Further east, at Warborough Hill, Stiffkey, 11 sherds of West Harling-type pottery were found in the face of a gravel pit.

MIDDLE IRON AGE SITES

We know of more sites which date from the Middle Iron Age, after about 450 BC. Unlike the earlier sites from the Thetford area, these later settlements were not surrounded by banks or ditches and can be described as 'unenclosed'. Evidence again comes from Thetford where, at London Road, excavation in 1989 revealed a cluster of 26 sub-circular and oval pits which contained pottery broadly belonging to the period between the 5th and 2nd centuries BC.[13] Elsewhere, in the south and west of the county, human remains have been encountered. At Bridgham human bone was found in association with pottery sherds. At Broomhill, Weeting, a cremation burial was found with a pot dated between 300 and 100 BC.

Further north, at Beeston with Bittering, gravel workings cut into a pit containing sherds of 3rd–2nd-century BC date. In the north-east, material of this date was found during the construction of the Aylsham bypass. On the north coast, Middle Iron Age pots were excavated in the cliff face at Cromer. Other sites of this broad date range have been recorded at Paston and Ken Hill, Snettisham.

In 1992–3 an unenclosed settlement was excavated at Park Farm, near Wymondham.[14] Pottery evidence provided a date of between the 3rd and 1st centuries BC for this site, which is atypical, having features quite different from those of the usual Iron Age farmsteads. Park Farm appears to have been a specialist industrial site. There is no evidence to suggest that it had a farming function or that it was even a permanent occupation site. Excavation revealed evidence for craft, industrial and agricultural activities, including quarry pits for the extraction of natural boulder clay. Quantities of slag show that iron smelting was undertaken and there was also evidence for antler and horn working. These activities had been allocated distinct, separate, activity zones within the site.

The early sedentary settlements of the Middle Iron Age avoided the heavier clays of central Norfolk. It was easier to cultivate the lighter soils on either side of the claylands until the use of the iron-tipped plough, or ard, was adopted. Park Farm was one of the first sites to be located on the heavier soils, but it was not a farm and was probably used only on an occasional, seasonal, basis.

As the population continued to grow, there was increased demand for the better soils across the region. People were forced to spread into less productive areas and the heavy claylands were some of the last to be properly exploited and settled. It is possible to see the use of Park Farm in this context. Some of the more adventurous individuals were moving beyond the better farmland and onto the clay, initially to undertake the less sociable and smellier activities described above. This may be seen as a very early specialist industrial site, used by Iron Age pioneers as they moved out into new lands.

Other Middle Iron Age sites were discovered during the construction of the Norwich Southern Bypass between 1989 and 1991.[15] These include a cemetery at Harford Farm, while a settlement was discovered at Valley Belt, Trowse, which revealed pits, ditched enclosures and quantities of pottery. These sites were located just off of the clayland, on free-draining sand and gravels. Settlements in general appear to have developed into open, unenclosed, farmsteads, which sprawled over wide areas and were not tightly defined or constrained in form. However, no complete settlements of this period have yet been excavated.

In 2001 the Norfolk Archaeological Unit excavated a settlement at Shropham, near Attleborough, to the north-east of Thetford, which is the most extensive area of Iron Age domestic occupation uncovered in the county to date.[16] The excavation team revealed three definite roundhouses, with evidence for a dozen other circular buildings, together with their associated enclosures. Preservation was remarkable and remains showed that the houses had originally been covered with thatched roofs.

BURIAL IN IRON AGE NORFOLK

Evidence for burial in the Iron Age is rare right across Britain. From the Late Bronze Age to the Middle Iron Age, the dead were disposed of in a manner which has left little or no trace in the archaeological record. They were being treated in a way that ensured they did not enter the ground intact, in the form of a complete burial. It is possible that excarnation, or the exposure of dead bodies, was being practised. This explanation, whereby bodies were left above ground – perhaps on raised platforms – to decompose and to be eaten by predators, seems to be the most likely explanation. Any remaining bones were not subsequently buried in any formal way.

Just fourteen examples of Iron Age human skeletal material have been recorded from Norfolk. Not all of these were complete skeletons and a number are just individual bones. Five are just skulls. This remarkably small sample is all that represents the population which inhabited the area for some 750 years. Even within this small group of human bones, not all appear to have come from conventional burials. Some represent something far more sinister. It has been recognised from other parts of Britain that human remains, together with parts of animals and domestic objects such as pottery, could be used for ritual purposes. Some of these examples appear to represent the practice of placing body parts within specific locations in a way that must be associated with ritual.

A single inhumation burial was discovered in 1944 during gravel digging in a ploughed field near the church of St Margaret at Shouldham.[17] The contemporary account mentions that an iron sword was found on the chest of a buried human skeleton. The sword, which has an anthropoid hilt, was donated to Norwich Castle Museum in 1949 but unfortunately the skeleton has not survived.

There are four recorded cases of Iron Age cremation burial from Norfolk. This practice spread over much of south-east England during the 1st century BC. Examples are known from Ford Place in Thetford and Weeting in the south-west.[18] Others come from the north-west, at Heacham and Stiffkey.[19] With the exception of the cremation from Ford Place, there is an absence of complete burials from settlement sites in Norfolk. There is also less recorded human bone from the county than from other parts of Britain, such as Wessex or the upper Thames valley.

The Harford Farm complex

Six unusual ritual or funerary enclosures were discovered at Harford Farm during the Norwich Southern Bypass excavations.[20] These were square enclosures arranged in a line running north–south and sited in an elevated position within the landscape. In each case, a ditch surrounded an inner bank. This is a unique form of burial site in Norfolk but it does bear a superficial resemblance to the Arras Culture barrows of eastern Yorkshire, which were also square in shape.[21] There are also similarities to the cemetery of Westhampnett in West Sussex, where four small square-shaped ditched enclosures were discovered, again in a line.[22] Other similar features of Iron Age date have been recorded at the site of Maxey in Cambridgeshire.[23]

THE IMPORTANCE OF BOUNDARIES

Land divisions and boundaries had started to appear in the landscape during the later Bronze Age. This was a significant development which showed the growing importance of land as a scarce resource. The population was growing and settlements were expanding. There was pressure on the better soils and the use of boundaries developed, taking many different visible forms.

Boundaries were significant places in the prehistoric landscape. They could take the form of artificially created monuments or earthworks which marked out areas that should be respected and not encroached upon. Boundaries could also be natural places of recognised significance, such as rivers. A location with water was often seen as a place of great significance, providing a boundary between land and sky – a place to commune with the gods. Individual finds, especially metalwork objects, are regularly found in these watery locations.

Fields were laid out across East Anglia during the Bronze Age in relation to pre-existing visible features in the landscape that had remained significant for centuries. The earlier landscape had been defined and marked out by the construction of barrows and henges. These landscape features served to identify symbolic and ritualised boundaries.[24]

In 2003–4 Michael de Bootman made a significant discovery at a location between Litcham and East Lexham in central west Norfolk.[25] A massive ditch some 2m deep was found to run for nearly 1km due east–west. This feature was made even more distinctive by its deliberate infilling with huge quantities of pottery for part of its length. The pottery collected comprises one of the largest assemblages of the later Iron Age to have come from Norfolk. The types in question were also unusual and included highly distinctive exotic imported material rarely found in this part of East Anglia. Human bone had also been placed in the ditch. This feature must have functioned as a boundary marker separating significant areas in the landscape, both through the defensive capability of the ditch and the construction of a symbolic boundary through the burial of special, possibly ritual, deposits.

As noted above, other forms of boundaries were defined in Norfolk by water. Rivers, such as the Waveney, provided significant natural barriers across the landscape. The number and extent of these natural features is, of course, difficult to assess but we now understand how some unaltered places in the landscape had great significance to the prehistoric population of Britain.[26]

NORFOLK'S LINEAR EARTHWORKS

As time progressed, the Iron Age saw the coming together of people within more nucleated communities. The population continued to grow and as pressure on the landscape increased, the spiritual boundaries that had been created were no longer adequate to prevent unwelcome encroachment. Areas needed to be defended physically and earthworks were constructed to define and reinforce the earlier boundaries.

Boundaries of Iron Age date, in the form of linear earthworks, are found in many places across southern England. Five such earthworks are known from west Norfolk and there may have been others that have been destroyed in more recent times. For many years, these earthworks were associated with the Saxon period, although an Iron Age date had originally been proposed some decades before.[27] Norfolk's linear earthworks consist of the *Launditch*, a single bank and ditch which runs for approximately 6km north–south between Wendling and Mileham; the *Panworth Ditch*, a single bank and ditch running north–south in the parish of Ashill; the *Bichamditch*, a single bank and ditch which runs from the parish of Narborough southwards for approximately 18km to a tributary of the River Wissey; the *Devil's Ditch*, an earthwork near Garboldisham, running north–south due south of Norfolk's central watershed; and the *Fossditch*, an earthwork which runs north–south for approximately 10km due south of the Bichamditch between the valleys of the Rivers Wissey and Little Ouse.

There is little dating evidence for these earthworks but that which does exist suggests a probable Iron Age origin.[28] Excavation in advance of gravel extraction at Beeston with Bittering in 1980 revealed an alignment of post-holes, some of which contained Iron Age sherds. The alignment ran the full length of the field examined and parallel with the Launditch, which lay 25m to the east. Excavation in 1992 which showed that the Launditch pre-dated a Roman road confirmed a prehistoric date for this earthwork.[29]

The only other dating evidence for any of the other examples suggests a similarly early date. The Bichamditch is clearly sited in direct association with the Iron Age enclosure at Narborough Camp. The coincidence of hillforts and large enclosures with focal points on prehistoric linear ditch systems has been recognised as a recurring feature within the Iron Age landscape of Britain.[30] The physical resemblance between the Panworth Ditch, Devil's Ditch and the Launditch suggests that these too may be of similar date.

Further south, in north Suffolk, there is an extensive linear earthwork known as the Black Ditches, which has a possible Iron Age date.[31] The projected alignment of the Black Ditches would meet up with the Fossditch and the Bichamditch, with Narborough Camp at its terminal. Could the overall alignments, in conjunction with the line of the watershed, as shown in Figure 62, be the remains of two extensive north–south linear boundaries isolating Breckland from the heavier clay lands to the east and from the fen-edge and greensand belt to the west? The central corridor defined in this way contains the important Iron Age sites and finds at Thetford and Saham Toney, which will be considered in the next chapter. However, at present, much fieldwork still needs to be done to confirm an early date for several of Norfolk's earthworks.

HILLFORTS

To use the term *hillfort* is particularly inappropriate in the context of Norfolk's relatively flat landscape. However, within today's county, there are, possibly, six enclosures which have similarities to the class of monument defined elsewhere in Britain by this term (Fig 57).[32] These sites, as in other parts, display differences in their methods of construction and in their locations within the landscape. In Norfolk, they may more comfortably be called medium-sized enclosed sites.

Warham Camp

The most spectacular surviving prehistoric site in Norfolk is Warham Camp, which is situated on sloping ground next to the River Stiffkey in north Norfolk. Marshes on three sides and a river to the west provided a measure of natural defence, while higher earthworks on the east side compensated for higher surrounding terrain in that direction. Warham's spectacular earthworks are circular and bivallate, and the inner bank encloses an area of 1.5ha (Fig 58).

Holkham

The site at Holkham, in contrast, was constructed at the southern end of a curving sandspit. Access was restricted to a narrow causeway in the north. Surrounded by marshes, it is sub-rectangular, partially bivallate, and covers 1.5ha.

Thetford Castle

The site at Thetford – the ramparts of which were later incorporated into the medieval castle – lies within a meander of the River Thet, on a chalk rise overlooking adjacent fords crossing the Rivers Thet and Little Ouse. It is roughly oval, bivallate in the north, and utilised the River Thet to complete a defensive circuit in the south. It encloses 6ha (Fig 59).

Narborough

This earthwork at Narborough forms an irregular oval. It was strategically sited on a low plateau close to the crossing of the River Nar by the Icknield Way. It is univallate and encloses 6ha.

South Creake

The site of Bloodgate Hill at South Creake is situated at the highest point on the valley edge overlooking the River Burn. Geophysical survey initially provided detail of the internal layout. Subsequently, acquisition by the Norfolk Archaeological Trust in 2003 provided the opportunity for a fuller insight into this site, to which end an evaluation excavation was carried out.[33]

The whole layout at South Creake suggests a ceremonial function. The site would have been a very imposing feature in the landscape, even more so when entering through the main gate; the surrounding earth bank had an external ditch 4m deep. A date for the site is

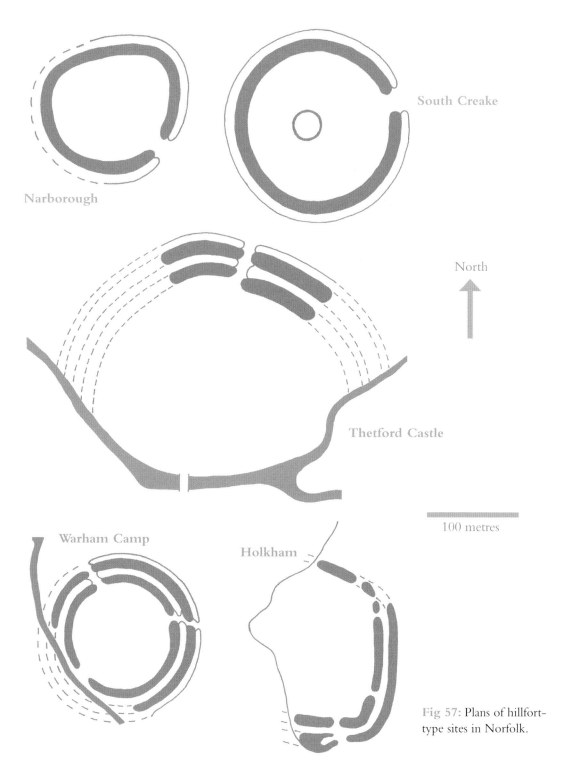

Fig 57: Plans of hillfort-type sites in Norfolk.

suggested by a cattle bone from the base of the ditch, which has been radiocarbon dated to c 280 BC.

Fig 58: Warham Camp's earthwork defences.

The site was laid out in symmetrical fashion in relation to a single elaborate entrance on the east side. An internal circular feature was identified by aerial photography, which lies back from the exact centre. Two linear features radiate away from this, serving to focus attention towards the centre when entering the site from the main gateway. The circular feature was recently thought to be the remains of a structure, possibly a large Iron Age roundhouse. However, the 2003 excavation obtained a radiocarbon date of c 1630 BC from its primary ditch fill, while OSL dating suggested an even earlier date, by some 230 years. So, the Bronze Age date for this feature may indicate the presence of a large barrow and ring-ditch of that date. This discovery is a most significant one which suggests a sequence of activity which respects this special location. This is a high point in the landscape and is visible from miles around. The barrow would have occupied a most conspicuous position. Its presence was clearly subsequently respected by the builders of the Iron Age earthwork, who gave it a central and focal position within their enclosure. In this way, this earlier feature appears to have been venerated and integrated into the workings and significance of the later earthwork.

Bawsey

A possible addition to this list of Norfolk enclosures is at Bawsey, next to King's Lynn, in the west of the county, where an undated ringwork surrounds a hilltop (Fig 60). This site was later used during the Anglo-Saxon period but significant Iron Age finds have been discovered there since 1941, including two electrum and two gold torcs (elaborate and substantial necklaces), a possible torc terminal and decorative harness and torc fragments (Fig 61). This was certainly an Iron Age site of some importance and it is possible that the earthworks here originated at that time.

Location, dating and function

Although Norfolk's enclosed earthwork sites display a measure of diversity in their construction and shape, they show more unity in terms of their location. All are close to rivers or, in the case of Holkham, the sea. They display a preference for valley-edge or valley-bottom situations and generally employ the natural topography to enhance the defensive potential of their entrances. Thetford Castle and Narborough also have strategic locations in relation to early routeways.

Once again, there is a frustrating absence of dating evidence from these sites. South Creake has been discussed above. Pottery from Thetford

Castle has been dated to the 5th–2nd centuries BC and a broadly Middle Iron Age date can be suggested for the use of that site. Excavations at Warham Camp yielded a mere 11 sherds dating from the 2nd or 1st centuries BC, together with Romano-British pottery. However, it is possible that the construction of the enclosure was earlier.

With the exception of Thetford Castle, all of these sites are located in the north-west of Norfolk. They occupy positions close to the boundary between the free-draining soils to the west and the heavier clay to the east. They were positioned in strategic locations and each would have been imposing in appearance. South Creake indicates an element of formal layout. Could this group of sites have collectively served as visible markers in the landscape to denote a boundary or boundaries? If so, it may be that these highly imposing earthworks had more of a symbolic role than a genuinely defensive one, emphasising territorial divisions in the landscape (Fig 62).

SNETTISHAM – A VERY SPECIAL PLACE

Snettisham is a place famous throughout the country for the spectacular nature of the archaeological discoveries made there over the last 60 years. The site of Ken Hill is located 2km inland, on the northern end of a prominent hilltop which dominates the surrounding landscape of north-west Norfolk. The profile of the hill itself bears a striking resemblance to the hillforts which similarly dominate the landscape across parts of southern Britain. The location of the site at Ken Hill

may have been chosen for similar
reasons to those which governed
the establishment of the southern
hillforts.

The site was located at the
highest point of the hill and provides
views right across the Wash, into
Lincolnshire, as well as far inland.
The spot was also very visible for
many miles around, across land and
sea. This was clearly a special place
with a unique strategic importance.
It also provided a defensible position,
which may or may not have been
significant.

Fig 61: Torc fragments
discovered at Bawsey.

The first discovery of gold jewellery was made at Ken Hill in 1948.[34]
Three hoards were subsequently excavated, containing complete and
fragmentary gold and bronze torcs, ingot rings, gold and potin coins
and other scrap metal. Subsequent finds were made in 1964, 1968, 1973
and 1989. These comprised additional gold and silver torcs and coins.

The nature of the Iron Age material buried at Snettisham consisted
of forms of jewellery, scrap metal and coins. Jewellery other than torcs
included smaller bracelet-sized rings. Most of the treasure was precious
metal, including gold, silver and electrum (an alloy of gold and silver).
Together, this all formed a concentration of enormous wealth, both in
ancient as well as in modern terms, dating from approximately 80 BC
(Figs 63–65).

It used to be thought that the Snettisham Treasure was the stock-
in-trade of a metalsmith, partly because many of the items were
fragmentary. More recent fieldwork has enabled the modification of this
interpretation. Excavation by the British Museum in 1990 revealed a
series of additional torcs, adding new significance to the whole deposit.
They comprised a series of discrete 'nests', cut into the ground and
carefully structured. Great care had clearly been taken when burying
these items. So what was their significance?

There are currently two schools of thought. Some think that
Snettisham represents a treasury – an accumulation of wealth over time,
buried for safe-keeping. As such, it would represent the possession of
more than a single person – perhaps of an extended family, or even the
whole tribe. Others think that it may have been a votive deposit. The
British Museum excavations showed that the individual hoards were
carefully structured, with a clear separation of contents by metal type
(gold/silver/copper). They were also ordered by their colour. The most

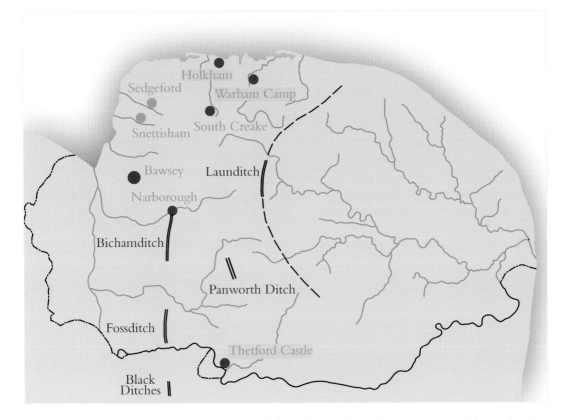

valuable torcs in some hoards were separated from the rest by a layer of earth. The careful way in which the items were buried has added strength to the belief that they were votive offerings to the gods.

Fig 62: The enclosed (hillfort-type) sites and earthworks of west Norfolk.

In addition to the hoards, another significant discovery at Snettisham was a large ditched enclosure.[35] It was polygonal in shape and covered 8ha in size. When the ditch was sectioned it was found to measure 3m wide by 2m deep. Finds suggest that this enclosure was constructed during the 1st century BC or 1st century AD, much later than the torc hoards. It was not a defensive construction; rather, it appears to have had another function. It is most likely that the ditch defined a sacred enclosure. Although constructed later, the origins of the sacred place may well have had roots and significance back in the Iron Age, and possibly even earlier.

Rumours have circulated since the early 1990s about the existence of another very special and unusual deposit that had been stolen from the hoard field. This deposit, which has been called 'the bowl hoard', is said to have contained over 6000 coins buried within a silver bowl, together with some 500 gold coins and ingots buried beneath the bowl, within the same pit. Richard Hobbs has written about the appalling loss to our knowledge and understanding of Snettisham which the theft of this unique deposit represents.[36] Its true composition will remain obscure and distorted by colourful and anecdotal evidence. However, it is possible to say that it must have been buried later than the torcs, adding to the growing picture of Snettisham having been a special place for many generations.

More recently, a number of pottery and artefact finds of Bronze Age date have also been recovered from the vicinity of the torc deposits; thus the chronology of the site is now also being projected backwards. We now know that this was an important focus – a special place – from the Bronze Age, through the Iron Age and into the Roman period.

WEALTH IN THE WEST – TORCS

Torcs, as noted above, were elaborate neck rings or very substantial necklaces. They are so-named because many were made from twisted strands of metal. Most examples have come from the site of Ken Hill at Snettisham. They include a range of many different decorative styles, all of great beauty; in particular, the torc ends, or terminals, exhibit an astonishing range of forms. Individual torcs were objects of significant value and they would have been worn by prominent people within society as symbols of status.

More torcs have been found in East Anglia than in the rest of Britain. They had a western and mainly north-western distribution,

Fig 63: The complete Snettisham treasure, before the 1990 excavation (*copyright Norfolk Museums and Archaeology Service*).

radiating away from the main site of Snettisham. Most examples have come from Ken Hill, while others have been found at North Creake, Marham, Bawsey and Sedgeford (Fig 66).

Most would have been extremely heavy to wear. Some were much lighter, such as the hollow tubular type, which were made of thin gold sheet (Fig 65). These examples were designed to come apart at their joints, to enable them to be worn easily on special occasions. However, it would have been extremely difficult to keep removing some of the weightier forms. Some of the more elaborate twisted examples may not have been repeatedly removed (Fig 67). Their significance may have been similar to that of modern-day wedding rings. They may have been continuously worn, following an initial symbolic ceremony.

Buried torcs have been interpreted on the continent as ritual offerings.[37] There are a number of observations which indicate that the Norfolk examples should also be considered in that context. A high proportion are incomplete, missing their terminals, which suggests that they may have been intentionally broken before burial, as often occurred with other categories of deposited prehistoric material. The carefully structured method of their burial at Snettisham also compares well to the way objects such as pots were placed within ritual shafts at this time.

Fig 64: The 'Great Torc', bracelet and incomplete torc with buffer terminal from the Snettisham Treasure. Torc diameter 200mm *(copyright Norfolk Museums and Archaeology Service).*

THE FOCUS OF POLITICAL POWER

By the early decades of the 1st century BC the focus of political power, as defined by the location of key sites, earthworks and material finds, appears to have been in west and north-west Norfolk. The basis of the power was the control of trade through maritime trade links with other parts of Britain and abroad, and especially the control of the flow of precious commodities – such as gold and silver – into the region.[38] Snettisham itself contained wealth unequalled anywhere in the country at that time and must be the prime candidate for that centre.[39] As a focus of religious activity, it would have exercised influence over a very wide region.

Another prominent western site of the earlier 1st century BC was Sedgeford, which has also yielded unusually rich artefacts over a number of years. These finds include several fine brooches and a hoard of 39 Gallo-Belgic E gold staters, which were excavated in 2003.[40] A magnificent but incomplete electrum torc was found there in 1965.[41] The missing terminal was discovered during excavation at the site by the Sedgeford Historical and Archaeological Research Project in 2004, almost 40 years later. This beautiful example bears close similarities with other examples from nearby Snettisham. Sedgeford was clearly another site of high status at this time.

The west of Norfolk as the focus of wealth, power and important sites was defined, and possibly defended, by the extensive north–

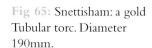

Fig 65: Snettisham: a gold Tubular torc. Diameter 190mm.

Fig 66: The distribution of torcs in Norfolk.

Snettisham

south line of hillfort-type enclosures and earthworks. These sites and boundaries, located at prominent places in the landscape, served to separate the region containing the political and religious foci from the rest of Norfolk.

This was the situation when contacts with the continent were revived during the 1st century BC and the Roman world began to reach northward into Britain. It was into this fascinating world – that of a supreme clash of cultures – that Boudica was born. In the next chapter we shall look in more detail at the final decades of the Iron Age, as those cultures came face-to-face.

Fig 67: An electrum torc discovered in south-west Norfolk in 2005. Diameter 200mm *(copyright The Trustees of the British Museum).*

Chapter 9
The age of Boudica
100 BC — AD 61

When the British warrior queen,
Bleeding from the Roman rods,
Sought, with an indignant mien,
Counsel of her country's gods
(William Cowper, *Boadicea*)

BOUDICA'S BRITAIN

We do not know exactly when Boudica was born but she was probably in her thirties at the time of the rebellion which she led against the Romans in AD 60. In that case, she would probably have been born between AD 26–7 and AD 30.[1] This was during the period we call the Late Iron Age.

At that time Britain was being drawn back into contact with mainland Europe following a prolonged period of isolation. Archaeology provides evidence for renewed long-distance trading with the Mediterranean world and we have traces of the exotic goods entering parts of Britain from far away. Members of British tribes also crossed the Channel to become mercenaries during the turbulent period of Julius Caesar's Gallic Wars. There were also political contacts between Rome and the tribes of south-eastern Britain.

A number of significant developments occurred during the Late Iron Age. This period saw the first use of coins. Concentrations of settlement known as *oppida*, which were much larger than anything previously seen in Britain, were developing in some parts of the country. Complex burials have been discovered in some places. However, it is becoming increasingly clear that not all of these developments happened everywhere; archaeology is recognising cultural differences between those living in different parts of Britain at this time. Nevertheless, the process of agricultural intensification continued everywhere and there was increasing exploitation of the better soils.

It was during this period that the Romans first invaded Britain, under Julius Caesar, in 55 and 54 BC. They did not stay. The main invasion came nearly 90 years later under the Emperor Claudius, in AD 43. This invasion normally serves to define the end of the Iron Age in Britain. However, the land of the Iceni – the tribal people who then lived in northern East Anglia – remained. This became a client kingdom under the Romans and Norfolk's Iron Age was to continue for a further 18 years, until the defeat of the Iceni, following their rebellion under Boudica.

Before going on to consider the rebellion itself we must look in more detail at the world in which Boudica herself lived. We shall look at the nature of society and the fascinating diversity of the material evidence. What does archaeology tell us about the land where Boudica lived?

LATE IRON AGE SOCIETY

The classical sources have presented a picture of a Late Iron Age Britain populated by separate warlike tribal states that were dominated by warrior nobilities. Writers such as Julius Caesar, Tacitus, Cassius Dio and Strabo write of Britain in terms that were familiar to them from elsewhere in northern Europe. Popular images of Boudica as Queen of the Iceni leading her army against the Roman invaders have done much to cement this conventional view. However, the picture now being revealed by archaeological investigation suggests that the situation described by Caesar in Gaul should no longer be used as a generalisation. The peoples of Britain were neither unified nor uniform. Local studies are revealing regional differences, with many communities and territorial groupings of varying sizes doing things differently from their neighbours, often with differences in their material cultures.

So, who were the Iceni? Caesar refers to a tribal group that was living north of the Thames called the *Cenimagni*, who may have been the people subsequently referred to as the *Iceni*.[2] The name used by Caesar may have been a version of the name, meaning 'Eceni Magni' or 'the Great Iceni'. There is a second historical reference to the tribe, relating to the military situation of AD 47. Tacitus, a Roman historian writing between AD 75 and 120, names the Iceni in that context and indicates that they regarded themselves as allies of Rome.[3]

We are told by Tacitus that the Iceni were the northern neighbours of the Trinovantes. We also know that this latter tribe was located in the modern counties of Essex and southern Suffolk, so the Iceni must have occupied parts of northern East Anglia. Precise boundaries are hard to establish but Norfolk comprised the heartland of the tribal land. The Iceni may also have extended south into northern Suffolk and north-east Cambridgeshire for part of this period.

The overall social, political and territorial structure of Late Iron Age Britain was far more complex than the standard 'tribal map' of Iron Age and early Roman Britain implies. We should envisage a more

decentralised pattern, in which the country was
divided into a large number of small-scale
groupings. At a local level, there was a
loose confederacy of small-scale
societies with their own leaders
and aristocratic elites. It may
be that Caesar's *Cenimagni*
were one of the smaller
social groups. These groupings
would then have come together under a single senior leader at times
of stress, coalescing into larger regional entities whose organisation was
based on kingship and associated client networks.

Fig 68: A La Tène
brooch from Feltwell.
Length 55mm.

With the recognition of an external threat from Rome, the loose
decentralised communities within northern East Anglia came together
as a single larger unit, under a senior chieftain or king. It was at that
stage the grouping recognised as the Iceni became identified by Roman
writers.

THE ICENI 'DID THINGS DIFFERENT'

The coat of arms of the University of East Anglia today declares that
'people in Norfolk do things different'. Archaeology shows that this
observation was just as pertinent in the Late Iron Age. Studies of sites and
artefacts indicate that the land of the Iceni was indeed a distinctive part
of Iron Age Britain, with its own strong identity. The unenclosed nature
of Icenian settlements and the hillfort-type enclosures of west Norfolk
are two manifestations of regional diversity. Aspects of local material
culture provide another. Not only does the quantity of metalwork items
produced at this time increase but their range and diversity is another
feature of this period (Figs 68 and 69).

The steady population increase and a growing pressure on the
landscape were accompanied by increased stress, unrest and even
warfare. The expression of identity within society is often manifested at
such times of escalating trouble and people of the Late Iron Age were
showing this through the way they dressed and the way they lived. The
peoples of Britain were increasingly expressing their local identities
and by the end of the period we see the emergence of a full tribal
society across Britain. They also expressed their identity through their
own traditions, laws and beliefs, although these are not visible in the
archaeological record.

THE KINGDOM OF THE HORSE

A high proportion of Iron Age artefacts found in Norfolk are horse-
related items, implying that horses were very important to the Iceni.

Metal-detector users regularly discover harness and cart fittings, bridle bits, terrets (rein-rings), linch pins (used to secure cart or chariot wheels to their axle (Fig 70) and harness decorations. The original owners invested much wealth in these elaborate fittings.

A most exciting discovery of such material was made in 1992, when a metal-detector user brought a box full of metalwork items for identification to the Archaeology Department at Norwich Castle Museum. Prominent among the items were five large bronze rings (see Fig 8). Although they initially appeared unspectacular within piles of lead and bronze waste, these distinctive D-shaped rings were in fact a set of terret rings, which had been attached to a chariot during the Late Iron Age period, serving as guide-rings for the leather harness. The group also contained two bronze bridle bits, a beautiful enamelled harness decoration and a linch pin.[4] Most significantly, the group had been found at Ashill, adjacent to Saham Toney, adding more vital clues to the growing evidence for an important settlement at that location (Figs 71 and 72).

Fig 69: A La Tène brooch from east Norfolk. Length 52mm.

Some years later, in 2000, an equally spectacular discovery was made, this time at Swanton Morley in central Norfolk, of a magnificently decorated bronze bridle bit. The condition was remarkable but the decoration even more so. Each of the rein-rings contained internal decorative mouldings, both of which were different (Figs 73 and 74). An asymmetrical design of this type is not unique but is rarely encountered, and is not previously known from this part of Britain.

Such items of horse harness are characteristic of the Iceni (Figs 75 and 76) but they are rare in some other parts of the country. For example, they are seldom found in the south-east of England, through from Kent to Hampshire. We may conclude that the raising and riding of horses appears to have played a very important role within Icenian society, which was not the case in all other parts of southern Britain. Horses were also depicted on almost all Icenian coins, which further identifies this to have been *the kingdom of the horse.*

Fig 70: A pair of linch pins. Length 47mm and 49mm.

SYMBOLS OF THE ICENI

It is becoming apparent that a number of specific symbols had significance for the Iceni. They may have served to reinforce tribal identity and their use was especially important in the absence of writing. In particular, one form of brooch, known as the 'rear-hook' type, has been associated with the Iceni area and can be considered a badge of the tribe. It is found across Norfolk, north Suffolk and east Cambridgeshire and has been tightly dated to the years AD 60–5.

Icenian coins carry a range of stylised designs which include symbols interpreted as suns, moons and stars. These symbols were originally seen in terms of decorative space-filling devices but careful study is now suggesting that these designs may have had meaning and significance, especially before the use of writing was adopted. One such motif is the back-to-back crescent, which is found on both gold and silver issues and is particularly prominent on the prolific Pattern-horse and inscribed coin series (Fig 77). The same motif is also found elsewhere within Icenian material culture. A bronze bowl or bucket fitting designed around the back-to-back crescent motif was found at Fakenham in 1993 (Fig 78). Another example from Tattersett, in the form of an enamelled disc, appears to have been purely ornamental and was perhaps worn as a form of badge by its owner.

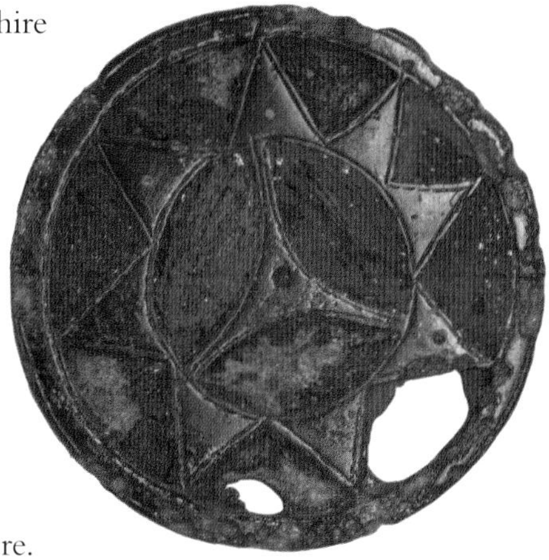

Fig 71: An enamelled disc from Saham Toney. Diameter 58mm.

Symbols which emphasise the number three, such as the Y-shaped symbol, trefoils and pellet triangles, are very common on items of material culture right across Europe (Figs 79 and 80). These symbols are all found on Icenian coins (Figs 81 and 82). The 'triplet' is sometimes positioned below a portrait and may have served as a stamp of authority or power for the issuer. Another bronze item which echoes the Icenian 'triplet' motif is a dress item, known as a button and loop fastener (Fig 83).

The use of recognised symbols served to distinguish the Iceni from their neighbours. Tribes to the south also used their own distinctive motifs. These societies were, however, more regularly exposed to Roman influences and, as a result, tribes such as the Trinovantes and Atrebates frequently used symbols from the classical world on their coins, such as the centaur, pegasus and the sphinx.

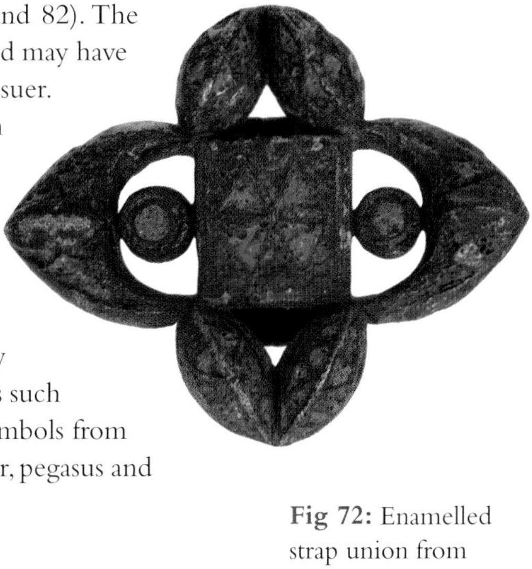

Boar figurines

Depictions of boars are prominent on the coinage of the Iceni and on that of their western neighbours, the Corieltauvi. Representations of boars are also known from elsewhere in western Europe, often in the form of figurines. The known corpus of such figurines from Britain stood at just 22 in 1977, with none at all recorded from Norfolk.[5] Since

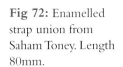

Fig 72: Enamelled strap union from Saham Toney. Length 80mm.

then, two remarkable examples have been found in the county by metal-detector users.

One was found in 1990, on the Norfolk fen-edge at Methwold (Fig 84). This beautiful tiny figurine, of the highest quality and realism, is set on a rectangular plinth. Another, more stylised, example was discovered in 1997 in south-east Norfolk (Fig 85-87). It is freestanding and has a high perforated crest along its back, which has been damaged. It has an elongated snout and damage on either side of the mouth, which may relate to the position of tusks now missing. It shows strong similarities to another example found at Hounslow, Middlesex, in 1864.[6] Both may have been helmet crests, as indicated by the angle of the feet, which are inclined inwards in the Norfolk example.

A deliberate feature on the new Norfolk boar was a tick-shaped symbol on its right shoulder. It is interesting to note that another boar figurine, found at Soulac-sur-Mer, at the mouth of the River Gironde on the southern Atlantic coast of France in 1989, had a similar marking on its left shoulder (Fig 87).[7] Could it be that these symbols perhaps indicate an association with a particular religious cult?

Figs 73–74: The decorated mouldings from the Swanton Morley bridle bit, also see Fig 9.

A VERY RELIGIOUS PEOPLE

People of the Iron Age had a very different concept of religion from that familiar to people living in Britain today. Everyday life was imbued with actions and activities that made reference to spiritual beliefs and to the gods. They attached great significance to sacred places, which could be natural places in the landscape or even locations within their homes and settlements. Sometimes special places were constructed within the landscape. People dug wells and shafts that penetrated deep into the ground, perhaps to serve as an interface with the underworld. At Fison Way, Thetford, an artificial woodland grove was constructed around this very special religious site.[8]

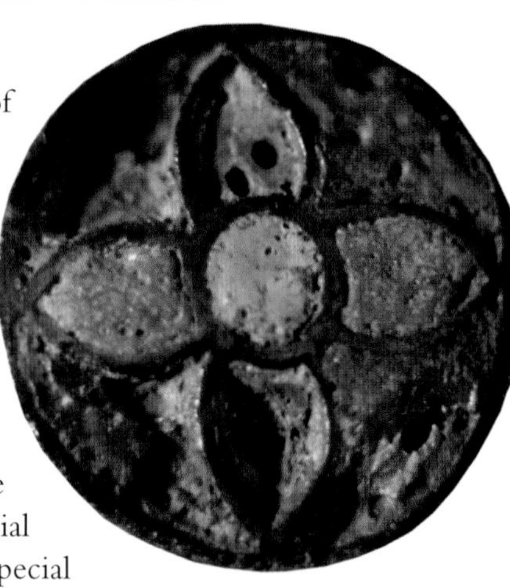

It has become increasingly apparent that a large proportion of Iron Age objects recovered in modern times had been intentionally buried or deposited and were not merely casually lost by their owners. They

Fig 75: An enamelled terret platform, from Saham Toney.

112

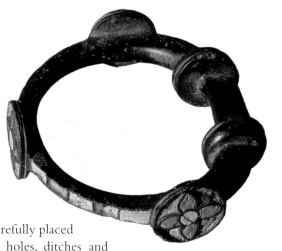

were carefully placed
in pits, holes, ditches and
watery places. Some were buried
in high places in the landscape, on the tops of hills. We may view
these as offerings to the gods. Votive objects were not always finely
made items. They could also be parts of people or animals – or even
quantities of carefully selected pottery. Representations of human
heads are also encountered.

A number of ritual locations have been identified in
Norfolk, which include the Fison Way grove, the Snettisham
torc field and a religious shaft at Ashill. Many offerings
were made in watery places, as they had been in earlier
times. These included slave chains, coins and weapons.
Depositing and throwing things into water was, as it is
today, associated with bringing good fortune.

The Ashill shaft was a carefully structured and
assembled deposit. Lined with oak timbers, it had been filled
with separate layers of pottery vessels, each of which had been
placed within a bedding of twigs and leaves.[9] Similar ritual shafts
have been found near to *oppida* sites right across Europe.

The burying of pottery in ditches and pits, along with parts of
human skeletons and parts of animals such as cattle skulls, is another
recurring feature of the period. Once again, people were returning to
the earth what had come from the earth, within a ritual context. These
deposits were placed at significant locations associated with territorial
and ritual significance.

Fig 76: Terrets from
Carleton Rode, with
detail of enamelled
decoration. Diameter
of terrets 76mm and
55mm.

Ritual coin deposits

Some coin deposits can also be interpreted as having a votive purpose.
Two coin groups from the south-west of the county contain an unusual
mixture of gold, silver and non-Icenian types. In both cases, these show

a selection of the very best, very worst and most unusual coins available. They appear to have been assembled as sacred offerings.

In August 2003, excavations at Sedgeford in the north-west recovered a hoard of 39 Gallo-Belgic type E gold staters.[10] Although an exciting discovery in its own right, it was the hoard container that was most remarkable. The majority of the coins had been hidden within a cow bone. Just why this bone had been chosen as a container is still a mystery. It had been placed within a specially dug pit at a carefully chosen high position overlooking the nearby river. These elements again point towards this being another deposit with religious significance.

Fig 77: An Icenian Pattern-horse type silver coin, carrying the opposing crescents symbol.

Feasting

The practice of feasting was important within Iron Age society as it had been in the Neolithic and Bronze Age. Feasts could have ceremonial and religious associations, and acted as an important focus for social gatherings, serving as a way of bringing together the wider community.

Several Iron Age finds from Norfolk can be associated with the practice of feasting and drinking. Bronze tankard handles have been found at three locations: examples are known from Morley and Billingford, and a third example from West Rudham was described as having an attachment plate shaped into 'ears' and rivet holes as 'eyes'. These bronze handles would have been fastened to wooden tankards. At Snettisham, part of another form of drinking vessel was found: a mount from a socketed drinking horn, which had been cast in the form of a bird's head.

Cult of the severed head

Classical writers have described the practice of 'taking heads' during battle within Late Iron Age societies. Warriors would cut off the heads of enemies, which may have served as trophies or been used in religious rites. They would fix severed heads to houses and shrines. Heads are often represented in the art of the period.

In Norfolk, miniature bronze heads have been found by metal detection at a number of locations: examples have come from Holme Hale, Sedgeford, Weybourne and Gillingham (Figs 88 and 89). What they were is not yet clear to us. Did they serve a function or were they symbolic? Some may have become detached from the hilts of anthropoid-type swords, like the example found at Shouldham. Alternatively, it is possible that these heads could have been used as miniature votive objects in their own right.

Fig 78: A fitting in the shape of opposing crescents, a symbol used by the Iceni. Height 34mm.

Fig 79: A pair of linch pins from Attleborough showing the triplet symbol on their ends. Diameters 28mm and 29mm.

As well as miniature heads, an even more quirky form of sword and dagger hilt attachment has been recognised, in the form of what appear to be miniature droopy 'Celtic' moustaches! An increasing number of these strange copper alloy pieces are being found, including one from Gayton Thorpe in 2004 (Fig 90).

COINAGE AND SOCIETY

Fig 80: The triangle symbol, a variant of the triplet, decorating a small dome-shaped dress item. Diameter 19mm.

The first coinage to be used in Britain was produced in Belgica, now northern France, during the early 2nd century BC. The first coinage produced in this country was a cast bronze type, which was made in Kent at the end of the 2nd century BC. Bronze coins of the Iron Age are rarely found in Norfolk. The powerful Iron Age kingdoms situated north and south of the Thames had more direct contact with Roman Gaul and produced early coinages which show a Romanising influence, an influence that can be detected throughout their society at that time. The tribes that were situated to the north and west of the Trinovantes, Catuvellauni and Atrebates, including the Iceni, are called the peripheral tribes. These peripheral tribes developed coins which lack the Romanised influences found within those of the south-east.

Gallo-Belgic uniface gold staters of the Gallic War period (the mid 50s BC) have been found at many locations in Norfolk, mainly through metal detection. These coins were produced in the north of Gaul by the Ambiani tribe and tend to turn up in hoards from around the coast of southern Britain, including Norfolk.

Fig 81: An Icenian Face-horse type silver coin, showing the triplet motif beneath the bust.

The coinage of the Iceni contains distinctive artistic content and innovation. It depicts a series of beasts which we interpret as wolves and wild boars, depictions which would appear to reflect the native fauna of Britain at that time. Human faces, ranging from naturalistic to highly stylised depictions, are represented in a wide range of issues. The coins also contain symbols, some of which appear to be astrological, such as the sun, moon and stars. We can only guess at the meaning of some other symbols. However, a constant feature of Icenian coins is the presence of a horse on the reverse. Although not unique to the Iceni, this feature appears to confirm the importance of horses within Icenian society.

Some Icenian silver coins bear strong stylistic resemblances to other tribal types from both Britain and Gaul. In particular, they bear close similarities to those of their western neighbours, the Corieltauvi, and of their southern neighbours, the Trinovantes. Others show strong similarity to coinage from northern France.[11]

There are around 90 recorded varieties of Icenian coins, including both gold and silver types.[12] The Iceni used a bi-metallic coinage, which also incorporated the use of quarter and half units. Until recently it was thought that the series started with the use of gold alone, which was later succeeded by the striking of silver coins (Fig 91). Now, work has shown that gold, silver and the sub-denominations were all used at the same time.[13]

Fig 82: Norfolk Wolf type gold coin, carrying the triplet motif on the reverse.

Coinage was first produced by the Iceni during the second quarter of the 1st century BC. The first gold issues were the Snettisham stater, a type which has been known since 1990, and the Norfolk Wolf stater. The Norfolk Wolf carries the head of Apollo on the obverse, coupled with a leggy animal, with snapping jaws, on the reverse (Fig 92). There are just two known examples of a Norfolk Wolf quarter stater, both of which are held at Norwich Castle Museum. Another form of gold quarter is known as the Irstead, which is again contemporary with the Norfolk Wolf and Snettisham series (Fig 93). This depicts a sheaf of corn on the obverse. Snettisham and Irstead types have distributions within western and central Norfolk.

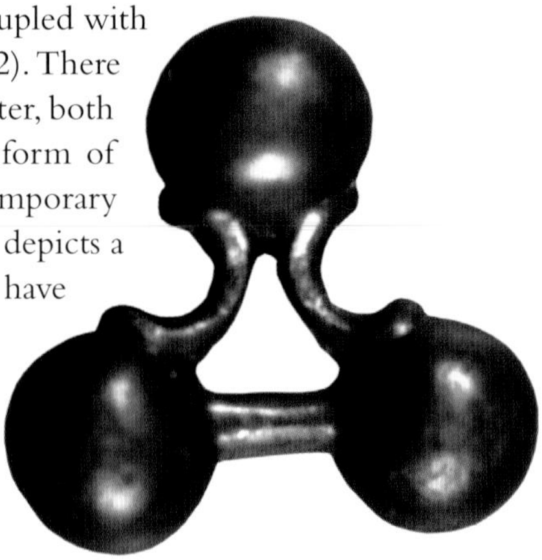

Freckenham-type gold staters were coins of great beauty (Fig 94). They were elegantly struck in high relief, with particularly finely engraved depictions of horses. The Late Freckenham type was broadly contemporary with the silver early Boar-horse (below). It carries a floral pattern on the obverse. The Irstead gold quarter stater was also broadly contemporary with the Freckenham stater.

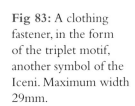

Fig 83: A clothing fastener, in the form of the triplet motif, another symbol of the Iceni. Maximum width 29mm.

The first silver coin type is known as the Early Face-horse (Fig 95). These were contemporary with the Snettisham, Norfolk Wolf and Irstead issues. Multiple examples turn up at some of the main sites of the period, such as Great Walsingham, Wicklewood and Ditchingham. Another early type, known as the Large Flan C, is specifically associated with the Breckland.[14]

Another distinctive early form, closely related to the Early Face Horse, is the Bury type (Figs 96 and 97). This was originally named thus because the first recorded examples were found in the vicinity of Bury St Edmunds in Suffolk. Types known as Bury A, B and C all have restricted distributions within Icenian territory. Bury A carries a naturalistic face, coupled with a horse motif, in high relief. These are mainly found in central west Norfolk. Bury B are evenly spread across the south of the county, while Bury C are much rarer and are concentrated around Norwich. All of the Bury types are absent from the far north. The site of Wicklewood, near Wymondham, appears to have had significance in relation to Bury coins. Types A and B are heavily concentrated there, although no C types have come from the site at all.

The first really large silver series was the Boar-horse (Fig 98). This issue depicts a creature with a pronounced row of hair along its back. Smaller examples of the Boar-horse have been found, which we call minims. Boar-horse coins are most common in the south of the county and many come from the vicinity of Saham Toney.

The second substantial silver coin issue was the Face-horse (Fig 99), which may have been struck between AD 0–30. This type depicts a very simplified human face, which was copied from Roman Republican denarii of the 1st century BC. Face-horses are most common in the west and south-east of the county, with larger numbers coming from the major sites, especially Saham Toney.

Fig 84: A boar figurine discovered at Methwold in 1990, courtesy Derek Woollestone. Height 47mm *(copyright Norfolk Museums and Archaeology Service).*

The most common type of Icenian silver is known as the Pattern-horse (Fig 100), which accounts for 70% of all Icenian silver coinage. This series may have been struck between AD 10–50. The obverse depicts two back-to-back crescents, while an early form of Pattern-horse is distinguished by smaller crescents. Pattern-horses are distributed right across the county.

The earliest Icenian silver units were uninscribed types, with no recognisable lettering. However, a major development occurred within the main Pattern-horse series when coins began to be inscribed with letters which appear to be the names of Icenian rulers. ECE and ECEN may be names of rulers, echoing that of the tribe. Another name used is ANTED. All three were in use, and were produced, at around the same time, probably after AD 30 (Fig 101). Just when the minting of Icenian coins ceased still remains unclear. Amanda Chadburn prefers an

Fig 85: Bronze boar figurine from south-east Norfolk. Length 88mm.

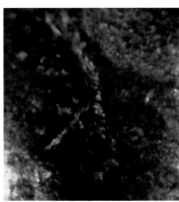

Fig 87: Boar figurine from Norfolk, showing mark on the left shoulder.

Fig 86: Boar figurine, detail.

end to production around the time of the Roman conquest in AD 43. An alternative might have been in AD 47, when there was a rebellion within the Iceni against the Romans.

The latest issue struck by the tribe, which has been attributed to King Prasutagus, is clearly Romanised in its design (Fig 102).[15] The style of the portrait is very similar to that used on contemporary Roman Julio-Claudian coinage and shows the ruler to have been under some degree of Roman influence during the period when the Iceni were a Roman client kingdom. The coin also carries a legend of Roman style. It reads SVB ESVPRASTO ESICO FECIT, which means 'made under Lord Prasto, by Esico'.[16] Esico was presumably the moneyer in charge of coin production.

All in all, it is now appreciated that staters, silver units and quarter units were being produced and used together. This suggests that there was more of a widespread and sophisticated use of coinage than had previously been thought possible at that time in eastern Britain. The recovery of types also shows that there were many local, sub-regional, coin types with localised distributions.[17] This may reflect the presence of sub-groupings within the Iceni tribe.

A small number of coin hoards from south Norfolk and Suffolk, including examples from Norton Subcourse, Scole, Weston Longville, Weybourne and Forncett, contain a mixture of Icenian silver units and Roman silver *denarii*.[18] It is possible that these different coinages were considered acceptable currency together, with the lighter Icenian units being used as sub-denominations alongside the *denarii*.

Evidence for Iron Age coin production has been found in the form of clay moulds which were used to prepare silver pellets which were then struck as finished coins. These moulds have been found at the major settlements of Saham Toney and Thetford, as well as at Needham (Fig 103), a place which has not been recognised as a significant Icenian settlement, although much of the evidence may have been removed by quarrying. All three sites are in central and south Norfolk.

WHAT DID THE ICENI LOOK LIKE?

There are no contemporary accounts which tell us what ordinary people of the Iceni looked like. However, the distinctive identity of the tribe is likely to have been reflected in their dress and fashions, especially that used on special occasions, such as feasts, ceremonies and when going into battle. The coinage, however, provides some clues to their appearance.

The Early Face-horse coin series includes types which are naturalistic representations of human faces. They presumably depict individuals of the Iceni tribe, probably chieftains or religious leaders. The head depicted on Bury A type shows a clean-shaven face and is wearing a head-dress with prominent head-band. Bury B shows a similar head-dress, with decorated head-band, above which twisted rope-like shapes flow up and twist back. An elaborate spiral-shaped decoration covers the ear. The whole effect resembles a Native North American feather head-dress. Or could this be an early use of dreadlocks?

The Early Face-horse B form is quite different. It appears to show a bearded (but not moustached) individual. The head is covered with pellets which could, again, depict a head-dress but may be a very full head of curly hair.

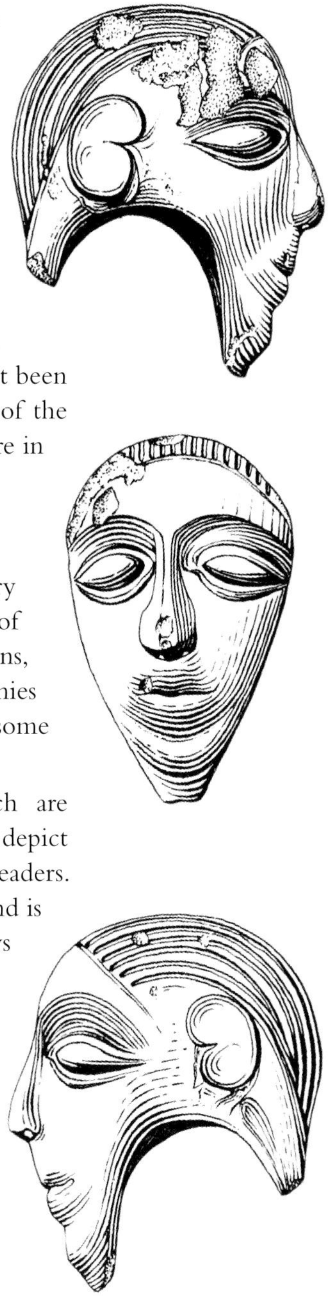

LARGER SETTLEMENTS IN NORFOLK

More substantial settlements known as *oppida* began to appear in Late Iron Age Britain. These sites were associated with trade and saw the first use of coinage; they were linked less by their form than by their function and while some could be undefended, others, like Sheepen at

Fig 88: Miniature bronze head from Holme Hale. Scale 4:1 (drawing by Sue White).

Colchester, Bagendon, and Chichester, were associated with systems of surrounding earthworks. Evidence of coin production is often found at some *oppida*, as at Silchester and Old Sleaford. There has been very little excavation on this category of site nationally.

Such *oppida* have not previously been recognised in Norfolk. However, the increasing range and scale of evidence coming from certain locations today shows that some sites within the county were different in size and function from the ordinary farmsteads which filled the landscape. Several sites sprawled over wide areas, each covering several square kilometres. Some have produced evidence of coin production, as well as coin use, and they are all found at strategic locations (Fig 104). Whether or not it is appropriate to term these more substantial Norfolk sites *oppida* may be questioned but, within the regional context, we can now identify significant settlements and centres of population within the Icenian area. Unfortunately, as with such sites more widely, there has been a lack of excavation on these Norfolk examples and a fuller understanding of their full significance and role within the land of the Iceni must await such investigative fieldwork. However, at this stage, I consider that the following sites should be considered within this category.

Caistor St Edmund

Caistor St Edmund, due south of Norwich, is a location where evidence for important Late Iron Age occupation pre-dating the Roman town has been steadily accumulating. The presence of inscribed coins provides a date, between AD 10–40, for the rise to prominence of this site. Excavations within the central part of *Venta Icenorum* between 1929 and 1935 recovered isolated examples of Icenian silver coins and bronze La Tène-style brooches. Similar material has continued to be recovered as surface finds, mainly through metal detection. Terret rings, gold and silver coins and other items continue to be found to the east, south and west of the Roman walls. The extra-mural temple on raised ground 600m to the east has also turned up Icenian coins. Just to the north, a cemetery comprising cremation burials and funerary enclosures was located at Harford Farm. A Roman fort defined by substantial triple ditches was constructed here, possibly in the aftermath of the Boudican uprising.[19]

Fig 89: Miniature bronze head from Sedgeford. Scale 2:1 (drawing by Sue White).

Thetford

A second location can be suggested at Thetford, which had been a strategic location of regional importance for the duration of the Iron Age: this was the crossing point of the Icknield Way

Fig 90: Miniature bronze moustache from Gayton Thorpe. Scale 2:1.

Fig 91: Hoard of
Icenian gold staters
from Heacham.

Fig 92: Norfolk Wolf
gold coins: a stater and
a rare quarter stater.
Diameters 17mm and
13mm.

Fig 93: Irstead-type
gold quarter stater.
Diameter 10mm.

Fig 94: Freckenham-type gold stater. Diameter 18mm.

Fig 95: Early Face-horse – large flan B type. Diameter 16mm.

Fig 96: Bury A type silver unit. Diameter 15mm.

Fig 97: Bury B type silver unit. Diameter 15mm.

Fig 98: Boar–horse type silver unit. Diameter 14mm.

Fig 99: Face–horse type silver unit. Diameter 14mm.

Fig 100: Pattern–horse type silver unit. Diameter 13mm.

Fig 101: Pattern–horse ECE type silver unit. Diameter 14mm.

with the Rivers Thet and Little Ouse. There was continuity of Iron Age settlement in the vicinity and substantial earthwork fortifications at Thetford Castle in the Early and Middle Iron Age. The religious enclosure at Fison Way would have had regional significance. Clay moulds for coin manufacture were also found at this site. Many individual finds have been made across the town since the eighteenth century, and many silver Icenian coins have been found, especially from the area between Thetford and Brettenham to the east. Increasing evidence shows that this was a widespread settlement. Just 5km to the south of Thetford Castle lies another Late Iron Age double-ditched enclosure at Barnham, in north Suffolk.

Fig 102: King Prasutagus silver unit. Diameter 14mm.

Saham Toney/Ashill

A significant concentration of settlement and activity was located within the modern parishes of Saham Toney and Ashill, to the north-west of Watton in central Norfolk, on the northern edge of the Breckland. This settlement developed as a strong economic centre between AD 0–30. The location is defined by the junction of the River Wissey and Watton Brook to the west and the River Blackwater in the east. These rivers demarcate the western boundary of the settlement spread. The natural crossing point was at Woodcock Hall, where a rich collection of Iron Age coins and pre-conquest brooches and coin moulds have been found. A Roman military presence was established here in the form of a Claudian fort, which was built on high ground overlooking the river.

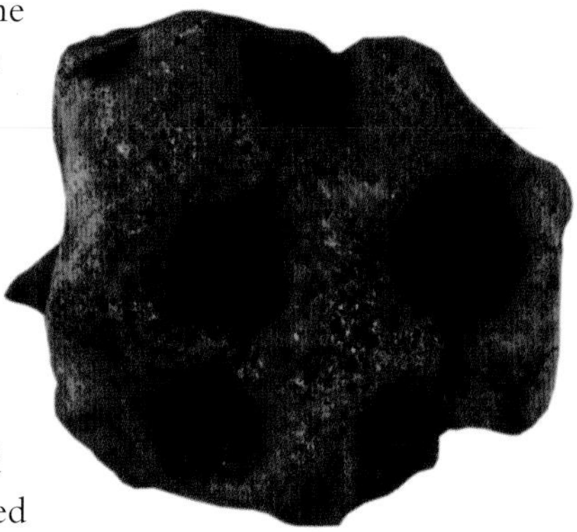

A second focus of settlement within this general area has been recognised just 5km to the north at Ashill, to the east of the Panworth Ditch. Surface finds have included terret rings, harness fittings, chariot ironwork, brooches, and gold and silver coins. Small-scale excavations in 1995 revealed pits containing slag, crucible sherds and clay mould fragments, indicating that metalworking, possibly terret manufacture, was being undertaken there.

Fig 103: Coin mould from Needham. Width 45mm.

The surrounding area has revealed mainly Late Iron Age artefacts within a triangular area defined by the convergence of the two rivers in the west and the watershed and Panworth Ditch in the east. The area immediately south-west of Saham Toney, adjacent to Watton Brook, in the parishes of Hilborough, Bodney, Great Cressingham, Little Cressingham and Threxton, reveals prolific activity. Another focus lay on higher ground above a loop in Watton Brook at Little Cressingham.

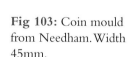

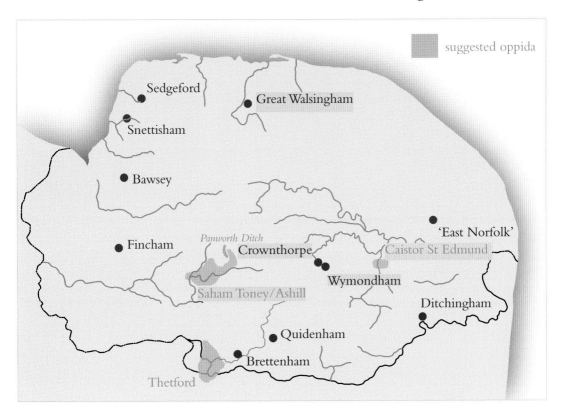

Fig 104: Sites of the Late Iron Age in Norfolk.

The entire settlement at Saham Toney/Ashill and the vicinity covered several square kilometres. The location is a concentration of all forms of artefacts and the settlement included a manufacturing and trading role. Numerous non-local coin types indicate long-distance trading contacts and emphasise the area's importance.

OTHER LATE IRON AGE SETTLEMENTS

Some earlier sites, such as Park Farm, Wymondham, remained in use but many new sites can also be assigned to this period, by which time settlement had spread onto the heavier boulder-clay interfluves. In the Fenland, too, there was an appreciable density of settlement on the southern islands and promontories, where the clays were exploited for settlement.[20] Pollen evidence also indicates extensive deforestation in parts of east Norfolk.[21]

Several smaller sites also appear to have had a role in relation to trade. We can detect how silver as a trading mechanism spread from the larger sites to smaller ones:[22] thus Brettenham, Burlingham, Ditchingham, Great Walsingham, Quidenham and Wicklewood have all produced appreciable numbers of Icenian silver coins, deposition probably reaching a peak between AD 10 and AD 60. These sites are distributed right across Norfolk and, together, they once again indicate that there was more of a widespread monetary economy across the area than has previously been appreciated. This network of smaller trading settlements served to complement the major foci at the *oppida* sites.

Many Roman sites in Norfolk can now be seen to exhibit continuity from the Late Iron Age. It is noticeable that Brettenham, Ditchingham, Great Walsingham and Wicklewood continued as small towns during the Roman administration. However, of the three areas of settlement identified as *oppida*, only Caistor St Edmund continued into the Roman period.

The Waveney valley was a major transport route and attracted settlement not only on the north but also on the south, Suffolk, side. At Homersfield (Suffolk), situated opposite Wortwell in Norfolk, Bill Holdridge has undertaken a metal-detector survey of a site which was partially excavated half a century ago; these investigations revealed a thriving settlement.[23] Material recently discovered includes domestic pottery, button-loop fasteners and cosmetic pestles, together with coins in gold and silver, and more exotic potin and Trinovantian issues from the south. This would have been a substantial settlement associated with water-borne transport and early trade. Coins also show an early Roman presence which developed in size during the Roman period, when its position on the clay facilitated the establishment of pottery kilns. There was also copper working on site. Finds indicate the presence of a shrine or temple which served the surrounding area.

A number of farmsteads have also been identified. One, at Spong Hill, remained in use from the Late Iron Age into the 4th century AD.[24] Another example was excavated at Runcton Holme, on the fen-edge, between 1931 and 1936; weaving and salt production were both undertaken there. Evidence for farming during the 1st centuries BC and AD was also discovered at Eaton Heath, Norwich,[25] including boundary ditches which outlined planned field systems, and a small number of pits. Another farmstead was discovered by Michael de Bootman at Great Dunham, near Castle Acre, in 2002. Pottery analysis has shown that this was in use between the 3rd and 1st centuries BC.

Crownthorpe

The Late Iron Age site at Crownthorpe, in Wicklewood parish, is known through a fascinating collection of artefacts recovered from the surface through metal detection. No excavation has been undertaken on the site and although as a result nothing is known about the structures below ground, this settlement would probably have been a small concentration of roundhouses and stock enclosures.

The association of this site with Icenian Bury type coins has been mentioned above; they may have been manufactured here. Other fine metalwork items recovered include several La Tène-style brooches and fittings with Celtic-style decoration. However, the most significant find was the Crownthorpe hoard of bronze vessels, mentioned in Chapter 1, which provides a direct association with the time of Boudica's rebellion in AD 60.

TRADE WITH THE ROMAN WORLD

This period saw important social and economic developments across parts of south-east England. There was a renewal of exchange contacts, which had lapsed during the Middle Iron Age, with continental Europe. Britain exported a range of goods, amongst which agricultural produce was prominent. The ancient writer Strabo tells that minerals such as tin, iron lead and copper, together with goods such as hides, hunting dogs and slaves, were also exported.[26]

The Iceni did not receive the same range of imports from the Mediterranean world as did sites further south, where there is evidence for imported pottery and amphorae. However, archaeology is now showing that Norfolk was engaged in significant trade, both with the continent and with other parts of Britain. There is now good evidence for the early introduction of continental material in the form of gold and silver and the use of directly recycled Roman coinage, confirming that East Anglian society was open to outside influences and imports from the 1st century BC onwards. Much of this metalwork was subsequently reworked into local-style vessels and coins, particularly before the conquest of AD 43; after this there was a more general acceptance of Roman style and imagery.[27]

Some direct evidence for contact with Gaul came in the form of foreign coins. In 1995 two silver coins of the Santones, of western Gaul, and the Aedui, from central Gaul, were discovered at Gayton in west Norfolk. The presence of Gallic coins confirms that there was a level of contact with those specific areas. Northern East Anglia has always had close ties with the continental regions of north-east France and the Low Countries. This natural axis for trade has continued into modern times. The length of the Norfolk coastline presents many potential locations for trading ports; one prime location is the mouth of the River Yare, where the Great Estuary provided access into the heart of Norfolk via a network of rivers. The importance of this location was certainly recognised by the Romans. Another major point of entry must have been located in the north-west, somewhere between Snettisham, Hunstanton and Brancaster, through which precious metals were imported during the earlier 1st century BC.

Burgh Castle

Today the site of Burgh Castle lies inland from the east coast, situated above an expanse of marshes which once formed the Great Estuary.

Before the silting-up of the estuary during the post-Roman period the location had high strategic importance and was chosen by the Romans as the location for a Saxon Shore fort. In 1994 an evaluation excavation was undertaken at Burgh Castle by the Norfolk Archaeological Unit.[28] They encountered a system of ditches beyond the fort which appeared to be outer defences. However, the ditches were notable for their lack of ceramics of a Roman or later date. Then, large sherds of Iron Age briquetage were found in one of the ditches, suggesting they might have been dug at an earlier date than had been anticipated.

Fig 105: Slave shackles from the River Wensum, at Worthing. Scale 1:2.

Although this evidence is very limited in extent, it suggests that these ditches may have served as a boundary, cutting off the promontory during the Iron Age. So, could the Roman site have had an Iron Age predecessor? These ditches are perhaps reminiscent of the Iron Age dyke system at Hengistbury Head, which served to cut off the headland from any landward approach.[29] Is it possible that there was an Iron Age coastal trading site beneath Burgh Castle?

This slight evidence may be an indication that the Roman fort was situated at this location *because* there had been an earlier trading settlement, of Iron Age origin. Only excavation will confirm or disprove this suggestion.

The evidence for slavery

The brutality of life in the Roman world is reflected in the writings of Strabo, who refers to slaves among the list of exports from Iron Age Britain. There is archaeological evidence from right across Britain which confirms the existence of this shocking trade. One silver coin (dated c 50–30 BC) of the Cantiaci, who inhabited the region of modern Kent, depicts two men shackled by slave chains and carrying a wine amphora.[30]

Slave shackles have been found at sites including Bigbury in Kent and Llyn Cerrig Bach on Anglesey.[31] Closer to Norfolk, examples have been found across Essex and Suffolk. In Norfolk itself, shackles have been found at Weeting and Hockwold, on the fen-edge, and at Worthing, to the north of Breckland. More recently, examples were found in the county, at Burnham Overy in 1994 and Bunwell in 1995, through metal detecting (Fig 105).

A number of these British finds have been associated with watery places, including Walbrook in London, Ware Lock in Hertfordshire, the River Tyne at Corbridge, the River Black (County Kildare) and Lough Sheelin in Ireland. To these may be added the Norfolk fen-edge examples from Weeting and Hockwold. Could it be that these custodial relics were intentionally consigned to watery sacred places as an expression of thanks to the gods when their owner had been fortunate enough to escape or be released from captivity?

Our evidence for Iron Age slavery comes not just in the form of these retarding chains. In 1991 a small bronze figurine was discovered at Dersingham, near King's Lynn. It has the attitude of a seated captive, bound at the wrists and neck (Fig 106). Once again, this item was associated with a wet place; it was found by the old course of the River Ingle. Its appearance is very similar to a small corpus of other known examples, ten of which are from Britain.[32] They include examples from the Roman fort at Brough-under-Stainmore, in Cumbria,[33] and, closer to Norfolk, from Harmston and Thonock in Lincolnshire.[34] Miranda Aldhouse-Green associated the attitude of the Brough figure with what she called deliberate humiliation and subjugation of the individual in question. She suggests that the person may have had a power so dangerous that it needed to be tethered to render it harmless. So, just who could the Norfolk figurine represent? Could it even be Boudica herself or one or her followers, symbolically shackled?

Fig 106: Bronze figurine in the form of a seated captive. Height 42mm *(copyright Norfolk Museums and Archaeology Service).*

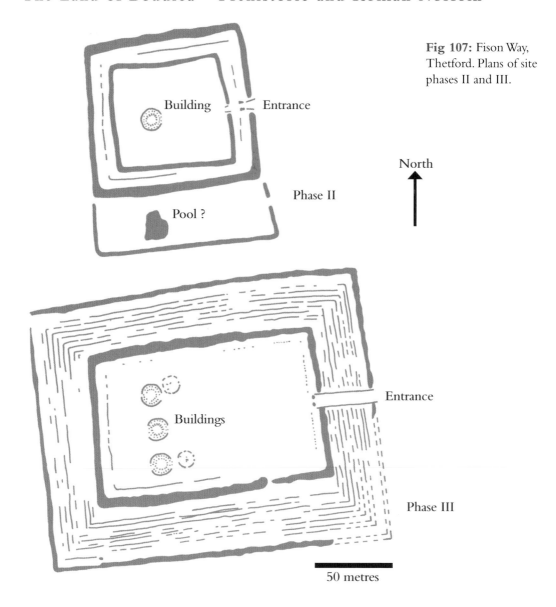

Fig 107: Fison Way, Thetford. Plans of site phases II and III.

FISON WAY, THETFORD – ANOTHER REGIONAL CENTRE

The site of Fison Way, Thetford, was excavated between 1980 and 1982. The grand and unusual nature of the final phases of the site originally led the excavator, Tony Gregory, to speculate that it might have been Boudica's palace.[35] The precise function of this long-used site is still not completely clear but Richard Bradley has explained how the site developed from a settlement at which some specialised activities took place into a grand ceremonial centre which became physically separated from its adjacent landscape.[36]

Gregory distinguished three main phases at this settlement. (Fig 107) The first phase lasted from the Middle Iron Age, perhaps as early as the 4th century BC, to the early 1st century AD, and consisted of a series of separate hilltop enclosures. The northernmost enclosure was constructed around a round barrow. Further south, an oval-shaped earthwork contained a grave, as did two of the ditched enclosures.

The second phase probably dated to the period of the Roman conquest. This stage was dominated by a large square-shaped enclosure defined by double ditches. A single massively constructed round building was positioned inside, on the central axis, and aligned with the entranceway which lay to the east. Other smaller enclosures surrounded the complex, one of which, a rectangular example, joined the main enclosure to the south. Clusters of graves were found to the north, while a workshop containing clay moulds for minting coins was an important discovery.

Soon after this, in the third phase, perhaps in the AD 40s to mid 60s, the main enclosure was enlarged to form a rectangle orientated east–

Fig 108: Reconstruction of Fison Way, phase III, (illustration by Sue White).

131

west and measuring 220m x 175m. (Fig 108) This time it contained five carefully positioned round buildings, again aligned towards a prominent entrance to the east. Three of the structures were positioned side-by-side, facing the entrance, with two others located in front of the outer pair. The central building was very substantial and may have had two storeys. This final enclosure was surrounded by parallel rows of close timber fencing which may have served as an artificial, ceremonial, oak grove.

The remarkable plan and size of the Fison Way complex suggests that it had an importance right across the region, perhaps way beyond the Breckland. The near-absence of domestic debris recovered during the excavation makes it more probable that this was a ceremonial, and possibly a religious, centre, particularly in its latest stages. Bradley suggests that it might have provided a symbol of native resistance to the foreign rule of Rome.

Fig 109: A harness mount from Fison Way, Thetford. Diameter 73mm.

POLITCAL FOCI IN THE LATE IRON AGE

Snettisham and Fison Way were prominent sites which undoubtedly exercised influence over wide areas. Both are situated in west Norfolk and each could have been a focus of religious activity of regional significance. Both may also have been associated with exercising political power across the region. However, it was Snettisham that had first came to prominence, as related in the previous chapter.

It was in later pre-Boudican years that the large sprawling *oppida* developed in the south and south-east of Norfolk. Saham Toney, Thetford and Caistor St Edmund all came to prominence somewhat later than Snettisham. This reflects a shift in power away from the western zone towards the sites in Breckland and the clayland further east which dates from the end of the 1st century BC.

This was the situation at the time of the Roman invasion of Britain. Political power lay in the south, centred on these large trading settlements. Boudica herself probably lived at one, if not all, of these larger sites, possibly moving from one to another in the way that our modern monarchy travel between their different homes across England and Scotland.

Chapter 10

The Roman invasion and the end of Iron Age Norfolk

Historical references to the people living in the area of Norfolk extend back to the mid 1st century BC, when Julius Caesar mentions a group named the *Cenimagni* among the eleven tribes who surrendered to him.[1] Neither of Caesar's two incursions reached East Anglia but there is evidence of social disruption in the area at that time, in the form of hoards of gold Gallo-Belgic coins which have been recovered from locations close to the north Norfolk coast.

Following Caesar's expeditions to Britain, Roman policy shifted from one of annexation to one of watching tribal leaders and exerting a degree of control through careful treaty relations. The area of Norfolk can no longer be considered to have been an isolated backwater at that time; archaeology is showing how trading links were developing with the world to the south, towards the north Thames region, as well as continuing with the continent. The shift in political power to the *oppida* in south and east Norfolk was based on their growing status as expanding economic centres and their control of the developing trade routes.

THE CLIENT KINGDOM

For a short period in the mid 1st century AD, the early history of Norfolk suddenly comes starkly to life through the writings of Roman historians. The Iceni were involved in a great drama during these years and the spotlight of world history briefly shone on this area. Our account of Norfolk's development through the early years of Roman Britain can be supplemented through these historical accounts.

It was in AD 43 that Claudius chose to invade Britain. His force consisted of four legions, each of 6000 troops. There were also 20,000–30,000 auxiliaries. In total, the army of invasion comprised 50,000 fighting men. It was accompanied by civil servants, support services, traders and a civilian retinue which amounted to a major incursion of personnel into Britain.

Once the conquest of the south-east seemed complete, Claudius himself travelled to Britain. The Emperor received the submission of eleven British chieftains, which is recorded on his triumphal arch in Rome. The historian Tacitus, writing between AD 75–120, indicates that the Iceni considered themselves as allies of Rome in the years immediately after the conquest and it is likely that Prasutagus, a king of the Iceni and husband of Boudica, was among those who submitted to Claudius.

The Iceni entered into a treaty relationship with Rome through the agency of a client king, a practice commonly used in other parts of the Empire. A client kingdom could retain many of its own laws and independence, while enjoying protection from external attack by Rome. It was also allowed to continue to strike and use its own coinage. In return, the king was expected to name the Emperor as his heir and generally to act in a pro-Roman way. In this way, the Iceni were ensured a period of peace and security, and the tribal area of the Iceni remained neutral during the main period of the conquest of Britain.

During this period Rome was exerting a strong influence on Iron Age communities at a subtle level not always manifested in an obvious way in the material record. There was steadily increased contact and Roman goods, tastes and styles were reaching the area and were being absorbed by at least part of the community. A good example is in the Crownthorpe hoard of drinking vessels, which shows a fusion of Roman and Celtic artistic styles.

THE REBELLION OF AD 47

By AD 47 the military governor Aulus Plautius had established a defensive line, known today as the Fosse Way frontier, between the Rivers Severn and Trent. In that year he was replaced by Ostorius Scapula, who was tasked with pressing ahead with the conquest of Britain. In order to achieve the advance beyond the Fosse Way, he needed to withdraw troops from the south but also ensure the security of his rear. He decided to disarm those living behind the military front, removing their weapons of warfare.

The removal of weapons was seen as a massive indignity by the conquered peoples of the south and east, and particularly so by the Iceni, who had neither been defeated in battle by nor surrendered to the Romans. Indeed, they considered themselves as allies of Rome. No doubt there had always been those within the tribe who were less than happy with the political alliance, with the invaders who were seen to be occupying the lands of their neighbours and subjecting them to unprecedented indignities as conquered peoples. However, the removal of Icenian arms was perceived as an open signal of mistrust and was enough to spark a faction of the tribe into open revolt sometime in AD 47.

An account of the events has been recorded by the Roman historian Tacitus.[2] He graphically describes the fierce battle and savage defeat of the Iceni, telling how the Iceni chose a defendable position for their action, which was protected by earthworks. Archaeologists have suggested that the location of the battle was Stonea Camp in the Cambridgeshire Fenland.[3] However, another possible site is Holkham Camp in north Norfolk. This site, defended by earth banks and ditches, was in a naturally strong position – surrounded by salt marshes on all sides and accessed by a single narrow causeway. The Romans stormed the fortification and restored order to the land of the Iceni. Following this revolt, the whole tribe was subsequently ruled over by Prasutagus.

THE REBELLION OF AD 60-61

King Prasutagus died in AD 60 (Fig 110). Under the agreement struck with the Romans in the creation of the client kingdom, the king was expected to name the Roman emperor as his heir. However, Prasutagus attempted to bequeath half of his estate to his family. Catus Decianus, Procurator of Britain (treasury officer), was sent to the kingdom to enforce the authority of the Emperor and to secure the whole estate for Nero.

Fig 110: Coin of King Prasutagus (drawing by Sue White).

Resentment was still simmering within part of the tribe following the brutal suppression of AD 47. Another cause of anger came when Catus Decianus attempted to reclaim monies which were termed 'loans' by the Romans. This money had been presented to leading members of the tribe under Claudius. It appears that the Iceni did not share the same concept of loans; the monies had been received in terms of goodwill gift exchange. The demand for their return was taken as a grievous insult to the tribe. Subsequent outrages by the Romans culminated in the flogging of Boudica, wife of the dead king, and the violation of her daughters. There could have been no greater insult to this proud tribal people. Their simmering anger, under the leadership of Boudica, ignited into open rebellion and lust for revenge.

The Iceni poured south and were joined by the adjacent tribe, the Trinovantes, who inhabited the area now covered by Essex, parts of Suffolk, Hertfordshire and Cambridgeshire (Fig 111). These people had their own grievances; some of them had been thrown off their own land to make way for the settlement of Roman veteran soldiers. The growing army marched on the capital of the new Roman province

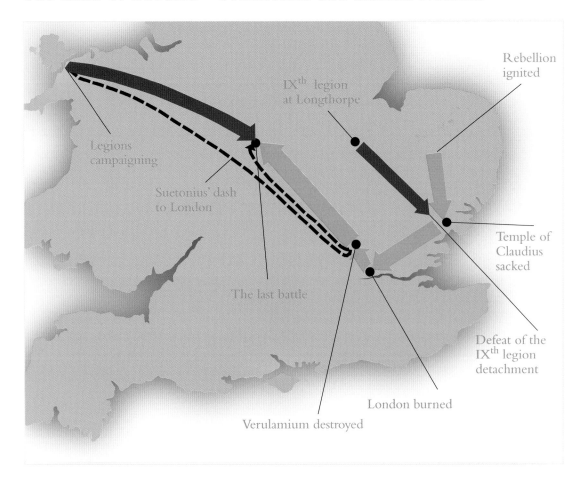

Rebellion
ignited

IXth legion
at Longthorpe

Legions
campaigning

Suetonius' dash
to London

Temple of
Claudius
sacked

The last battle

Defeat of the
IXth legion
detachment

London burned

Verulamium destroyed

at Camulodunum (Colchester). It is at this point in the story that the statue of Claudius was torn down and the horse's leg, later deposited at Ashill, was carried off as a trophy (see Fig 6). The town was still under construction and remained relatively defenceless. It was razed to the ground, and was followed by the other new settlements at Londinium (London) and Verulamium (St Albans). The Roman governor Suetonius Paulinus eventually lured the native army to battle at the site of his choosing, near Mancetter in the Midlands.

Tacitus tells how the Roman forces used the terrain to their advantage. They stood their ground despite being heavily outnumbered and launched their javelins at the advancing British army with devastating effect before bursting forward in a wedge formation. The cavalry then broke up all remaining pockets of resistance. The Romans showed no mercy and many thousands of Boudica's followers, together with their animals, were slaughtered as they tried to flee, being boxed in by the baggage train which blocked their escape. It was in the aftermath of this decisive action that Icenian territory came under full Roman rule.

Fig 111: The course of the Boudican rebellion.

Fig 112: Crownthorpe hoard – the strainer bowl. Rim diameter 205mm.

Fig 113: Crownthorpe hoard – the patera bowl. Bowl diameter 216mm.

WHAT CAN ARCHAEOLOGY TELL US ABOUT THE REBELLION?

Evidence of the rebellion is not restricted to the pages of Tacitus. A series of spectacular archaeological finds have been made, bringing us into direct contact with the people who took part in these dramatic events. Some of the discoveries, including the fragment of Claudius' statue from Colchester and a group of drinking vessels from Crownthorpe, were related in Chapter 1.

The Crownthorpe hoard

Although the discovery of the Crownthorpe hoard was discussed in Chapter 1, this spectacular and important group of objects deserves fuller description. The hoard contained seven individual items, all

Fig 114: Crownthorpe hoard – the two tinned bowls. Diameter 106mm.

Fig 115: Crownthorpe hoard – the saucepan. rim diameter 88mm.

made of bronze. The largest item was a strainer bowl which had been repaired in a rather crude manner, with the application of a spout in the form of a stylised lion's head (Fig 112). The other six vessels had been packed inside the strainer bowl prior to burial. They consisted of a patera bowl with a form of handle made in southern Italy (Fig 113); two shallow bowls with everted (out-turned) rims, which had been tinned on the interior, giving the appearance of silver (Fig 114); a deep-pan saucepan of standard Roman type, another import, possibly from Capua in southern Italy (Fig 115); and, most special within the hoard, a charming pair of Roman-style drinking cups (Fig 116). These last items form a closely matching pair, each carrying handles decorated with Celtic-style swimming ducks, which are unparalleled outside this hoard (Fig 117). The eyes of the ducks are inlaid with red enamel. It is likely

Fig 116: Crownthorpe hoard – the two cups. Height 89mm.

that these cups were made locally, in the style of Roman silver imports; the handles are definitely not in the classical tradition. Together, this group of vessels formed a drinking set of the type used within a Roman household. There is some debate as to whether it would have been used to strain and serve wine or beer,[4] but whichever was the case, it shows the adoption of Roman ways of doing things at the settlement of Crownthorpe during the mid 1st century AD. It had been deposited in a high position, a location which still provides views right across the local landscape.

The Crownthorpe hoard had been hidden in the ground as the Iceni rose in revolt against the Romans under Boudica. It may have been owned by a prominent local person who had been hoping to enhance his status by adopting Roman modes of behaviour, a strategy that must have backfired, because the hoard had been buried in some haste. The owner may have been fleeing from Boudica's rebels, who were intent on revenge against the Romans and their friends. And he was presumably caught, as he never returned to recover the items.

Fig 117: Crownthorpe hoard – a cup handle, showing the duck-shaped decoration.

Another deposit has been associated with the instability surrounding the rebellion. A hoard of five Roman silver drinking cups was discovered in 1962 at Blackdyke Farm on the south-eastern fen-edge. They were of exceptional quality and had been elaborately decorated in a style associated with continental late Hellenistic vessels of the 1st centuries BC and AD.[5] They had been deliberately buried and may have been loot, hoarded for temporary safe-keeping during the upheavals.

Coin hoards are another form of evidence which graphically shows the extent of instability in Norfolk as the rebellion took hold. Ten hoards of the period have been recorded, nine of which comprise silver coins and one bronze metalwork. Five of the former comprise Icenian

Fig 118: Portrait of Boudica, painted by Ivan Lapper *(copyright Norfolk Museums and Archaeology Service).*

silver units and four are of mixed composition, also containing Roman *denarii*.[6] Significantly, they cluster in the south of the county and can be seen to form three main groups. One centres around *Venta Icenorum*, while a second group clusters around Thetford and spreads along the Waveney valley. The third concentration is found beyond Norfolk, in north-east Cambridgeshire – between March, Stonea and Chatteris. That part of the Fens was part of Icenian territory and this appears to have been an important focus for the western part of the tribe. Together, these hoards suggest that the centre of the rebellion was in the vicinity of Thetford and Caistor St Edmund, perhaps pointing to the location of the events of AD 60 as described by Tacitus.

FOCUS ON BOUDICA

How much do we really know about Boudica? In some ways we know a lot and she unquestionably remains one of the most recognised figures in world history. The historical account by Tacitus is both descriptive and memorable, but tantalisingly limited. Today, archaeology is increasingly shedding new light on the period of the rebellion but we still know little about Boudica as a person, and the historical glimpses add to the sense of mystery surrounding her (Fig 118).

So, she remains a shadowy figure. We don't even know the name she was given during her lifetime. The name Boudica derives from the Celtic word *bouda*, which means 'victory' (*buddog* in modern Welsh), and was probably a title conferred on her during or resulting from her successes in battle against the Romans. The name itself has been spelled in different ways, which is the source of concern to generations of people to whom the version *Boadicea* became familiar. Tacitus called her *Boudicca*, mistakenly adding a second 'c'. The error was later compounded by a medieval copyist who inscribed an 'a' instead of a 'u' and an 'e' instead of the second 'c'. However, the most correct form carries just one 'c'.[7]

The Roman historian Dio Cassius, writing in the late 2nd–early 3rd century AD, provided the following description of Boudica:[8]

> *She was very tall and severe.*
> *Her gaze was penetrating and her voice was harsh.*
> *She grew long red hair that fell to her hips*
> *And wore a large golden torc*
> *And a vast patterned cloak with a thick plaid fastened over it.*

We cannot prove nor disprove this physical description. However, our developing knowledge of the period can suggest more about her probable personal appearance. Boudica was an important individual and an aristocrat. Both she and Prasutagus, as rulers of the pro-Roman client kingdom, would have been receptive to Roman culture and would have been influenced by Roman modes of dress and behaviour. They would have been elegantly groomed and attired in a way that reflected Roman fashions. They would have worn elaborate jewellery and fine clothing, as prominent people had done since the Bronze Age. At the same time their tribal identity was important, and their jewellery would have been fashioned by local craftsmen in local forms, carrying tribal motifs which expressed Icenian identity.

Boudica would have worn a form of brooch called the rear-hook, which is a form we now know was made within Iceni territory and served to identify those who lived and came from there. She would also have borne the tribal symbols of the back-to-back crescents and triplet symbols somewhere on her dress.

She would have taken great care of her appearance. Prominent people were well-groomed and used toilet implements, including nail cleaners and tweezers, to clean their bodies, especially the face and hands. The women used cosmetics. Many small 'cosmetic grinders' have been found in Norfolk and Suffolk, which were used to grind coloured powders that were applied to the faces of wealthy women, like modern-day make-up. Boudica would have been familiar with this practice (Fig 119).

What actually happened to Boudica after the final battle remains a mystery and has become the subject of folklore. Suetonius failed to capture her and according to Tacitus she took poison rather than be taken back to a Roman triumph. Dio Cassius, writing over a century later, says that she died of a disease and that she received a grand and costly burial. However, her burial site has never been discovered.

BOUDICA'S LEGACY

What was Boudica's legacy? Some consider that she is mainly remembered because of the way writers in modern times have promoted her as an embodiment of the national character and a symbol of resistance against oppression and potential invasion. Portrayed as a champion of the underdog, her image has a particular resonance with the British psyche.[9]

In truth, Boudica achieved far more. She showed extraordinary strength and leadership at a time of great crisis. Her charisma was such that she united not only the Iceni but also factions of other neighbouring tribes. Militarily, she was able to identify and exploit weakness in the greatest military machine of the ancient world, a feat that was achieved by few others. The Roman army was often poorly led by incompetent generals but was usually saved at such times by the quality and training

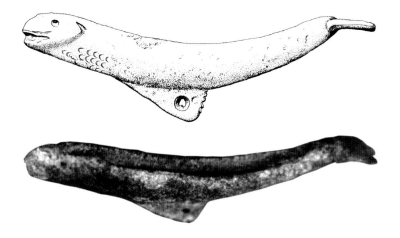

Fig 119: Cosmetic palette. Unusual example in the form of a sea mammal, possibly intended to represent a dolphin or whale, from Hindringham. Length 85mm (drawing by Sue White).

of its fighting men. Boudica repeatedly overcame this foe. She ultimately came close to ejecting the Romans from the whole of the recently won new province.

The native culture of Boudica's people did not just disappear after their military defeat. In AD 61 her conquerors arrived in the land of the Iceni and imposed full Roman rule across the area. Roman civilisation was introduced but today archaeology is showing how many aspects of the native way of life continued largely unchanged beneath a surface veneer of Romanisation.

Chapter 11
The establishment of Roman Norfolk

But the Roman came with a heavy hand,
And bridged and roaded and ruled the land
(Rudyard Kipling, *The River's Tale*)

THE ROMAN COASTLINE

Before we start to investigate the developments associated with the establishment of Roman Norfolk it is important to consider the physical differences in the shape of the coastline which defined the study area at that time. Both the north and east coasts were markedly different to those of today. It has been calculated that, between Holme-next-the-Sea and Happisburgh, the coast lay approximately 2km to the north of its present position.[1]

In the west, the coastline ran south from where King's Lynn now stands. There were marine transgressions and recessions during the period and some people were able to move westward into the Fenland, onto what are known as the Terrington Beds. In the south, the River Waveney was a more substantial feature than today and served both as a physical barrier with the land that is now Suffolk and a transport link to the sea.

The Roman landscape of east Norfolk was dominated by a great estuary which extended some 20km inland, fed by rivers which included the Yare and Bure, as well as the Waveney. Where Great Yarmouth stands today was open water and the region of Flegg was a large island, while Lothingland, to the south, formed a long peninsula.[2] Between about 5500 and 2500 BC the sea had risen, extending up river valleys and flooding what is now the Halvergate triangle.[3] Then, during the Bronze Age, the sea began to retreat from the lower valleys of Broadland, and they became dominated by fresh water once again. The sea was kept out during this time by a sand bar which had formed along the east coast between about 3000 and 2000 BC. This barrier was eventually breached during the Iron Age and major flooding occurred across Broadland. Some time before the Roman invasion the sea level rose and saltwater

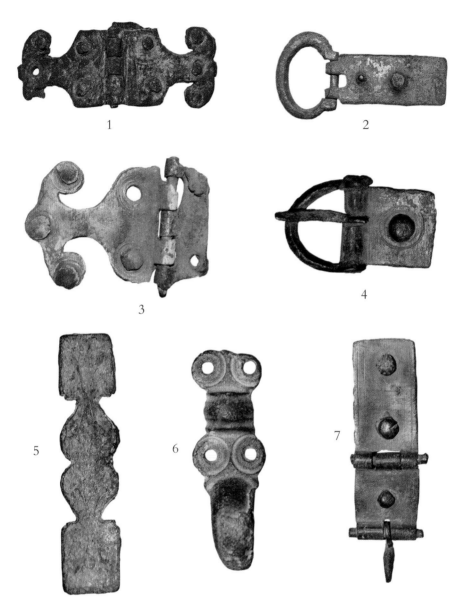

Fig 120: Items of military metalwork: fittings from Roman armour found at Norfolk sites. **1:** 60mm, **2:** 30mm, **3:** 39mm, **4:** 32mm, **5:** 46mm, **6:** 44mm, **7:** 55mm.

conditions penetrated still further up the valleys and wider out into the floodplains, leaving clay deposits above the preceding peat, covering the vegetation and replacing it with salt marsh and mud flats.[4]

An insight into the extent of the Great Estuary is provided by a document known as the Hutch Map – so called because it was kept in Great Yarmouth's town chest, or 'hutch'. This map was produced much later, in Elizabethan times, but provides a view of the situation which still remained around AD 1000. The Hutch Map shows Lothingland and Flegg as islands, with a large sand bank forming in the mouth of the estuary where Great Yarmouth now stands.[5]

MILITARY NORFOLK

The Romans spent the immediate post-conquest years strengthening their control of Britain, placing garrison forts at strategic intervals across the countryside. Aerial photography in Norfolk has identified several forts in recent years. However, it is not always possible to be certain whether sites are pre- or post-Boudican in foundation.

The Norfolk sites are part of a pattern of military garrisons situated right across south-east Britain. To the south, there was a legionary fortress at Colchester. Forts have been discovered at Coddenham and Pakenham in Suffolk, while another military site has been suggested at Hatcheston.

Evidence for the presence of the Roman army in Norfolk also comes in the form of early military metalwork finds, which are widespread. They include tunic fittings, armour, weapons and some types of coin which can be specifically associated with use by soldiers (Fig 120). Finds of early Roman Republican and imperial coins are often, if not invariably, interpreted as evidence for the presence of Roman troops at a site.[6] These include bronzes of Claudius I – *asses*, *dupondii* and *sestertii*. In particular, it is 'irregular' bronze coins of Claudius – crude copies of the official coins – that are discovered in greatest numbers (Fig 121). There was a substantial demand for coins by the invading army and associated personnel which could not be satisfied by the limited injection of money sent to Britain by the Roman authorities. No official mint existed in Britain at that time and it was the lack of coinage which led to the striking of the 'irregular' coins by the invasion army. They must have received official sanction as an emergency coinage for a limited period during the mid 1st century.

One group of military finds can be associated with the Pye Road, in eastern Norfolk, in the vicinity of Scole, Caistor St Edmund and Horstead. Others have been found to the north of Thetford, in the area around Ashill and Threxton. Some other finds, especially coins, appear to have been associated more with the coast. It may be that the role of the navy in subduing this area has been overlooked in the past. In contrast, these early Roman coin finds are not found in association with the Suffolk or Essex coastlines.[7] Landings between Burgh Castle in the east and Heacham in the west may have served to supply and reinforce troops advancing north overland in the aftermath of the Boudican rebellion.

Fig 121: Claudian imitation coins from Swanton Morley. Diameters 25 to 28mm.

147

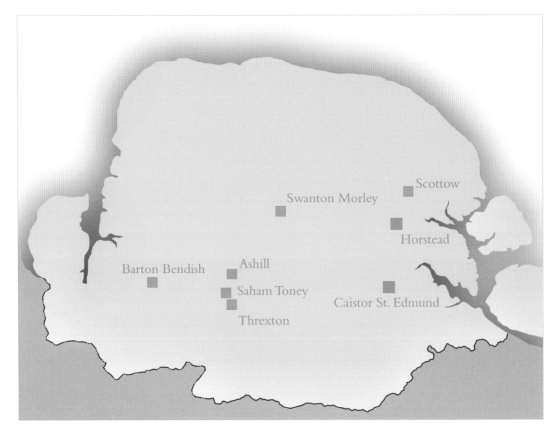

Early forts in Norfolk

Surface finds from the site of Woodcock Hall, Saham Toney, revealed the presence of a 1.6ha Roman fort of the Claudian period (Fig 122).[8] The fort had been constructed on a bluff south of the River Blackwater, and had been positioned to safeguard the river crossing, possibly in the period following the first Iceni revolt of AD 47. It then appears to have been abandoned after about 10 or 12 years.

Aerial photography now shows a second fort nearby, to the south, at Threxton. It was larger, covering 5.6ha, and surrounded by triple ditches. The size of the fort suggests a garrison of approximately 800 troops and it was probably constructed in the aftermath of the Boudican uprising.

Another potential military site has been identified nearby at Ashill, north-west of Saham Toney. This roughly square-shaped enclosure covers some 5ha and is enclosed by a ditch and bank.[9] Tony Gregory considered that this could be viewed as another possible early fort.

In 1984 aerial photography revealed the location of another early fort at Swanton Morley, next to the Romano-British small town of

Fig 122: Early Roman forts in Norfolk.

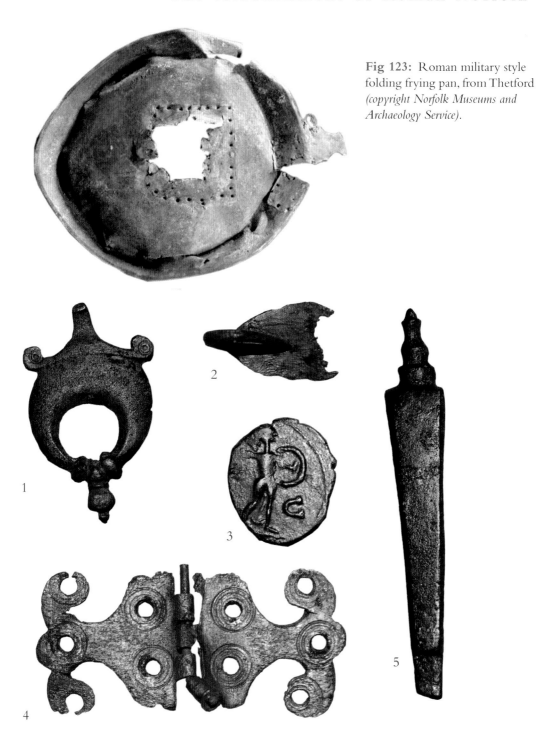

Fig 123: Roman military style folding frying pan, from Thetford *(copyright Norfolk Museums and Archaeology Service).*

Fig 124: Early military items from Venta Icenorum. **1:** harness pendant, 40mm **2:** armour hook, 26mm **3:** coin (as), 28mm **4:** armour hinge, 61mm **5:** scabbard mount, 88mm.

Billingford, in central Norfolk. The characteristic 'playing card' shape was clearly outlined, as was a defensive triple-ditch system, a feature which has been associated with several forts of this date across East Anglia. A metal-detector survey was carried out by Barrie Sharrock, which recovered a range of finds including early Roman coins, pottery and military-style metalwork. Some items of native metalwork and coins of the Iceni were also recovered. These may have found their way to the fort for the purpose of metalworking by the army blacksmiths.

A further cropmark enclosure has been identified to the west of Horstead, north of Norwich, by aerial photography. It takes the form of a large playing-card-shaped feature which has been identified as a Roman military fortification.[10] The size suggests that a detachment of legionary size could have used this, possibly as a temporary marching camp. It is likely that a very substantial force would have been involved in pacifying the area following the Boudican troubles.

In 1996 aerial photography revealed another playing-card-shaped cropmark at Barton Bendish in the south-west, to the west of the Devil's Dyke earthwork. This, again, was identified as a Roman marching camp. Fieldwalking in the vicinity has revealed 1st-century material, providing a likely date for the site. The fort also lies next to a large Late Iron Age settlement at Fincham. Another cropmark feature that may be additional evidence for military presence lies to the north of Norwich at Scottow, where an enclosure surrounded by several ditches has been identified.

Fig 125: Pilum head from Caistor. Length 130mm *(copyright Norfolk Museums and Archaeology Service).*

A number of pieces of Roman military equipment were found during excavations at Fison Way, Thetford. These may have been lost by soldiers involved in the demolition of the main site. In 1992 a military-style skillet, or frying pan, was found nearby. It was made of bronze, with a folding handle, enabling it to be carried inside a soldier's pack during marches (Fig 123). It also had an ancient repair on the base.

Military artefacts have also been turned up during excavations at Scole, on the Norfolk–Suffolk border, while substantial numbers of coins of military type have been found at the sites of Great Walsingham in the west and Burgh Castle on the east coast.

Caistor St Edmund

Artefacts recovered from the centre of the Roman town of *Venta Icenorum* at Caistor St Edmund confirm an early military presence. They include harness and tunic fittings, together with Claudian coins (Fig 124). Two individual *pilum* heads have recently been identified within the archive from the excavation of 1929–35 at Norwich Castle (Fig 125). Samian ware pottery dating from the reign of the emperor Nero (AD 54–68) and earlier Claudian (AD 41–54) pottery from east of the town may have been used by military personnel. Pottery kilns of a similar date, which were identified as a military kiln complex for the benefit of the army, were found immediately north and south of the north wall and south of the southern town ditch.

Further evidence of a military presence has come from aerial photography, which shows a triple-ditch system running roughly parallel to, and outside, the line of the later town walls on the south and east sides.[11] Although these features have not been closely dated, excavation showed the inner ditch to be V-shaped and of probable military type. These defences might have originally joined with the River Tas in the west and north to form a roughly square-shaped defensive enclosure. Triple ditches, as noted above, were a feature of early forts across this area; in addition to the Norfolk examples mentioned here, they have also been found at Pakenham and Coddenham in Suffolk. The area enclosed by the Caistor ditches is approximately that of a full-sized legionary fortress. There was a strong necessity to keep a close watch on the defeated tribe and the temporary stationing of a legion at this key location may have been required to ensure the peaceful transition to full Roman administration.

A Claudian 'irregular' *as* which had been countermarked with the stamp 'BON' (meaning 'bonus' or 'good coin') was discovered at the site in 1995 (Fig 126). This countermark has been closely dated to the

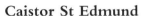

Fig 126: Claudian imitation coin, with a countermark 'BON'. Diameter 24mm.

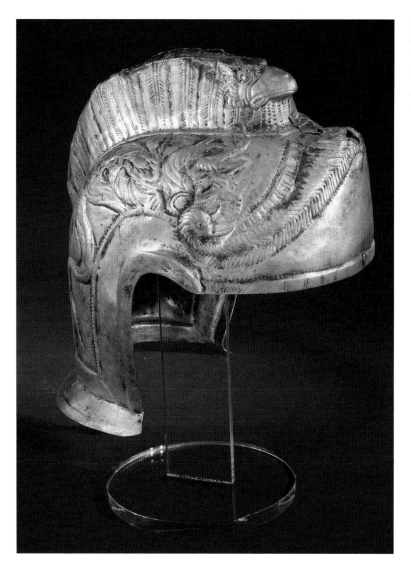

Fig 127: The cavalry parade helmet from Worthing. Height 250mm *(copyright Norfolk Museums and Archaeology Service)*.

mid to late AD 60s and there are only five other examples known from Britain, two of which come from the forts at Swanton Morley and Saham Toney. However, this countermark is well known outside Britain, from Rhenish frontier posts in the Roman province of *Germania Inferior*.[12] With half of the known British examples coming from Norfolk forts there is now a clear association between the military units operating in the upper Rhineland/Netherlands and this area in the post-Boudican years.

Later military evidence

In 1947, during dredging of the River Wensum at Worthing, a beautiful piece of Roman armour was recovered, in the form of a bronze, gilded, cavalry parade helmet (Fig 127). It had been made from a single sheet of metal and the crest was elaborately decorated in repoussee with feathered eagles. It had been made in the Danube valley during the first half of the 3rd century and was too delicate to have ever been used in battle.

In 1950, further dredging in the vicinity produced another remarkable find. Again made from gilded bronze, this visor mask from a cavalry parade helmet carried elaborate repoussee decoration depicting Mars on one side and Victory holding a wreath on the other (Fig 128). Both finds are evidence for a continued military presence in the area during the 3rd century AD.

In 2002 two individual fragments of a Roman military diploma were discovered at Great Dunham in central Norfolk by Michael de Bootman. The original small lead diploma dates from the 3rd century. It would have been awarded to an auxiliary soldier upon his completion of 25 years' service in the Roman army, confirming the grant of citizenship. Although this example is incomplete, specialists have been able to tell

Fig 128: Visor mask from the River Wensum. Height 198mm *(copyright Norfolk Museums and Archaeology Service).*

that the owner had served with the first cohort of Aquitanians, who are known to have served in Britain.[13] Unfortunately, the name of the soldier has not survived.

The changing picture

So, archaeological finds and aerial photography have transformed our understanding of early Roman military Norfolk. These forms of evidence have confirmed that there was a substantial mid 1st-century military presence in the land of the Iceni. Some of this can be associated with the subduing and monitoring the tribe during the post-Boudican years, with forts located close to centres of native population.

The overall distribution of finds also points to a military strategy of support and supply from the coast. Similar military finds are absent from the Suffolk and Essex coastline, and it appears that the role of the Roman navy in subduing the Norfolk area may have been overlooked in the past. Sea-borne landings between Burgh Castle in the south-east and Heacham in the north-west may have served to supply and reinforce troops advancing overland, perhaps in the aftermath of the Boudican rebellion. This observation again serves to confirm the continuing importance of maritime routes in relation to the area.

The effects of the second Icenian revolt lasted for generations. The scale of casualties meant that the native population was reduced, which in turn had an effect on agricultural production. There were no longer enough hands to work the land and the tribe struggled to produce enough food in the years after the defeat.

The imposition of full Roman administration brought a number of new ideas and ways of doing things to the area. Although daily life in the countryside was to change very little, some of these innovations were to have an impact on the development of the tribal area – the *Civitas Icenorum* – and its relationship with other parts of Britain and the continent, as a distinct region within the Roman Empire.

ROAD AND RIVER TRANSPORT

One of the most widespread and visible legacies of the Roman occupation is the network of roads. The routes of many have survived, providing several of our modern lines of communication. In the years after the invasion the Romans strengthened their control and constructed these roads in order to speed up the movements of troops and supplies and communications with other parts of the province. The network would have been largely established between the conquest and the end of the 1st century.

The roads which ran between major settlements were substantially built, with raised banks and ditches on either side. The construction comprised a base of rammed flint, clay or chalk and a cambered surface of stones. However, not all roads were built as thoroughly. Some less important routes were little more than trackways and were neither raised or surfaced. Sometimes natural obstacles were avoided, meaning that Roman roads were not always completely straight. However, the engineers were highly skilled and could cope with most situations; examples include the situation in the Fens, where the subsoil was too porous to support the road, and needed to be replaced by finer soil to prevent flooding.[14]

Evidence for Roman roads in Norfolk is contained in the Roman document known as the Antonine Itinerary, which outlines journeys planned by the Emperor Caracalla (AD 211–17). *Venta Icenorum* stood at the hub of the road system in the east, as well as being at the centre of a network of river routes stretching east to the Great Estuary and the sea beyond. Route IX describes a road from *Venta Icenorum* to London, which is listed as 127 Roman miles. Route V also runs through East Anglia, from London to Cambridge, but mentions the Norfolk sites of *Villa Faustini* (thought to be Scole) and *Venta Icenorum*. No Roman milestones have been identified in Norfolk. The route connecting *Venta* with Colchester and London has been known as the Pye Road since the 18th century. It passed through Long Stratton before reaching the town of Scole.

Another arterial route, which is known as the Fen Causeway, ran directly west from *Venta*, passing through Crownthorpe, Threxton and Denver. Work during the Fenland Survey Project and Fenland Management Project allowed the course of this road, which is still visible as a band of orange gravel in places, to be scrutinised in that sector. The initial construction is thought to have been undertaken in the 1st century. Some time later, probably in the 3rd century, this part of the Fens was flooded and a replacement road was built on higher ground, which was formed as a natural levee of silt.[15]

In central west Norfolk the Peddars Way ran up from Bildeston in Suffolk, cutting through Breckland and passing through Threxton towards Holme-next-the-Sea in the extreme north-west. It is thought that this location must have been a ferry point for vessels, perhaps of military origin, to cross the Wash.

The movement of goods by road was slow and expensive, while water transport was quicker, much more efficient and also safer. Norfolk's extensive network of rivers and its long coastline were therefore considerable assets. The Great Estuary in the east allowed penetration far inland by fleets of medium-sized boats and barges, while *Venta Icenorum* acted as a redistribution centre, where goods were transferred from barges to land transport.

RELIGION

Religion played an important part in everyday life in Roman Britain, just as it had in the years before Roman rule. Local Celtic gods became associated with their Roman counterparts, becoming combined in a 'Romano-Celtic' religion. The picture normally accepted is that the Romans pursued a policy of religious tolerance which helped the more general integration between themselves and the conquered peoples of Britain. However, it is also possible to envisage a situation whereby the Romans in fact forced the people of Britain to change their concepts of their own deities and re-mould them to fit within the Roman system, or pantheon.[16]

Fig 129: Bronze bust of Venus from Tharston. Height 70mm.

In this interpretation, which views the Romans as culturally arrogant rather than tolerant, native deities are likely to have undergone degrees of alteration to fit the mould of their classical counterparts. The local population probably would have attempted to resist this process.

A wide range of objects associated with religious practices has been found right across Roman Norfolk (Figs 129–132). Evidence for worship of the major Roman gods, such as Jupiter, is widespread in the county. Other gods, such as Mars and Mercury, were also represented in the form of figurines. The Romans introduced the practice of making representations of human and animal deities, which are occasionally found at sites of religious significance in the county.

A number of Iron Age sites associated with religious sanctuaries or ritual behaviour, such as Ken Hill, Snettisham, had sacred associations of long standing. Some continued to be used as religious centres during the Roman period.

Romano-British temples have been found at Caistor St Edmund, Crownthorpe, Great Walsingham and Hockwold-cum-Wilton, all of which were towns.

WRITING IN ROMAN NORFOLK

There was no tradition of writing in Britain prior to the conquest. The Romans introduced the Latin alphabet, initially through trading and early political contacts, as manifested on Late Iron Age coinage. The adoption and spread of literacy can be traced through varied forms of inscriptions and artefacts. In Norfolk, most evidence of writing has come from the largest town, *Venta Icenorum*, and it remains slight elsewhere in the county.

Stone inscriptions are very rare in Norfolk. One such fragment was found during excavations at *Venta* in 1929. Inscribed in two lines, the letters '-ADAT-'/'-SVPE-' are insufficient to allow a meaningful translation.

Fig130: Bronze Pan head mask from the Thetford area. Height 82mm.

Official documents recording legal issues are another form of evidence for writing. Military diplomas are exceptionally rare in Britain but two have now been found in Norfolk, one of which has already been mentioned in this chapter. Another came from the south gate at *Venta Icenorum*, and reads '…and are in Britain under [missing name of the governor] who have served for twenty five years and more'. The style of the text indicates that it was issued after AD 91 and before 24 September AD 105.[17]

Writing is also found in the form of spells and curses. People would scratch messages to specific deities on a small sheet of lead known as a *defixio*. This would be folded up and offered at a temple as personal messages to the gods. One such *defixio*, dedicated to the god Neptune, was found in the bank of the River Tas at *Venta Icenorum* (Fig 133). It requested the help of the deity to seek out a thief and recover a list of stolen items, including a wreath, bracelets, a cap, a mirror, a head-dress, a pair of leggings and ten pewter vessels. This discovery, associated with the sea god, also serves to highlight the importance attached to the role of the river and to continental trade across the North Sea by the town's inhabitants.

Lamellae were charms made of thin sheets of gold. Magical protective spells were written on one side and they were then rolled up to contain the magic. In 2003 only the fourth *lamella* to be recorded from Roman Britain was discovered in west Norfolk (Fig 134).[18] The writer of this example signed himself as 'Similis, son of Marcellina'. Similis had used the charm to call on the protection of Abrasax, who was an eastern deity, often depicted as having the head of a cockerel and snakes for legs. Abrasax was a popular god in Roman Britain.

People used iron styli for writing on wax tablets. Examples have been found at Caistor St Edmund, but not from other parts of Norfolk (Figs 135 and 136). Important documents would have seal boxes tied to them, which held an impression of the personal seal of the sender. These were often highly decorated, reflecting the use of seals as a mark of status. Seal box lids, again, mainly come from *Venta Icenorum*, although examples are known from smaller towns such as Crownthorpe (Fig 137). Lettering is occasionally found on trade-related objects, such as lead weights, again found at *Venta*. A lead bag seal was found at Brettenham, stamped with the letters 'C.BFEC'.

Evidence for literacy also comes from some temple sites. Votive letters have been found at sites such as Hockwold-cum-Wilton; worshippers

Fig 131: Pan head box mount from Elsing. Height 54mm.

Fig 132: Lead Mercury plaque from Brampton. Height 30mm.

Fig 133: A lead defixio from Venta Icenorum. 105mm x 65mm.

were able to purchase these items, which were made of bronze, and nail them to a wooden board to make personal dedications at the shrine.

Eye troubles in the Roman period were treated by a range of salves and ointments. The treatment of these ailments has left us with another form of written inscription known as 'oculists' stamps', which can provide us with written information, including details of specific treatments and the name of the doctor. These details were impressed onto sticks of ointment by the stamps, which were often made of soft stone. These stamps are rare finds in Britain but two have been found in Norfolk. One, which contained lettering which recorded that it was 'the stamp of Publius Anicius Sedatus', came from *Venta Icenorum* in 1927.[19] A second example was reported in November 2006 from the Roman town at Hockwold cum Wilton. It is inscribed with the letters CAELIBANVM, which have been translated as 'salve of frankincense'.[20]

Fig 134: The gold lamella from west Norfolk. 42mm x 30mm.

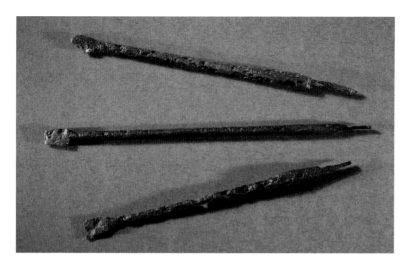

Fig 135: Iron styli from Venta Icenorum. Length of middle stylus 142mm.

COINAGE

The Romans introduced a mature multi-denominational system of coin use to Britain. This system was an essential medium to facilitate trade with the array of new markets. The use of coinage at certain sites during the Late Iron Age is now being seen to have been greater than previously envisaged, but the Roman system presented a deeply embedded single currency for the whole Empire.

Vast numbers of Roman coins circulated in Britain. They are generally the most common type of Roman artefact discovered today and have been found in prolific numbers from right across Norfolk (Fig 138). Official mints operated in Britain for only very brief periods and the economy of Britain relied on occasional injections of coin from imperial mints situated on the continent. Neither were all types of Roman coin sent to Britain. The smallest denominations – the *semis* and the *quadrans* – were not used here and are extremely rare finds in this country.

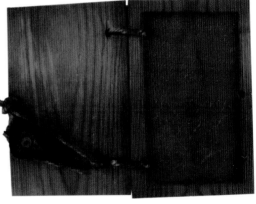

Fig 136: Reconstruction of a wax tablet used for writing.

Many thousands of Roman coins have been recovered from Norfolk, mainly by metal-detector users. Viewed collectively, they have contributed significantly to our understanding of the extent, development and chronology of Roman settlement.[21] In the absence of opportunities for excavation the study of the coins found at different locations can suggest the presence of a whole range of settlements and help elucidate their histories.

The bulk of the coin circulating in Norfolk up to AD 60 was Icenian rather than Roman. After this date, the presence of the Claudian types

Fig 137: A seal box with enamelled lid from *Venta Icenorum*. 31mm x 22mm.

provides a major source of evidence for the extent of early military activity. A subsequent general increase in site and casual finds shows that Norfolk benefited from the stimulus of Romanisation seen elsewhere in Britain during the Flavian period (from AD 69–96).

Coin use remained rare in the countryside during the first two centuries of Roman rule; only in the second half of the 3rd century did the use of coins take off more generally. The native farmsteads would not have experienced coin use perhaps until the mid to late 3rd century, and it still remained slight in some parts, notably on the fen-edge, within the area of what has been recognised as a large imperial estate. However, in some places, such as temple sites, as at Hockwold cum Wilton, there was intense coin use. Temple sites across Britain provided *foci* for seasonal fairs and markets for the surrounding rural population, who would have travelled many miles across the surrounding countryside. Large quantities of small denomination coins were lost at these religious sites in the later Roman period.

Fig 138: The Mattishall Roman coin hoard: 1080 silver denarii and antoniniani dating from AD 154 to 260, found in a greyware pot.

Unofficial coin production in Norfolk

There was no official mint in Britain until the late 3rd century, under the Emperor Carausius (AD 287–93), and unofficial coin manufacture was carried out throughout the duration of Roman Britain. Following the episode of irregular coin striking by the army, there was a small but persistent presence of counterfeit Roman coins in circulation. Most of these were imitations of silver *denarii* and they were made by casting the originals in base metal and applying a thin silver plating over this.

In 1995 a very unusual hoard of over 100 imitation plated *denarii* was discovered just over the border in Suffolk and reported to archaeologists at Norwich Castle Museum.[22] These coins were probably buried shortly after their 'terminal date' of AD 51, indicating that they belonged to the immediate post-conquest period. They were buried in the client kingdom between the rebellion of AD 47 and the uprising of Boudica, and appear to be very early good-quality forgeries. It is uncertain whether there was a link with military personnel in their production.

In 1990 a very unusual item was discovered at North Creake by metal detector. It initially appeared to be a small foil milk bottle top. Closer inspection showed it was made of gilded silver. It was a thin metal plating found to have been part of a counterfeit gold *aureus* of the Emperor Severus Alexander. This plating would have adhered to a base-metal core and was intended to make it look like a gold coin. The obverse legend IMP SEV ALEXAND AVG, a form used between AD 222–34, is still readable (Fig 139).

Fig 139: Plating from a Roman counterfeit gold aureus of the Emperor Severus Alexander (AD 222–35) from North Creake. Diameter 16mm.

Irregular coins produced in the late 3rd century are the most prolific type of Roman coin found today. These contemporary imitations, sometimes known as *barbarous radiates*, copied official radiate issues (*antoniniani*) of the 270s and 280s (Figs 140 and 141). They were produced at a time when there was a growing demand for coin and an insufficient supply from the official mints. More people wanted to use coins at this time and readily accepted these imitation coins alongside the official ones. Despite being manufactured on such a widespread basis, archaeologists have, until now, struggled to identify

Fig 140: Late 3rd-century barbarous radiate coin hoard from Scole (a total of 60 minims). Diameters 7 to 16mm.

their sources of production. Metal detection is now beginning to provide important evidence about some of the unofficial mint sites in Norfolk.

During the mid 1990s a prolific spread of Roman material associated with metalworking was found by metal detection at Rocklands, on the edge of Breckland. The presence of 29 barbarous radiates, all of minim size, provided conclusive proof that this was part of a coin producer's workshop. There were also 24 copper alloy rods, together with metal bar fragments, finished blank coin flans, which had been hammered smooth, ready for striking as coins, and also a lead lump covered in saw marks (Fig 142). This object may have been a source of lead, which the coiners would have added to the alloy in order to achieve the correct mixture. Other coin blanks would have been cut from the rods and bars. This workshop was situated at a small settlement, away from any major roads or major settlement.

Fig 141: A group of late 3rd-century barbarous radiate coins fused together in the 'peardrop' shape of a Roman cloth bag or purse, found at Bale. Length 38mm.

In December 1985 a group of 1 regular and 19 barbarous radiates were discovered at West Acre, a minor Roman rural site on the Peddars Way,[23] and in early 1988 a further 61 barbarous radiates were found there. All the coins are smaller than official issues and over half measure just 10mm diameter or less. More fascinating was the presence of three small bronze pellets, each containing just enough metal to produce a small blank flan.

More and more sites producing bars, blanks, pellets and cut *sestertii* (raw material for melting down) are now being discovered through metal detection. At the time of writing, nearly 50 of these workshop sites have been identified in Norfolk and Suffolk from just a two-year period of recording.[24] A picture is emerging of small-scale coin workshops located at very small settlements, away from the main settlements and towns.

Fig 142: Bronze rods and blank coins used in the production of barbarous radiates, found at Rocklands. All 7-12mm diameter.

THE DEVELOPMENT OF THE LANDSCAPE

Professor Frere has pointed to features across Roman Norfolk which suggest the possibility that there may have been a large-scale formal layout imposed within the Roman landscape in the aftermath of the Boudican rebellion.[25] Lengths of Roman road, lanes, agricultural trackways and some field boundaries which may indicate intentional alignment have been traced. Frere suggests that, if such a system did exist, it would have had a short life.

Soon, a network of towns, villages and rural buildings developed right across Norfolk. The evidence coming to light today is increasingly showing that there was in fact a high level of continuity within the landscape from the late prehistoric period through into Roman Norfolk. Such continuity can be seen in many towns, villages and rural settlements. The establishment of the towns and occupation in the countryside will be looked at in more detail in the next two chapters.

Chapter 12
The towns

Roman Norfolk, like its modern counterpart, was essentially a rural area. However, prominent within this agricultural landscape was a network of small towns and large villages. These medium-sized settlements grew up at key strategic locations, usually at places where a road or track crossed a river. They provided the functions that were necessary to ensure the well-being and development of the local farming communities, and also provided a link with Roman administration and, very importantly, with the wider Roman trading network.

There was just one major town, which the Romans called *Venta Icenorum*. It was situated towards the east, and sat at the hub of the network of major road and river routes. Today, *Venta* lies just three miles to the south of the modern city of Norwich, within the parish of Caistor St Edmund.

VENTA ICENORUM, THE TRIBAL CAPITAL

Venta Icenorum was not only the largest town in Roman Norfolk but it also served as the major Roman town for the whole of northern East Anglia. It provided administration and represented Roman authority within the region (Fig 143).[1] Situated next to the River Tas, it lay just to the north of the heavy central clayland. Today this site is identifiable by its well-preserved walls, which lie within a most picturesque and natural setting.

Early interest

Interest in the site can be traced back to the time of Elizabeth I. William Camden, who lived between 1551–1623, recognised that this was the site listed as *Venta Icenorum* in the Antonine Itinerary. At that date, much more of the town still survived and Camden wrote that 'the faces of

Fig 143: *Venta Icenorum*: the late Roman walled town (reconstruction by Sue White).

the four gates are still manifestly to be seen', as well as 'platforms of the houses and other buildings'. In the early 18th century John Kirkpatrick described the visible remains as 'monuments of a castle in it invironing fifty acres of ground, and ringbolts in the walls, whereto ships were fastened', thus confirming the presence of a wharf adjacent to the town's west gate.

Aerial photography transformed our understanding of the town during the 20th century. In 1928 photographs taken by the RAF showed the street layout in spectacular detail, which enabled an accurate plan of the town to be drawn (Fig 144). This led to the planning of excavations which were carried out between 1929 and 1935 by Donald Atkinson of Manchester University (Fig 145, 146 and 148).

The location and foundation

The situation of *Venta* provided some geographical advantages. Here, the River Tas was wide and deep enough to allow medium-sized boats to transport trade goods to and from the coastal ports. *Venta* was also far enough up the Yare/Wensum river system to allow roads

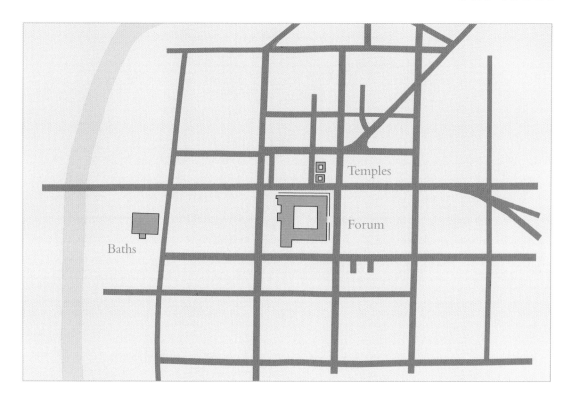

Temples

Forum

Baths

to access it easily. Its position in relation to the Great Estuary was particularly significant.

The area surrounding Caistor St Edmund, at the confluence of the Rivers Yare and Wensum, was a focus of settlement from the Neolithic period onwards. Arminghall henge is situated just 1.5km to the north-east and the Iron Age ritual or funerary enclosures at Harford Farm are just 800m to the north. This had been a focus of native settlement during the years of the client kingdom.

The Romans turned their backs on the other major native settlements in the Breckland and chose this as the *civitas capital*. It may be that those people living to the west were considered to have been pro-Boudican, while those at Caistor acted in a more pro-Roman way.

The layout

So *Venta Icenorum* became the *civitas capital*, the equivalent of today's county town. It served the area between other such centres at *Camulodunum* (Colchester), *Ratae* (Leicester) and *Lindum* (Lincoln). The layout of the Roman street grid has been dated to about AD 70. Judging from evidence of aerial photographs, this originally covered an area twice the size of that covered by the later town walls. The rectilinear street grid was laid out on a NNE/SSW alignment, with the streets

Fig 145: Small finds being washed at *Venta Icenorum* in 1929.

running parallel to the original course of the Tas. There are also streets which radiate from a nucleus just beyond the north-east corner of the walled area, which do not align with the main town grid. They may have been constructed earlier than the street grid. The street layout was the only major development at *Venta* before AD 100.

Buildings

The earliest constructions were simple timber structures and open spaces were left for the later addition of a forum and public baths. The remains of simple wattle and daub houses were found in the central location labelled Insula IX, beneath later town houses. Other buildings of similar construction and of 2nd-century date were found during the excavation of the Anglo-Saxon cemetery to the east of the walled area.

Fig 146: *Venta Icenorum*: aerial photograph showing the forum during excavation in 1929.

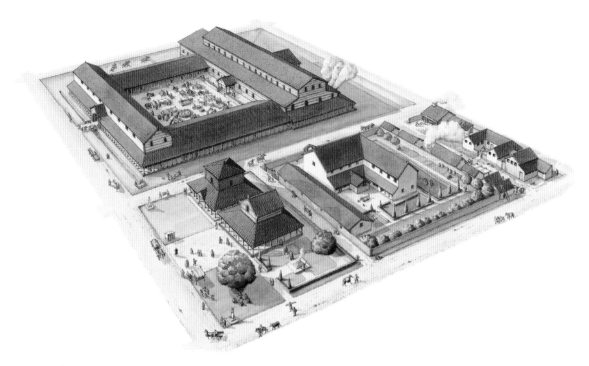

The forum, or market place, lay in Insula X, in the centre of the town (Fig 146).[2] Originally constructed during the reign of the Emperor Hadrian (AD 117–38), it was replaced during the Antonine period (AD 138–80) and was later burnt down, probably early in the 3rd century. It comprised three sides of a square and stalls were erected within the centre on market days (Fig 147). At the west end of the courtyard was the basilica or town hall. Building costs were reduced by using brick and flint just for the main walls and a combination of chalk blocks and unfired clay bricks elsewhere.

A bath complex was constructed in Insula XVII, next to the river, at the same time as the forum, during the Antonine period.[3] People entered the baths from the street on the east side. There was a *frigidarium*, or cold room, a *tepidarium*, or warm room, and a circular *laconicum*, or heated room. The large scale of this bath complex suggests that it originally supported a grand barrel-vaulted roof.

An amphitheatre has been identified by aerial photography, 90m to the south of the town walls. It shows as an oval cropmark, the long axis of which is aligned north–south. It has not been excavated but further evidence of the original plan has been revealed by geophysical survey, showing the dimensions of the arena to be 40m x 33m. There was a gateway in the south and outlines of rooms below the seating banks have been traced around the arena.

Fig 147: *Venta Icenorum*: the early forum, with two temples in the foreground (reconstruction by Sue White).

Two temples were excavated in Insula IX, immediately to the north of the forum (Fig 148). Romano-Celtic temples such as these consisted of a square central building (the *cella*) surrounded by a concentric wall which created a walkway. Both of those at *Venta* are very similar in plan but one had thicker walls and could have supported a more substantial superstructure. Both were built in the later 2nd century but we cannot tell whether they were in use at the same time. Neither do we know which gods were associated with them. Another temple, which also had a square plan, is known to the north-east of the town. It lay within a designated sacred area, or *temenos*, and there was a monumental gateway to the west.[4] This temple saw its main use in the years before AD 200.

In 2007 new fieldwork directed by William Bowden of Nottingham University discovered evidence of another significant construction not previously recognised, even by aerial photography. Geophysical survey has revealed, due east of the intra-mural

temples, a semi-circular feature:[5] only the fifth theatre known from Britain. So *Venta* can be seen to have been a highly civilised town, as manifested through its full range of public buildings.

Fig 148: *Venta Icenorum:* the temples during excavation.

Fire was a recurring hazard during the life of the town. Timber buildings beyond the eastern wall of the forum were destroyed during the 2nd century. Then, late in the 2nd or early in the 3rd century a major part of the town, including the forum and baths, was also badly damaged by fire. The forum remained derelict and was not rebuilt until the end of the 3rd century. The second forum was a smaller and simpler structure.

The walls

When *Venta's* walls were constructed, the town was reduced in size by about a half, to 14ha. (Fig 149) Although they are not dated archaeologically, it is likely that *Venta's* walls were built during the early AD 270s and originally stood to a height of 7m above ground level. The

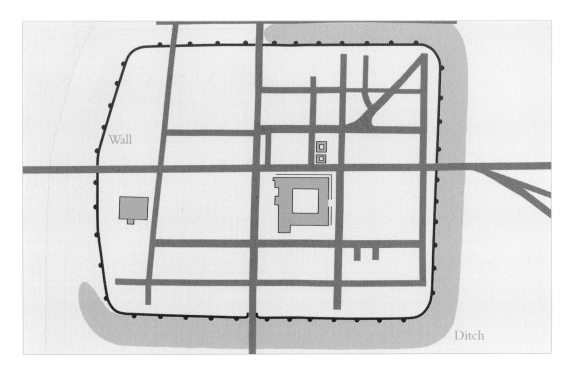

Wall

Ditch

Fig 149: *Venta Icenorum:* the later street layout.

outer wall was faced with dressed flint. There was an external ditch which measured 24m wide and 5.2m deep. No ditch was dug to the west of the town, as the River Tas came right up to the walls.

Today, the western half of the north wall (Fig 150) is visibly narrower than the eastern half. Although this section may have been more severely robbed of its flint in post-Roman times, the surviving masonry is remarkably slighter than the adjacent stretches of wall and may have been constructed less substantially. It is possible that an artificial channel was cut from the River Tas, running just outside this stretch of wall, which would explain why the wall did not need to be as strong in this sector.

A single gateway was positioned in the centre of each wall. In the south, Atkinson discovered a single opening 4m wide set between curved inturns in the curtain wall, with square guardrooms on each side. The most remarkable feature of the defences was the bastions (Fig 151). Two forms of these projecting towers have been identified at *Venta.* Rectangular and semi-circular bastions were arranged alternately, and just one of the U-shaped types has survived, while none of the rectangular examples has survived above ground level.

Trade and industry

The earliest industrial activity was pottery production. Four kilns, which operated between the reign of Nero and the early years of Vespasian (AD 54–70), supplied the requirements of the military

garrison. Commerce then played an increasingly important role in the everyday life of the town, through both local and long-distance trade. Local agriculture and, in particular, sheep farming provided the raw materials and the processing and export of woollen goods was a major industry in the town. A large iron woollen comb, spindle whorls and iron shears have all been discovered during excavations. Leather-working needles and carbonised cereal grains have also been found. To the north of the forum a glass maker's workshop, probably for window glass, was constructed around AD 300 from the rebuilding of two earlier town houses. A bronze-working furnace was also discovered to the north-east of the walled area.

Roads connected *Venta* with the agricultural area of the Fenland in the west and the pottery manufactories at Brampton in the north. A road just to the west ran due south through the small town of Scole and on to Colchester. By river, the town was connected to the Great Estuary, the east coast and beyond. Remains of timbers and substantial iron fittings have been described and found adjacent to the river, where a wharf once existed.

Trade with foreign parts is evidenced by finds of samian ware and Argonne ware from Gaul. Trade with Germany is shown by the presence

of Rhenish and Mayen wares. Amphorae, which are rare elsewhere in Norfolk, have been excavated at the town.

Roman *Venta* remained in use right through to the end of the Roman period. Moreover, accumulated evidence now points to a continuation of settlement into post-Roman years: Anglo-Saxon cemeteries have been found in the immediate vicinity, suggesting the existence of a local community around the Roman town which continued at least as late as the 6th century and probably into the 7th. However, there was no subsequent substantial building within the town, ensuring that it has survived as a green-field site to the present day.

SMALL TOWNS

A number of settlements that have been classified as Romano-British small towns have been recognised across the Norfolk countryside (Fig 154). They are found at regular intervals of between 15km and 20km and were frequently situated at route intersections, especially where rivers were crossed by roads. Some of the locations can be seen as natural stopping points for journeys through and across the region. Several of these small towns had originated as settlements in the Late Iron Age, as had been the case with *Venta Icenorum*.

Fig 151: *Venta Icenorum:* the 'west tower' – a U-shaped bastion.

173

The small towns played an important role in the day-to-day life of Roman Norfolk, providing the main infrastructure for the operation of the region. A recognition of the small town network is crucial to any interpretation of how Roman Norfolk operated.

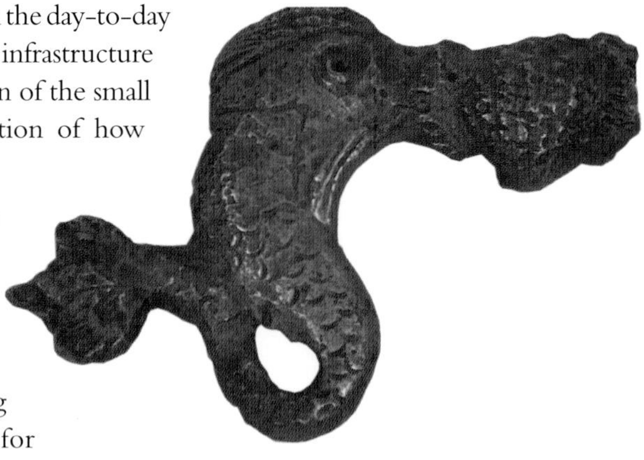

These sites display a range of common functions. They served as markets for the buying and selling of local produce and for the purchase of more unusual wares from itinerant traders. They were religious foci for the surrounding countryside. They also provided facilities for travellers, perhaps an inn and bathing facilities, and were foci for small-scale industry. These functions and services were generally small-scale, for local communities, although on occasions such roles could have regional importance.

Fig 152: Part of a drop handle for a military helmet in the shape of dolphins, from *Venta Icenorum*. Height 51mm.

Although they are classified as towns, their buildings would not have appeared very grand. Building stone was rarely used in construction, although flint and chalk were employed in some instances. Structures were more normally made from timber, wattle and daub. Today we can find spreads of roof tile at these sites, betraying a degree of Romanised construction methods. Some evidence of modest wealth is also occasionally encountered in the form of flue tiles, used for the central heating of buildings.

There has been very little excavation on these sites and the level of information available varies widely in each case. Much of our evidence has, once again, come from metal detection, and is in the form of individual artefacts and quantities of Roman coins recovered from the plough zone.

Brampton

Brampton, the largest of these small towns, is situated south-east of modern Aylsham, immediately south of the old course of the River Bure (Fig 156). There has been limited excavation and some fieldwork around the Roman settlement, making it one of the better-studied and published of Norfolk's small towns.[6] Iron Age activity is attested by a small number of coins. Roman occupation began in the later 1st century and carried on right through to the end of the 4th.

The town emerged as ribbon development along roads from the east, south and south-west directions. The centre is defined by a ditched enclosure which covers about 6ha and which has been clearly shown

Fig 153: Lead mend on a samian ware vessel, from *Venta Icenorum*. Height of sherd 85mm.

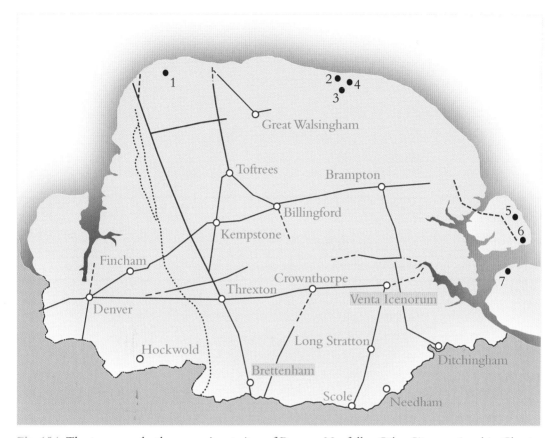

Fig 154: The towns and other prominent sites of Roman Norfolk. *Other Sites mentioned in Chapter 14* **1:** Brancaster **2:** Gramborough Hill, Salthouse **3:** Warborough Hill, Stiffkey **4:** Muckleborough Hill, Kelling **5:** California **6:** Caister-on-Sea **7:** Burgh Castle.

by aerial photography. There was access to a wharf in the north and an industrial zone to the west. A key feature in the centre was a bath house, which had cold, warm and hot rooms. The walls were of flint and mortar construction, with tile bonding courses, and were plastered and painted; there were *opus signinum* (a mixture of crushed brick and tile mixed with mortar) floors. Elsewhere, excavation has also revealed evidence for simple timber buildings and workshops; their superstructure probably consisted of wattle-and-daub infill and thatched roofs, although some roof tiles were recovered. A few buildings in the central area and in the southern suburbs had flint wall footings.

Religious life at Brampton is reflected by miniature votive objects and figurines of Minerva, Jupiter and Venus. Ritual pits which contained dog skeletons, an ox skull and a cat skull were also found. No cemetery has been located, but individual cremations have been discovered across the town.

Brampton's prosperity was based on pottery production, which was concentrated along the road leading to the south-west, where 132 kilns have been identified. A further 13 are known from the rest of the site. All excavated examples are of the updraught type, with a single flue. Some potters were involved in specialist mortaria and flagon production, for export to a wider market. Mortaria ascribed to the potter *Aesuminus*, dating to between AD 160–200, have been found as far north as Corbridge. Other products, including greywares and rusticated vessels of the late 1st and early 2nd centuries, were for more local use.

Other evidence for industrial activity included a number of industrial wells, which were lined with oak planks, and many pits and gullies containing smithing slag and furnace lining, which related to iron working. A 3rd-century iron- and bronze-working workshop was identified in the vicinity of the wharf. Elsewhere, leather offcuts from shoe-making were found. The industries declined and ceased during the 4th century and although the town remained in use the intensity of activity declined after about AD 380.

Fig 155: Key handle in the shape of a lion astride a person from Brampton. Length 85mm *(copyright Norfolk Museums and Archaeology Service)*.

Billingford

Billingford is situated just 1km to the north-west of the 1st-century fort at Swanton Morley, in central Norfolk. The town grew up at a strategic crossing point, where the Roman road which linked Brampton with

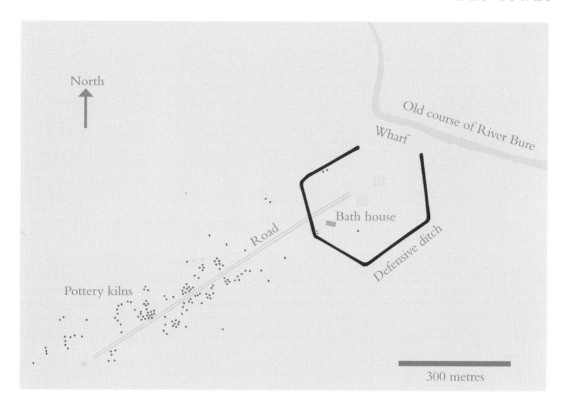

North

Old course of River Bure

Wharf

Bath house

Road

Defensive ditch

Pottery kilns

300 metres

Fig 156: Plan of the Romano-British small town at Brampton.

Denver, on the fen-edge, passed over the River Wensum. The fort had been strategically positioned in relation to the crossing and a local native community, evidenced by the presence of Icenian silver coins, developed into the Roman small town in the years following the Boudican uprising.

Excavations were undertaken here between 1991 and 1992 and again in 1997.[7] Although this provided a large open area for study, no evidence for substantial buildings was found. Some posthole structures were excavated and buildings at the settlement appear to have been made of timber and lath. Excavation also revealed evidence for some industrial activity, including iron smithing.

The density and extent of finds from the site indicate that this was a compact and busy roadside settlement. The southern extent of the town was defined by two substantial, possibly defensive, ditches. Part of an associated cemetery was also identified. There was evidence for extensive suburban activity stretching beyond the main settlement, which developed into a landscape of field boundaries and trackways.

Over 1500 coins have been recovered from Billingford. They provide a full chronological range covering the duration of Roman Britain. The period of most substantial coin loss was the mid to late 4th century, but, like Brampton, the town declined after about AD 380.

Long Stratton

Some 11km due south of Caistor St Edmund a small settlement grew up as ribbon development at Long Stratton, on the Pye Road, the main route to the towns of Scole and Colchester. Evidence for the settlement has come in the form of pottery, tile and coin scatters. This settlement may have developed as a resting place for travellers en route to and between these towns.

Scole

Roman Scole also became established on the Pye Road, a further 14km south of Long Stratton, where the road crossed the River Waveney. There is little evidence for Iron Age occupation at Scole, although a mixed hoard of Icenian and Roman coins was discovered there in 1982–3. Once again, the town grew, in the form of ribbon development. It expanded southwards across the River Waveney, as its role within the regional transport and communications system became more important.

Excavations were undertaken by the Norfolk Archaeological Unit in 1973, and by the combined forces of the Norfolk and Suffolk Units in 1993–4, in what has been one of the most extensive small town excavations in the region.[8] However, excavation has been limited to peripheral areas of the town and the centre of the settlement, which remains buried under modern housing estates, has not yet been investigated.

The Roman town underwent a process of formal planning during the 2nd century. A rectilinear pattern of housing grew up in the angles between the roads and land along the roadside was formally subdivided. Properties were formed into regular plots which fronted both the main roads and side lanes. Timber-lined wells were constructed within the individual plots, and there was also at least one communal roadside well.

Despite its size, Scole was neither ditched nor walled. Neither have any public buildings been identified, although this site would have been an ideal location for a *mansio* (an inn). We know that building methods used in the town were basic. The earliest structures were roundhouses and more complex building styles appeared during the 2nd century. The most substantial buildings had clay floors. One strip building was constructed using a timber frame with lath and mud walls, and had a commercial outlet to the front. An absence of roof tiles suggests that buildings were thatched or possibly shingled.

The excavations revealed widespread evidence for craft and industrial activities on the periphery of the town. There was iron smelting, while a maltings complex and a tannery occupied riverside locations. Ovens and hearths were widespread. Extensive coin evidence shows that the thriving commercial activity peaked during the early 4th century.

Ditchingham

Ditchingham, like Scole, was situated on the River Waveney, midway between Scole and the mouth of the Great Estuary. Its establishment appears to have been related to its location in relation to river communications and trade. A strong presence of Iron Age finds, especially coins, indicate that its origins lay in a pre-Roman settlement. It developed further as a settlement in the early years of Roman Norfolk and continued to grow in size through the late 3rd and 4th centuries, as shown by coins recovered from the site.

Crownthorpe

The small town of Crownthorpe is situated within the parish of Wicklewood, some 15km west of *Venta Icenorum*. Its initial development as an important settlement during the Late Iron Age has been described in Chapter 9. Not only have we found large numbers of Iron Age coins there but the predominance of Early Face-horse types shows that the site's floruit was earlier than at other Late Iron Age settlements, such as at Caistor St Edmund, Great Walsingham and Saham Toney.[9]

The early settlement developed into a Romano-British small town through its position on the road from *Venta Icenorum* to Denver, on the fen-edge. There has been no excavation on the main area of the site but we have extensive knowledge of the town through a very substantial metal-detected small find assemblage collected by Derek Woollestone and acquired by Norwich Castle Museum during the 1980s and 90s.

Some 1150 Roman coins give us some insight into the life of the town. There was strong early coin use, which started during the Flavian period (after AD 69), which was the time when *Venta Icenorum* was also becoming established. There was also markedly strong coin use through the 3rd and 4th centuries which continued onwards until about AD 380, after which life in the town declined.

The metal-detector finds have also revealed fascinating information about all aspects of the daily life of Crownthorpe's citizens. They include personal dress items such as bracelets, finger rings, an ear ring and cosmetic mortars. A delightful Mercury figurine showed the importance of religious activity, while spoons represented domestic life. There were also items associated with trade and commerce, including a steelyard weight, other lead weights, a quern and metalworking debris.

However, the most fascinating aspect of life at Crownthorpe was revealed through the recovery of over 600 Romano-British brooches in many different types and styles. They are all ordinary brooch forms which were used by people living in the town, and they all show signs of having been used and worn before being thrown away and replaced.

This evidence clearly shows how everybody commonly wore both plain and colourful brooches as a common form of daily dress. Some metal analysis was undertaken on these brooches during the 1990s and it has been suggested that many of them were made at a workshop situated within the town.

A military presence?

Scrutiny of the metal-detected assemblage has revealed a group of 20 items such as buckles, most of which are incomplete, of military type. Provisionally dated to the 2nd to 3rd century, these fittings indicate that military personnel were present in Crownthorpe at that time. No military structure has been identified and military personnel may just have been passing through the town, or were visitors, perhaps returning on a routine basis.

The temple

The first feature of the town to be identified was recognised nearly 50 years ago – before the days of metal-detector use on sites. A Romano-Celtic temple was first noted as a cropmark in July 1959 by the local farmer, who described the marks as 'a square within a square'. At the end of 1959 a trial excavation was organised by the Castle Museum, although the results were never published.[10] Substantial remains were discovered. The *veranda* wall measured 49 feet by 56 feet and the inner *cella* walls were 28 feet long. The construction had been in natural flint, set in mortar, while tile bonding courses were employed. Timber had also been used, as indicated by prolific quantities of nails.

A substantial concentration of fragmentary painted wall plaster was located, which had originally decorated the inner *cella* wall. Excavation notes say that this was red, with black and yellow designs, although there are no surviving sketches to show the pattern. Coarse tesserae made of tile were found all over the site, although no actual floor levels were located. It can be presumed that the floors were constructed with tile tesserae.

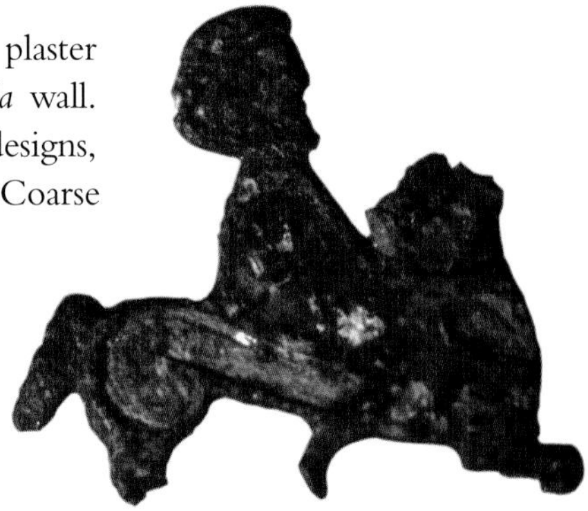

The excavation notes speculate that the temple dated from the 2nd or 3rd century AD, although the only dating evidence discovered was pottery with wide possible date ranges.

Modern aerial photographs show that the temple was aligned with a road to its south, which has a rough west–east alignment.[11] The metalled surface of the road is intermittently visible over a stretch of some 465m. Further to the north-east, another stretch of road is visible as a parchmark, together with ditches on both sides, which show as cropmarks.

Fig 157: 'Horse and Rider' brooch, from Great Walsingham. Length 35mm.

Great Walsingham

Great Walsingham is situated in central north Norfolk, to the north-east of Fakenham (Fig 161). A Roman settlement became established where a Roman road, running from east to west, passed over the River Stiffkey. Earlier activity of Iron Age date is evidenced by a substantial number of Icenian coins.

The extent of the Roman occupation is clearly indicated by a prolific scatter of pottery and tile, which extends over an area 1.5km from north to south and 750m from east to west. A combination of roof and flue tiles, together with some window glass, indicates the former presence of substantial buildings. Today, the impression gained from walking the site is of a town which had tiled roofs throughout, but with the majority of structures built from timber, lath and plaster, which have not survived.

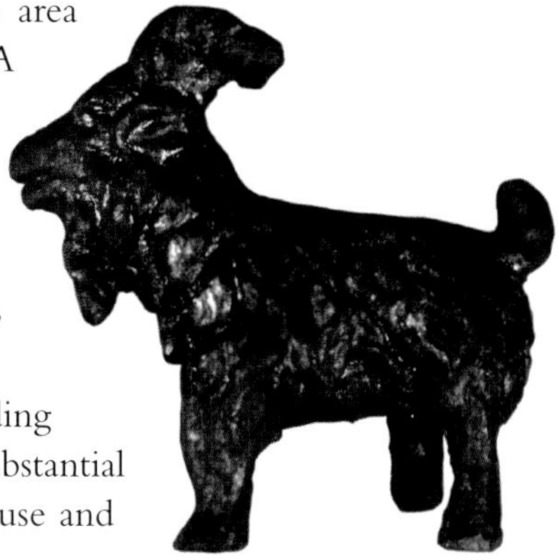

David Gurney has identified seven distinct scatters of building remains within the town, five of which may have been substantial masonry structures. One of these is interpreted as a bath house and another as a temple.[12]

At the northern extent of the settlement is a 9ha oval defensive earthwork enclosure that was constructed in the late Roman or early post-Roman period. This is the only part of the site to have been excavated:[13] fieldwork in 1974 revealed building debris, a cremation and two hearths. Five inhumations were also discovered, sealed beneath a bank.

Fig 158: Votive figurine in the form of a goat, from Great Walsingham. Length 57mm.

Metal detecting has once again added substantially to our knowledge of the settlement. A remarkable assemblage of metalwork has been recovered, including over 200 Romano-British brooches and in excess of 7000 coins. The coins cover the whole period of Roman Britain, but the most substantial coin loss occurred between AD 260 and 378. The period from AD 330 to 378 is particularly prolific, possibly coinciding with the construction of the earthwork.

Perhaps the most remarkable feature of Great Walsingham is the outstanding assemblage of religious objects, which serves to confirm the presence of a temple (Fig 157-59).[14] It includes some important figurines, and most are of outstanding quality. There are three statuettes of Mercury, two goat figurines (Fig 159) and three cocks. There is also a portrait bust of Minerva and another of a three-horned deity, together with masks of Cupid and representations of satyrs, a figure of Minerva and a mount in the form of a head of Jupiter. These spectacular votive items also include finger rings dedicated to Mercury, Toutates and the Matres

Fig 159: Votive miniature axe, from Great Walsingham. Length 36mm.

Fig 160: Head from a bronze figurine, from Hockwold. Height 51mm *(copyright Norfolk Musums and Archaeology Service)*.

Transmarini. Other objects include model wheels, and a miniature axe (Fig 159), mattock head and spear. Mercury appears to have been the most popular deity, while the presence of finds relating to Cupid and the satyrs suggest that there was also a cult to Bacchus.

The overall scale of finds reflects a large and thriving settlement of some affluence, which experienced a floruit during the later 4th century and possibly beyond. There is evidence for industrial activity, including bronze and iron working and pottery manufacture. The most remarkable element, though, is the evidence for the town's pre-eminence as a religious centre. Could it be that the temple or shrine provided a religious focus of regional status, similar to the later pilgrimage centre which became known in medieval England and which continues today? Such a continuity of religious association over a period of two millennia would certainly be remarkable, although a situation of complete coincidence is perhaps even more unlikely.

Brettenham

Brettenham is situated in the far south of the county, where the Peddars Way crossed the River Thet. Located just 6km east of Thetford, this site, once again, had origins back in the Iron Age. Finds of Roman material have been reported for centuries: Blomefield, for instance, mentioned the discovery of samian ware and a coin of Vespasian in the early 18th century. Aerial photographs taken by Dr J K St Joseph during the 20th century showed linear and rectangular cropmarks associated with the settlement.

There has been some limited excavation. In 1932–5 a section of the adjacent Peddars Way and four refuse pits were investigated. No structures were discovered but roof tiles, mortar and window glass were found. Rainbird Clarke concluded that that the method of construction used at Brettenham had been wood, wattle and daub, although none has survived. The extent of the site is still known mainly from surface finds. In recent years there have been additional finds of pottery, coins, brooches, querns and domestic metalwork, all indicating that the main period of occupation was in the 4th century.

Old Buckenham

The Roman site at Old Buckenham has been known since 1990 as a result of metal-detecting activity. So far there has been no evidence for any pre-Roman Iron Age activity, although there has been no excavation to confirm this. The first known occupation belongs to the very early post-conquest years. Artefacts, including coins, show that this continued through the 1st and 2nd centuries and that the town grew into a more substantial settlement in the later 3rd century. The assemblage of over 200 metal-detected Roman coins mainly date from the years after AD 260.

A small coin hoard was discovered adjacent to the site in 1994;[15] this contained 14 Roman silver *denarii* which date from between 124 BC and AD 45. Early post-conquest hoards such as this have been found elsewhere across East Anglia:[16] another was found adjacent to the small town of Needham, just ten miles south of Old Buckenham. Other metalwork items from Old Buckenham include 1st- and 2nd-century brooches, jewellery and personal objects such as decorated knife handles.

Despite the restricted nature of the evidence from the settlement, some craft activity, evidenced by material indicating brooch production, is known; this important material will be considered in Chapter 13.

Pentney

A settlement of uncertain status has been recognised at Pentney in west Norfolk. Limited excavation has revealed boundary features, including a series of ditches, and also industry, in the form of pottery kilns.[17] The extensive scale of the remains so far identified suggests that this may have been a major factory site, with as many as 120 kilns. The pottery recovered shows that mortaria were being manufactured there.

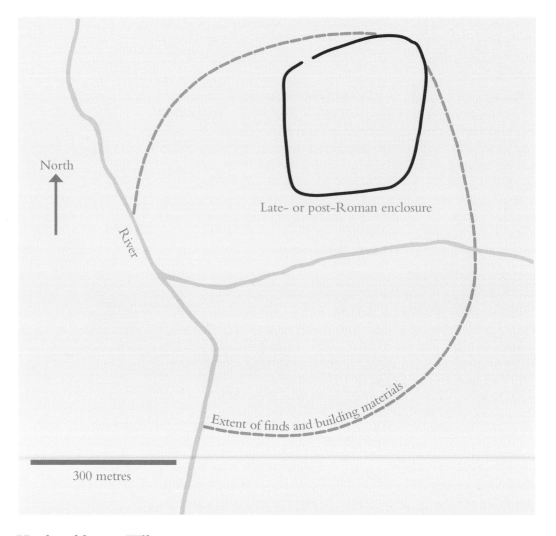

North

River

Late- or post–Roman enclosure

Extent of finds and building materials

300 metres

Hockwold cum Wilton

The small town of Hockwold cum Wilton is located on the fen-edge in south-west Norfolk, to the north of the Little Ouse River, and extended in a linear fashion, east to west, for approximately 7km. There is very little evidence for Iron Age or 1st-century activity; rather, discoveries show that there was an increase in occupation during the 2nd and 3rd centuries. A major focus for activity, particularly in the later Roman period, appears to have been provided by two temples.

The Hockwold temple sites were discovered at Leylands Farm (excavated in 1957 by Charles Green) and Sawbench (excavated in 1962 by F Curtis, Barbara Green and Col Kelly).[18] Each produced rich collections of religious material and large coin assemblages (Fig 160). Both temples would have served as major regional centres for periodic fairs and festivals and provided locations for markets and commercial

Fig 161: Plan of the Romano-British small town at Great Walsingham.

transactions within their complexes. This is confirmed by the large numbers of small late Roman bronze coins found at these sites, which are more representative of frequent monetary transactions than of votive coin deposition.

The far western extent of the Hockwold settlement contains an area of cropmarks extending over some 40 acres.[19] Excavations by Peter Salway revealed an enclosure and evidence for buildings constructed from wattle, daub and timber. There were storage pits and ditches of 1st-century date, with occupation extending through to the early 3rd century. Evidence for structures was also found at the eastern end of the settlement, together with a possible cremation cemetery. There are scatters of Roman tile, tesserae, pottery – including coarse wares, samian and mortaria – and animal bone. Aerial photography shows a complex series of roads and tracks, within which the enclosures and structures can be identified.

Kempstone

Kempstone grew up on the east–west road which connected Denver in the far west with Billingford and Brampton in the east. A Roman settlement is evidenced by a spread of pottery, tiles and iron slag over an area of some 12ha.[20] Considerable industrial activity is suggested by the extent and quantity of the slag. The pottery covers the 1st to 3rd centuries and possibly later. The site has also produced a quantity of coins, which group tightly between the years AD 260 and 364.

Denver

Denver was situated on the southern fen-edge, at the south-west extent of the southern greensand. Fens lay to the south and west. This settlement was located at a strategic position in relation to the Fen Causeway. Excavations by Charles Green in 1960 revealed an industrial area adjacent to the road, where the main activity was found to be salt production.[21] A number of substantial buildings were also revealed.

Although it served as a local market, Denver has not produced the same richness of finds, such as coins, which were found at Hockwold, further south. Its proximity to the fenland imperial estate (see Chapter 13) may explain why Denver did not develop into a more thriving settlement.

Needham

Needham is situated on the Norfolk side of the Waveney valley. Its presence was first revealed in 1921, when gravel working uncovered evidence of a Romano-British settlement, initially a series of pits and ditches containing material of Roman date.[22] The location appears to have been associated with a Roman road which crossed the river at this point, running north-west to join the major Scole–*Venta Icenorum* road.

Clay moulds for making Iron Age silver coins suggest that this may have been an Icenian settlement of some standing, although other evidence of that date is still to be discovered. Samian ware and Gallo-Belgic imported pottery indicate that there was a degree of early Roman prosperity during the reign of Claudius, in the years after AD 43. Other dated material is mainly of the 1st and 2nd centuries. Finds have included a pottery kiln, rubbish pits and inhumation burials. However, no buildings have yet been discovered.

A hoard of 29 silver *denarii* was discovered less than half a kilometre from the settlement in 1992 and 1993 (Fig 162).[23] The deposit can be assigned an early date through two coins which were struck in AD 63–4; these serve to confirm that the settlement was in use during the early post-conquest period.

Fig 162: Silver denarii from the Needham mid 1st-century coin hoard.

Small towns in the landscape

Despite the thriving network of small towns and villages, Roman Norfolk essentially remained a rural area. Coin evidence from right across greater East Anglia shows that there was much more of an urban infrastructure across Lincolnshire in the west and Essex to the south.[24] The extensive areas of countryside which existed between the towns in Norfolk were infilled with farmsteads, country houses and estates of varying sizes, all of which will be considered in the next chapter.

Chapter 13
Beyond the towns

We have evidence for activity right across the landscape of Norfolk throughout the period of Roman Britain. The network of country houses, farms and rural estates penetrated into every remote corner. Some of the more basic farmsteads are sometimes difficult to date as they show little or no material signs of Roman influence. However, Norfolk was a highly productive area and as the decades passed the degree of cohesion provided by the Roman network of towns, administration and improved communications ensured the development of a thriving agricultural region. This chapter will look at our evidence for life beyond the towns and will lead on to a consideration of other trades and industries, and how this all came together into a strong local economy which had importance across the region and way beyond.

RURAL BUILDINGS

The remains of many Roman buildings have been found right across Norfolk's countryside. Throughout the Roman period most of the landscape was filled by small farmsteads; we have evidence for well over 200 rural buildings in the form of spreads of building materials, including fragments of brick, flue and roof tiles, tesserae, flint wall footings and even wall plaster and window glass in some cases. These remains are complemented by cropmarks shown by aerial photography. However, archaeological attention has often focused on the grander farmsteads, known as villas. These impressive structures were the result of the integral links that existed between the acquisition of political status and land ownership throughout the Roman world: those in political power showed off their status by building these grand houses in the countryside.

Some 40 rural villas are recorded in Norfolk. The term 'villa' can embrace a range of building types but, generally speaking, villas were country houses which were usually associated with conditions of luxury and relaxation, while exhibiting an appearance and decoration that was recognisably Roman. They were normally associated with farming. The scarcity of building stone in Norfolk has meant that Roman country houses needed to make more use of timber, wattle, clay and flint than their counterparts in other parts of the country. Where possible, however, they used building stone, had solid floors and sometimes contained mosaics and, in the case of more elaborate constructions, some stone was imported from beyond the county. Some Norfolk villas incorporated hypocausts and baths.

In some parts of Britain, clusters of villas grew up around towns. In other areas, such as London and Canterbury, there were few villas in the immediate vicinity of urban areas. The situation in Norfolk provides an interesting contrast, with very different situations in the west and east of the county.

NORTH-WEST NORFOLK

There is a bigger concentration of substantial Roman rural buildings in north-west Norfolk than in any other part of the county. Villas were concentrated on slopes overlooking valleys at Hunstanton, Heacham and Snettisham. There has been no substantial excavation on this group of sites; rather, they were discovered and interpreted through limited excavation, fieldwalking and aerial photography.

This western part of the county, bordering the Wash and the fen-edge, comprises a belt of greensand which runs north–south and is cut through by a series of watercourses which flow towards the west. To the east of the greensand is chalk, which is covered in the north by boulder clay and in the south by Breckland sands. Villas tended to be constructed at the junction of the chalk and greensand. Their economy was based on mixed agriculture, although there was greater emphasis on the rearing of livestock on the higher chalkland to the east. North-west Norfolk has also always been acknowledged as an exceptional area for growing grain. A combination of the lightish sandy soil and localised light sea mist (known as a *sea fret*) create unique conditions for producing the very best barley.

These farming operations supplied markets by way of routes and lines of communication directed towards the north-west rather than towards *Venta Icenorum*, the Great Estuary and the east. A site at Brancaster may have played a major role in relation to the economy of these villas: this late Roman Saxon Shore fort possibly served as a regional trans-shipment centre for agricultural produce destined for more distant markets. The Icknield Way was also situated nearby, leading north to the sea.

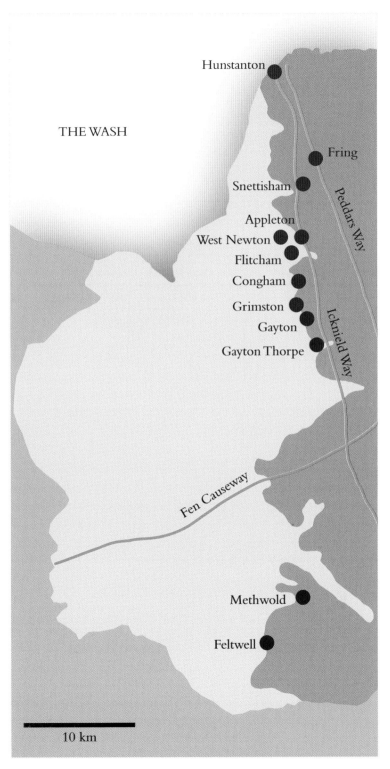

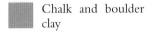

Fig 163: Map showing the location of villas in west Norfolk.

Chalk and boulder clay

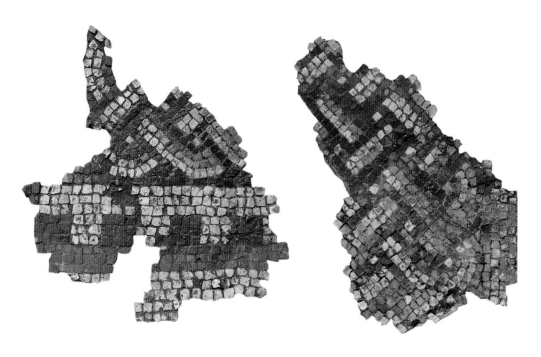

Fig 164: Gayton villa mosaic during re-excavation in summer 2006.

Fig 165: The Roman villa at Gayton Thorpe (reconstruction by Sue White).

It is noticeable that the whole of north-west Norfolk does not contain any Romano-British small towns, which are present throughout the rest of the county. The economic structure of this area clearly differed from that evidenced in the rest of Norfolk and appears to have been specifically based on large-scale farming operations centred on the villas and in the nearby fenland.

THE ICKNIELD WAY VILLAS

There are ten villas close to the Icknield Way, all situated between Gayton Thorpe and Heacham, and all close to springs and watercourses (Fig 163). Archaeological work has been sporadic and little has ever been published.[1] Very limited dating evidence suggests a floruit for these sites during the 3rd and early 4th centuries AD. They all show a modest level of luxury and individually appear to have been at the heart of small agricultural estates.

A scatter of building materials was recorded at West Newton, where a 3rd- to 4th-century bath house was identified. The Den Beck villa lies 2km to the east, at Appleton, where excavation in 1947–8 located a tessellated floor and a walled yard with a cobbled surface. At Flitcham, a building was evidenced by a scatter of pot sherds and flue tiles. Further south lies Congham villa, where painted wall plaster and coins ranging from Postumus to Valentinian I again provide a 3rd- and 4th-century

Fig 166: The mosaic at Gayton Thorpe villa *(copyright Norfolk and Norwich Archaeological Society)*.

date. Another substantial villa was excavated at Grimston in 1906; here, a major building incorporated a bath suite in its east wing.

Two separate villa sites are known at Gayton, near King's Lynn. The example at Well Hall is defined by 2ha of surface finds and a spread of substantial building materials, while that at Gayton Thorpe was excavated by Atkinson in 1922–3 (Figs 165 and 166).[2] His plan shows two conjoined winged-corridor buildings and a detached bath house to the south. The northern building had tessellated floors and a bath suite and its decoration was very fine, finished with painted wall plaster and marble veneer. The southern building was far simpler in both construction and finishings. Dating evidence shows occupation here spanned the late 2nd to the 4th century. Aerial photography shows a complex of enclosures and linear features extending for 100 hectares around the villa, while fieldwork between 1982 and 1985 revealed evidence for a further three buildings, including another possible detached bath house.[3]

ROMAN SNETTISHAM AND BRANCASTER

The area around Snettisham was a focus of activity in the Roman period. Although no town was to develop there, the landscape to the east of Ken Hill (where Iron Age torcs had been buried) was rich in agricultural and rural settlement.[4] A series of land divisions relating to individual dwellings was established between the mid 1st and mid 2nd centuries AD. However, in contrast to evidence from the villa sites, only small quantities of building materials have been found, usually in the form of roofing tiles and ceramic flooring.

A villa estate was discovered at Park Farm, towards the eastern extent of this settlement spread. It had access to upland grazing and was engaged in arable farming on the valley slopes. Excavations in the 1930s revealed a villa building with signs of wealth, which included painted wall plaster and a mosaic floor. The limited excavation records described a walled yard with carrstone and chalk floors.

A dense system of cropmarks, representing settlements and field systems, can be traced for over 3km to the south and west of this villa. These individual plots and allotments appear to have been laid out on a piecemeal basis. Settlements grew up by the 1st century AD on either side of the River Ingol, which drains westward into the Wash. There was a decline in activity during the 3rd century which coincides with the period of villa construction on the edge of the chalk escarpment.

Excavations at Strickland Avenue and Station Road in Snettisham revealed evidence for industrial activity. A pottery kiln was initially established and roads were then constructed during the mid 2nd century, which helped further industry, in the form of large quarry pits, to develop. Ironstone was extracted and smelted locally, and a second kiln was constructed. Other industrial evidence included wells and a metalworking hearth.

The Roman road system enabled the transport of the pots and smelted iron, together with other fenland produce from nearby, such as grain, meat, reeds and salt, to markets and redistribution centres. These local roads would have provided access to the Icknield Way and Peddars Way further east.

Further north, at Brancaster, there was a landscape that once again combined domestic, industrial and agricultural functions.[5] This was a formally planned system, with regular trackways and ditched enclosures forming house plots. Excavations showed that the ditches contained quantities of domestic rubbish. Occupation began here before the end of the 2nd century, pre-dating the construction of the Saxon Shore fort. A main east–west trackway formed the spine of the settlement and went out of use during the 4th century, after the settlement had declined.

THE FENLAND ESTATE

A vast imperial estate was established across a large part of the Fenland proper. This extended from Denver in south-west Norfolk through into Lincolnshire and was administered for the Emperor Hadrian and his successors from a headquarters at Stonea near March in Cambridgeshire.[6] Many of the sites of the Norfolk fen-edge would have come within its control, sharing an economy based on intensive stock rearing and wool production. The lack of development at the small town of Denver may have been due to the fact that many of the essential functions for the region were undertaken by the estate and its administration.

Roman coins are scarce finds on Fenland sites. Other than the two temple sites at Hockwold cum Wilton, very few Roman coins tend to be found there.[7] Excavation at Denver produced just four Roman coins. Gayton Thorpe villa produced just three and the total excavation of the Feltwell villa and bath house yielded just a single coin. Grimston villa and the two sites at Grange Farm, Hockwold, produced no coins at all. This may be associated with the presence of the estate and its influence across the area. Unlike the developing situation elsewhere in Roman Norfolk, estate farmers and those involved in Fenland industries probably saw little profit from their labours and their homes and settlements saw little coin use. The imperial estate may have supplied the needs of the workers, so that they did not require, or have the opportunity to earn, money. Indeed, luxury items in general are scarce on these sites.

THE NORFOLK FEN-EDGE

The southern fen-edge saw a marked expansion of settlement during the Roman period and it became a rich landscape. However, little is known about the earliest Roman occupation and there are no certain military sites. The Fen Causeway, which David Gurney has suggested may have been constructed in response to the Boudican uprising, was in use by AD 70 and provided Norfolk with a link to the Midlands.

The fen-edge provided a wide range of resources to exploit. There was cereal cultivation on the uplands and stock rearing further into the Fenland proper, which was drained in the early Roman period. Fishing, fowling and reed cutting were all important. Salt production was practised all along the fen-edge at sites such as Denver. Salt was important for feeding to cattle, for the preservation of meat and fish and for tanning hides.

A villa was excavated at Little Oulsham Drove, Feltwell, in 1962 and 1964.[8] This was a simple corridor type, with a range of five rooms. A rectangular bath house was situated nearby, with a *frigidarium*, *tepidarium* and *caldarium* arranged in line. A cold plunge bath was attached to the *frigidarium* and there was a timber-built lean-to entrance or changing room. Finds suggest a 4th-century date for both constructions. These two buildings may have been at the heart of a holding within the imperial estate, perhaps as the residence of a prominent estate administrator.

Remains of an extensive Iron Age and Romano-British rural settlement have been excavated at Watlington, on the Norfolk fen-edge, since 2004.[9] The site is defined by ditches, linear boundaries and enclosures, all of which were associated with stock rearing and agriculture. Accumulated evidence for a 'low order' settlement, representing activity over a period of 400 years, included the remains of domestic, agricultural, horticultural and limited industrial activity. Three Late Iron Age/early Roman pottery kilns were excavated, which were in use during the 1st century AD. The settlement expanded during the later 2nd and 3rd centuries, when a regular field system was also established.

RURAL LANDSCAPES IN THE EAST

On the other side of Norfolk, the landscape around *Venta Icenorum* has yielded evidence for late Roman rural settlement resulting from the movement of some of the wealthier citizens of the town out into the surrounding countryside during the later Roman period. These people, whose wealth was based on commerce, were able to build comfortable country houses away from the increasing hustle and bustle of the trading and industrial centre. Remains of one such high-status villa have been revealed on high ground some 2km to the south of *Venta*, a location which (although it must, regrettably, remain confidential) would have provided a splendid view of the Roman town. A combination of geophysical survey and fieldwalking has revealed a rectangular structure with side rooms leading from a corridor some 20m in length. Coin finds suggest a floruit for the occupation of between the mid 3rd and mid 4th centuries.

Further east still, in 1994, excavation in the churchyard extension to the east of the late Roman Saxon Shore fort at Burgh Castle revealed a complex sequence of 3rd- and 4th-century fields and enclosures.[10] These features, together with surface finds and rectilinear cropmarks east of the Church Loke and also to the south, represent an extensive agricultural landscape and show that Roman occupation was spread over an area of up to 40ha around the fort.

To the south-east of Burgh Castle, the remains of another Roman landscape, straddling the modern A12 road, are apparent at Hopton-on-Sea. Aerial photographs clearly show the boundaries of a system of

Romano-British farms and fields linked by double-ditched trackways. Their dating has been corroborated by fieldwalking and metal detection on the ground.[11]

Fig 167: The corn drier, excavated at the Roman farm at Hethersett. Photograph Andy Shelley, Norfolk Archaeological Unit.

OTHER TYPES OF RURAL SETTLEMENT

Agricultural features, such as ditches and field boundaries, are often difficult to date. However, other forms of Roman rural settlement can be identified across the Norfolk landscape, and many others no doubt remain undetected by archaeology. Roman rural sites could vary profoundly in size and status. In some instances, there was little change in the lifestyle from that of the Iron Age. It was during the 3rd and 4th centuries that many of the larger farming operations emerged.

Spong Hill

Spong Hill, at North Elmham in central Norfolk, is one settlement which changed little from the preceding prehistoric period.[12] An enclosure which had been constructed during the Late Iron Age was still in use during the mid 1st century AD, and a stock enclosure was added at this time. Then, after AD 60, the landscape was completely remodelled and a new enclosure, several paddocks and a droveway were laid out, together with a pottery kiln. A new farmyard enclosure was constructed during the early 2nd century and the farmstead, with its outbuildings and fields, then continued in use through to the end of the 4th century.

Environmental evidence shows that crops were being processed and that flax had been cultivated nearby. Animal species were mainly cattle and horses, while farmyard activities are represented by the presence of honestones, sharpening stones and quernstones. Iron was also being smelted. Modest wealth is indicated by the recovery of some 80 Roman coins and the presence of fragments from a range of domestic glass vessels.

Hethersett

In 2005 a substantial Roman farm was identified at Hethersett, in central Norfolk, and was partially excavated by the Norfolk Archaeological Unit.[13] A central farmyard enclosed by a series of ditches was revealed. Stock enclosures were identified to the north and south, and there was also a pond and a large well, which had been filled with domestic refuse in the 3rd and 4th centuries.

The eastern end of the yard contained a large square-shaped building, the walls of which were built of clay. A twin flue ran through the centre of the floor, allowing heat to be drawn through the building below ground level before exiting via chimneys. This building had been used to dry cereals during the 2nd and 3rd centuries (Fig 167).

Complete farmsteads of such a large scale are seldom recognised, although this type of farm was probably widespread across Roman Norfolk. However, Hethersett was probably one of the larger farming units in central east Norfolk. This particular operation clearly specialised in grain production, the activity which underpinned the developing prosperity of Roman Norfolk.

THE ECONOMY OF ROMAN NORFOLK

It was with the Roman period that the population moved beyond an existence based on subsistence towards one structured towards the production of surpluses and the accumulation of wealth. Merchants played a significant role in the opening up of the new province and traders accompanied the army as it advanced. The arrival of the military immediately created an increased requirement for food, pottery vessels and services. Coin use was also introduced within this context. As time progressed and the army moved away, economic functions became focused on the towns and villages.

Basic service industries, including metalworking, leather and bone working, carpentry and baking, were conducted in the small towns. Spinning and weaving were an integral part of domestic life; cloth was then bought and sold in the towns. Shops sold meat and farm produce, including fruit and vegetables, while the markets provided a trading focus for the local area. They were also able to facilitate trade over greater distances. Local produce was integrated into the imperial economy through the improved communication network, with water transport playing a particularly important role both within the area and beyond.

The economy of rural areas initially continued much as it had during the Late Iron Age, being geared towards food production; agriculture was of the greatest importance. However, tools available for farming improved during the Roman period: better ploughs allowed farmers to cut through heavier soils and it was then possible to increase field sizes. Extensive field systems have been identified in many places, often by aerial photography. As the period progressed, farms and villa estates were increasingly geared towards the production of surpluses and profits.

Fig 168: Iron ox-goads from Saham Toney. Scale 1:1.

Herds of cattle and goats, and flocks of sheep, together with pigs, formed the basis of the mixed farming regime (Fig 168). Sheep were kept for their wool and milk, rather than for meat. The production of wool was a particularly important local industry, as evidenced by wool combs and loom weights on sites. Crops grown included wheat and barley, rye and oats, and grain production was another major component in the local economy. Corn driers, similar to the example discovered at Hethersett, were commonly used on farms across the region.

As the economy continued to develop, people became more familiar with coin use. Most agricultural workers were initially unfamiliar with coins; their needs were provided for by the grain, meat and wool that they produced. By the late 3rd century, coin use was adopted more universally, even in more remote settlements in the countryside. Unfortunately, much of the agricultural activity that characterises Roman Norfolk remains invisible to archaeology, with the evidence that we do have being inevitably biased towards activities which leave more durable traces.

COASTAL AND MARITIME ACTIVITIES

Norfolk's extensive coastline supported a thriving fishing industry. Unfortunately, changes in the coastline since Roman times and the organic nature of the materials used have ensured that this has left little trace in the archaeological record. Shellfish, notably freshwater mussels, were also exploited. Oysters were an important food, and not just a luxury, as they are today. Oyster shells are found in large quantities on Roman settlements and their discovery is often good evidence for Roman occupation.

Another important industry was the production of salt, an activity which was certainly underway during the Iron Age.[14] Salt was essential

for the preservation of meat and fish, for treating hides and for feeding to stock animals. Production sites have been excavated and recorded in adjacent areas of Lincolnshire and are known from the extreme east and west of Norfolk.[15] Some are known on the east coast around the entrance to the Great Estuary. However, they are more prolific in the Fenland to the far west. Many sites investigated during the course of the Fenland Survey Project in the 1980s and excavated in the 1990s as part of the Fenland Management Project produced evidence for salt production. One such site in Norfolk was excavated at Blackborough End, and produced the largest assemblage of material from a Roman saltern site in East Anglia.[16] Another saltern was excavated at Denver by Charles Green in 1960 (Fig 169).[17]

Salt production at the fen-edge sites took advantage of the network of natural streams and creeks which ran several miles inland; at every high tide the water would flood up these and was then directed into a series of artificial ditches and tanks, where it was allowed to settle. Next the water was ladled into pottery troughs set over peat fires, where it evaporated, leaving salt crystals behind. Fragments of these troughs are regularly found at many locations along Norfolk's fen-edge.

Most salt production sites appear to have declined in the 2nd century. Another fen-edge saltern at Middleton flourished somewhat later, during

Fig 169: Roman salt-making at Denver (reconstruction by Sue White).

the 3rd and 4th centuries. Middleton, like Blackborough End, is a large site which seems to have operated on an industrial basis, rather than merely as a subsistence operation.

INDUSTRIAL ACITIVITES

Evidence for a range of activities has come from excavations at several sites, providing a detailed picture of the industrial landscape of Roman Norfolk. The excavations at Scole during the 1990s revealed evidence for leather working and tanning. Such activities would probably have been widespread at the small towns. More generally, developments in construction methods saw an increased use of bricks, tiles, shale and stone alongside the more traditional building materials of wattle, daub and timber.

There is evidence for iron working at a number of sites along the Holt–Cromer ridge in north Norfolk, such as Aylsham and Hevingham. This includes heaps of slag, bowl hearths and cinder deposits. An iron smelting site at Ashwicken, near Kings Lynn, was identified in 1958 by a spread of iron slag and Roman pottery which dates it to the 2nd century.[18] Excavation also revealed shaft furnaces made of clay. Some 350 tons of slag still remained within the working hollow. The process employed was a highly inefficient one which left a large amount of iron in the slag.

Evidence for a blacksmith's workshop was discovered at the 1st-century fort at Swanton Morley. This find included a very rare set of Roman iron tools.[19] Although such workshops must have been present at most settlements, iron objects do not survive well on archaeological sites.

There was a long tradition of bronze vessel production on the fen-edge. This local specialisation, which can be traced back to the Bronze Age Feltwell cauldron (Chapter 7), was still in operation during the Roman period. Several hoards of Roman bronze kitchen vessels have been discovered in the area, indicating that a bronze making workshop was active during the 3rd and 4th centuries.

Fig 170: Romano-British colour coated jar found at Burgh Castle. Height 150mm (copyright Norfolk Museums and Archaeology Service).

The pottery industry

Pottery is the most durable and prolific form of archaeological evidence and provides information about settlement and trade throughout the Roman period. Its production was widespread before the conquest but the arrival of the Roman army provided the stimulus for an increased number of kilns and the expansion of industrial production. Pottery manufacture took place right across Roman Norfolk and kilns are

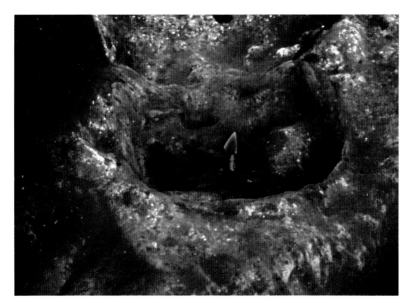

Fig 171: A pottery kiln during excavation at Pentney in 1981 (reconstruction by Sue White).

known from over thirty locations,[20] spanning the whole period of Roman Britain. Most of the pots were made to supply a local market but some Norfolk products did travel much further afield within Britain.

Early pottery production took place at Thorpe St Andrew, to the east of Norwich, where two kilns were investigated in 1938–9. This centre was supplying a local civilian market with a restricted range of vessel types during the period from the Roman conquest until about AD 70. A similar industry was supplying the area around Needham, in south-east Norfolk, at the same time. Further north, on the coast, a slightly later kiln was discovered at Upper Sheringham by local council workers erecting a boundary fence.[21] This industry had been active during the 2nd century. The clay walls of an updraught type kiln were exposed, together with a quantity of clay fire bars, which had been arranged radially within the chamber. Some broken pot sherds were also found.

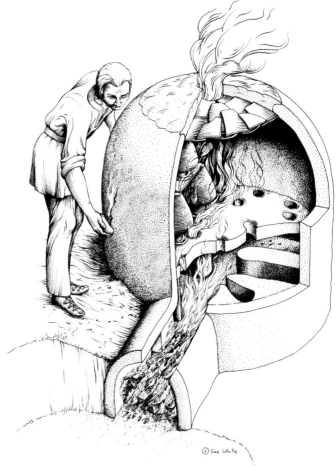

The largest pottery industry in Roman Norfolk was at Brampton. An industrial suburb was discovered to the west of the Roman town, in which the remains of over 130 pottery kilns have been found. The town had access to a local source of good-quality clay which was still being exploited at late as the 19th century.[22] Brampton's kilns were in use between about AD 100 and 300, and possibly even later. The main vessel types produced were coarse grey utilitarian vessels for the local market; these are found up to 30 and 40 miles from the town. However, some of Brampton's more specialist vessels were traded much further afield. Shipped from the town along the River Bure and to the east coast ports, they were then carried to the north of Britain by sea. Brampton pots have been found as far north as the Antonine Wall, near Edinburgh.

Venta Icenorum, the *civitas capital*, had a number of kilns, located just inside the north wall and to the south of the southern defences. Once again, this was a local industry, supplying everyday greywares for the community. Specialist pottery vessels were produced at some other locations. Kilns which produced mortaria have been discovered and excavated at Pentney, in south-west Norfolk (Fig 171).[23] Their period of use was between about AD 100 and 250. Sherds of mortaria made at Pentney have been found at a number of sites in Norfolk, almost all in the west of the county.

The Nar Valley

During the Fenland Survey Project of the 1980s, a number of industrial activities were recognised in the Nar valley, an eastern offshoot of the main Fenland basin some 5km south of King's Lynn.[24] This location appears to have been the centre of significant Roman industry which provided goods and services for a wide area, with a range of specific activities being carried out at individual sites. Pottery production is known at Shouldham, Pentney and Blackborough End:[25] 120 kilns are known from Pentney alone and this industry rivalled that at Brampton in the east. Iron smelting was discovered at Wormegay and, as noted above, salt production took place at Blackborough End.

Evidence for activity in the Nar valley is increasingly coming to light but, although awareness is growing, its significance is still not widely appreciated. However, it is already clear that this area was an important industrial focus unlike anything else in Roman Norfolk. Its significance would have been more than local, and was probably regional in nature.

Brooch and jewellery production

Evidence for the manufacture of Roman brooches is exceptionally rare across the northern provinces of the Roman Empire, and a disproportionately large amount of evidence has been recorded in

Norfolk during recent years. All of these new examples have come to light through the reporting of metal-detector finds.

Controlled metal detection during the 1980s at the Romano-British small town of Crownthorpe, at Wicklewood, has produced a superb assemblage of Roman brooches (see Chapter 12). This remarkable collection of over 600 individual items, which was acquired by Norwich Castle Museum, includes a whole range of different types, many of which were probably made at a workshop at the settlement.

In November 1999 a bronze brooch mould was found at Felmingham. This was one half of a two-piece mould which had been used to produce a form of brooch known as the 'rear-hook' type. Rear-hook brooches were a regional type which can be associated with the population of northern East Anglia and were the main type used by the Iceni before AD 60. Remarkably, another very similar lower mould for a rear-hook-type brooch was found in the county in June 2006. This second discovery came from Brancaster, in the civilian settlement adjacent to the area of the later fort.

Fig 172: The brooch mould, with brooch, discovered at Old Buckenham. Length 51mm.

In 1993 an even more remarkable discovery of brooch production material was made close to the Roman settlement at Old Buckenham in south Norfolk. The find comprised four incomplete brooches, each of which combined the foot and catch-plate with a metal sprue from the casting process. There was also a brooch head and one complete brooch. Most astonishing were five pieces of metal brooch mould, including a complete two-piece mould with a brooch fused inside it (Figs 172 and 173). The form of brooch in question is known as a Colchester derivative, which dates from between AD 60/65 and AD 100.[26] In addition to the more diagnostic items, there were pieces of sprue left over from the casting process and many pieces of scrap metal.

The inner surfaces of the moulds needed to be lined with tallow, oil or soot before the two halves were tied together and the molten metal poured in. After cooling, the mould sections were knocked apart and

the brooch released. The casting was then trimmed of the sprue and casting flashes, polished and attached to a spring. In the case of the Old Buckenham mould, this process went wrong. The mould cannot have been effectively greased or lined and the brooch became fused.

Fig 173: The brooch mould from Old Buckenham. Length 70mm.

Whether this group of material was discarded or lost is impossible to say. The metal may have been intended for reworking. Perhaps

Fig 174: The Snettisham jeweller's hoard.

it was swept up during rubbish collection and dumped away from the settlement.

There is no parallel for such a group of material from Roman Britain – nor from the western Roman Empire as a whole. Indeed, elsewhere, there is only limited evidence for brooches having been cast, and those examples have been in clay moulds. This collection, together with the other Norfolk evidence cited above, is the only evidence for the casting of Roman brooches in metal moulds yet discovered.

A very special jewellery hoard

A very spectacular find was made at Snettisham in north-west Norfolk in 1985. Specialist products intended for sale, such as jewellery, were sometimes carried around by itinerant craftsmen as they travelled from settlement to settlement during the Roman period. This amazing new discovery contained the stock of one such jeweller and gives us a unique insight into how such tradesmen operated at that time.[27]

The hoard was discovered during building development, when a mechanical digger revealed the rim of a small pottery vase. This near-complete greyware vessel was carefully lifted from the ground. As the contents were emptied out an amazing treasure was revealed: 356 items, including a stunning array of bronze and silver coins, gemstones, finger rings and bracelets, all in varying stages of completeness (Fig 174). The silver coins (*denarii*) and pieces of scrap would have served as a source of silver, while the brass coins may have been used for alloying the silver. There were also engraved gemstones ready to be set into rings.

This collection of material, which was dated to the 2nd century AD, provided the first ever direct evidence for the process of precious-metal jewellery manufacture in Roman Britain. It appears to be the complete stock of a craftsperson who made and sold silver and bronze jewellery. The manufacture of small items of jewellery on a mobile basis was not impossible for an itinerant smith, although they would probably have needed to return to their permanent workshop from time to time.

This single deposit from Snettisham shows the way that jewellers and other specialist craftspersons, including vendors of fine pottery and metalwork vessels, travelled from town to town to sell their wares. It provides a charming and very personal insight into the world of one such trader who was travelling the roads and trackways between the villages and settlements of north-west Norfolk during the mid AD 150s.

Late Roman glass vessels from east Norfolk

One small and relatively insignificant-looking fragment of glass from *Venta Icenorum* provides evidence of how international trade between the *civitas capital* and other northern provinces continued through the late Roman period. The sherd in question, which was discovered within the site archive at Norwich Castle, came from a deep tubular rimmed bowl with a tubular base.[28] No more than a dozen such vessels are known from Britain. They are a particularly late type and were introduced in the second half of the 4th century, continuing in use possibly into the 5th century. It is thought that they were produced in Gallia Belgica.[29]

Two additional complete examples have been identified from Burgh Castle.[30] Harriet Foster has undertaken analyses of this type of bowl and found that the form of glass used may have been made in the Near East – possibly Egypt. From there, the glass would have been transported to the north-western provinces for remelting and shaping into glass vessels.[31]

These rare glass vessels from east Norfolk reflect the continuing importance for sites on and around the Great Estuary of continental trade right through the final decades of Roman Britain.

Chapter 14
Late Roman Norfolk

> Legate, I had the news last night – my cohort ordered home
> By ship to Portus Itius and thence by road to Rome.
> (Rudyard Kipling, *The Roman Occupation*)

Roman Norfolk continued for 350 years after the death of Boudica, a period equivalent to the span of time between the reign of King Charles I and today. This long period, spanning many generations, inevitably saw continuous development and change. We should be cautious before generalising about life in Roman Norfolk as if it were a single brief episode.

Nevertheless, the key factors which determined the region's prosperity and development remained. As the years progressed, Norfolk's agriculture became important well beyond the boundaries of the *Civitas Icenorum*. Water, too, continued to have a significant influence, the efficient transport system provided by the extensive rivers and long coastline supplying the key that unlocked the region's trading potential.

THE IMPORTANCE OF THE GREAT ESTUARY

The importance of the waterways of east Norfolk, and especially the Great Estuary, cannot be underestimated in terms of the area's economic development and prosperity. The major rivers – the Bure, the Yare and the Waveney – together with the Ant and Bure, all drained eastwards. By the late Roman period, settlements across the east were thriving as a result of their positions on and near these rivers, which provided access to the sea beyond.

The successful development of the town of Brampton was based on its position adjacent to the River Bure. A wharf, which comprised a platform of reused timbers along a side channel adjacent to the main course of the river, was discovered there during excavations in 1973.[1] Long-distance water transport played a significant role in the development of the town's pottery industry.

The Iron Age and Roman settlements at Caistor St Edmund were located at a key point on the River Tas, which flowed into the Yare.

Water-borne communications again facilitated the growth of the town and its development as a regional centre of trade from an early date. The evidence for Roman wharves again attests to the site's role in relation to the export of agricultural produce from across the region.

Although the Great Estuary and its tributaries supported and nurtured trade from the earliest times, the archaeological evidence that we might expect to have found for this activity has not yet come to light.* Archaeological finds remain hidden beneath the silting of the estuary itself. Some important evidence may still be present within known archaeological sites across the area, which have not been excavated to modern standards.

In 1976 timbers were excavated at the point of an ancient ford of the River Ant at Smallburgh, in Broadland. A Roman road runs eastward from the fens and turns north towards the River Ant here, where Wayford Bridge is known to mark an ancient crossing point. The timbers were radiocarbon dated and found to belong to the late 2nd or early 3rd century AD.

Other sites have been recognised adjacent to the River Yare as a result of the recovery of large timbers. A possible port was identified at Brundall. Another such site was located during the early 1960s at Trowse, at the confluence of the Rivers Yare and Wensum, by Rainbird Clarke, Barbara Green and Donald Atkinson.

The settlements that were located along the banks of the River Waveney included Scole, as well as smaller places like Ditchingham and Homersfield; the latter lay on the south side of the river. Both of the smaller sites appear to have grown in relation to an early trading function, as indicated by quantities of Iron Age coins at each of them, but both continued to thrive in later centuries.

Exciting evidence of shipping and trading must lie beneath the marshes of east Norfolk for future generations to discover. However, with the fortification of selected sites in the late Roman period, there is more evidence for the river-based trading network and its importance to the economy of Roman Norfolk.

THE SAXON SHORE SYSTEM

The Saxon Shore is a major feature of late Roman Norfolk, with various impressive sites remaining today; some of these are well-known, while others are less so. The term Saxon Shore was introduced into the historical vocabulary by a document called the *Notitia Dignitatum*, which was drawn up in about AD 408, at the end of Roman Britain. It is referred to in that document primarily as a list of army units stationed at sites in south-eastern Britain. The earliest version of the *Notitia* dates from the 11th century, and comes through a document

Fig 175: The forts of the Saxon Shore.

known as the *Codex Spirensis*, which is now lost to us. It is via this much later document that scholarly studies and interpretations of the *Litus Saxonicum* have been developed.

The name 'Saxon Shore' was not explained in the *Notitia Dignitatum*, and its meaning has remained somewhat ambiguous. It could be interpreted as 'the coast settled by Saxons', or perhaps 'the shore on the Saxon Sea'. However, the favoured explanation has traditionally been 'the Shore threatened with attack by Saxons'.

The Saxon Shore comprised a system of forts built around the coast of southern England, between Portchester in Hampshire and Brancaster in Norfolk, in the 3rd and 4th centuries AD. Similar forts were also constructed on the continental shores, from Mardyck near Calais as far south as Blaye, on the estuary of the Garonne in south-western

France. Most of these were situated on the coast, on navigable rivers and estuaries. The British system as a whole faced towards the east and the sites appear to have been positioned around the approaches to major estuaries on the south-east coast (Fig 175).

The *Notitia* is a difficult document to use because it is potentially misleading, apparently conflating events and information which in fact occurred at and relate to disparate dates within the late Roman period. It is, in effect, a copy of a late Roman handbook prepared for the use of officials, within which the basic information is relatively accurate for around the year AD 395. Additions were then made, until about AD 430, to parts of the text in an effort to keep it up to date. A major problem with the document is that it lists only nine British forts. Eight forts beyond Norfolk have been associated with the system, while two Norfolk sites have been traditionally classified as part of the Saxon

Fig 176: Plan of Brancaster Saxon Shore fort.

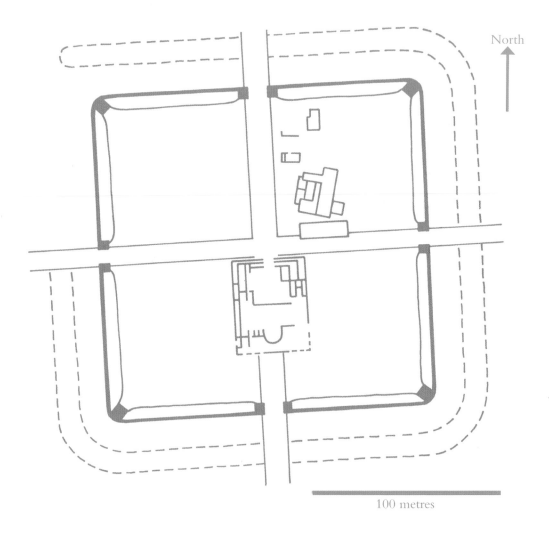

North

100 metres

Shore.[2] To this list we can now add one, or perhaps two, additional candidates from Norfolk, which will be discussed below.

Fleets and land garrisons, including cavalry units, were based at the British forts. A large body of literature tells how these forces were designed to counter a threat which was coming from the Jutes, Frisians, Angles and Saxons, peoples who began to harry the coasts of Britain, northern France and the Low Countries during the 3rd century.[3] The forts acted as strongholds and naval bases for sailors and flotillas whose duty was to control pirate raids. They were garrisoned by mobile troops who were ready to combat pirate landings. As they were sited on the principal river estuaries, they also acted as an active discouragement to penetration into inland areas by pirates.

Norfolk contains some important and spectacular physical evidence relating to the Saxon Shore, which contributes to a developing interpretation of the system.

Brancaster

The fort on the northern extremity of the system is at Brancaster, in north-west Norfolk. Today, it lies on a slight elevation above salt marshes. There has been considerable silting of this part of the coast since the medieval period: a combination of salt marshes, creeks and dunes has formed between the site and Brancaster Bay. In the Roman period the fort would have stood beside a navigable inlet with a sheltered anchorage, protected from the North Sea by a spit of land. Unfortunately, nothing of the fort remains standing above ground today, although a historical record by Spelman states that the walls were standing to a height of 12 feet as recently as 1600.[4] Today, this site has been revealed through aerial photography and partially explored through excavation.[5]

Fig 177: Church of St Mary the Virgin, Brancaster.

The site plan and construction

Aerial photography has been particularly important in understanding the overall site plan (Fig 176). There was an outer defensive ditch. Cropmarks indicate the layout of a *principia* facing the north gate at the centre of the fort, just south of the east–west road. This building has a courtyard surrounded by rooms and, to the south, a range of offices off the basilica hall. Two other buildings can be identified within the fort, north-east of the *principia*.

Excavations in 1974 and 1977 were confined to examining the defences. The fort was almost square, with rounded corners, and enclosed 2.6ha. There is no evidence for bastions. Building materials came mainly from local sources. The walls were built of sandstone, with a flint, ironstone and chalk rubble core; the chalk came from quarries in the west of the county or from the shores of the Wash, while flint came from coastal parts of north Norfolk.

The fort was faced with sandstone which had been cut into squared blocks. Originally white, this stone weathers to a steel grey colour. Today, grey stone blocks from the fort can be seen built into the chancel of the nearby church of St Mary the Virgin at Brancaster (Fig 177) and in other local churches, including St Mary's at Burnham Deepdale and St Mary the Virgin at Titchwell. It is also found in houses, farm buildings and walls in the villages of Brancaster and Brancaster Staithe.[6] Samples of this stone have been analysed and are now known to derive from west Norfolk. The Roman fort would have originally looked very striking from a great distance, the freshly cut sandstone endowing it with a bright white appearance.

Dating and occupation

The earliest fort at Brancaster can be dated before AD 200. This was replaced by a second construction, slightly further south, erected around the start of the 3rd century. This, in turn, was replaced by a larger construction around AD 225–50.[7] Occupation continued to the end of the 4th century.

This fort has been identified as the site of *Branodunum*, which is listed in the *Notitia Dignitatum*: the *Notitia* mentions a garrison stationed there called the *Equites Dalmatae Branodunenses*, who were an auxiliary cavalry unit from the Balkans.[8]

Stamped tiles recovered from the excavation also provide remarkable evidence for a military unit which served at Brancaster. They confirm the presence of the *Cohors I Aquitanorum*, which is the first unit to be identified through archaeological evidence at a Saxon Shore installation.[9] These two forms of evidence perhaps suggest that at some stage there was a change of garrison, perhaps with the *Equites Dalmatae* replacing the *Cohors I Aquitanorum*.

The civilian settlement

We also have evidence for a substantial civilian settlement, or *vicus*, which extends beyond the fort to both the east and west. A combination of excavation and aerial survey show the fort to be placed within an area of regular ditched enclosures and trackways of Roman date, covering an area of at least 23ha. Rectangular plots were probably linked to a settlement which was laid out in the 2nd century.

North

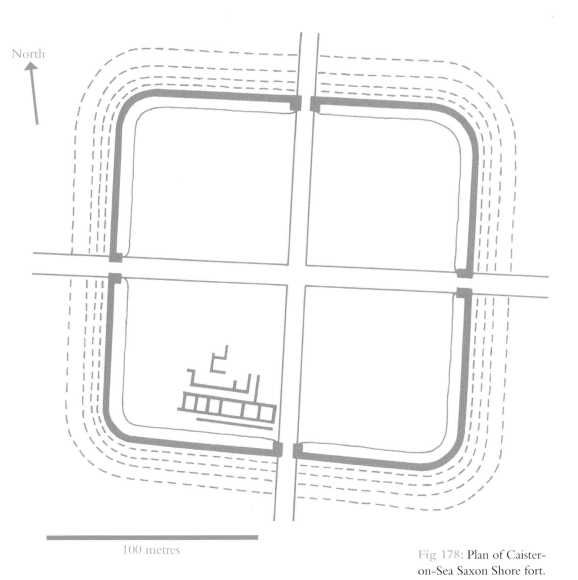

100 metres

Fig 178: Plan of Caister-on-Sea Saxon Shore fort.

Industrial and economic activity

A very large animal bone assemblage was recovered during excavation, representing the remains of domestic creatures raised and slaughtered for food.[10] There was a predominance of cattle, with sheep, pig and horse also represented. A paucity of younger animals suggests that they might have been shipped off to other sites, such as the northern forts, for consumption, while meat eaten at Brancaster came from more mature animals raised for milk and wool production.

A range of industrial activities is evidenced from the surrounding *vicus*. These include woodworking, stoneworking and various activities associated with agriculture.

Caister-on-Sea

The remains of the fort at Caister-on-Sea are located on the east coast, 7km north of Great Yarmouth and now 1km inland. In Roman times the fort sat adjacent to an embayment on the northern side of the Great Estuary. That Caister-on-Sea is considered to be part of the Saxon Shore system has still not been fully appreciated beyond East Anglia; until very recently it was classified as a coastal small town and civilian port. For years, however, archaeologists in Norfolk have argued that Caister should be considered as part of the Saxon Shore system. It is now believed that this fort may have controlled the northern side of the Great Estuary, while another fort at Burgh Castle controlled the water on the opposite side.[11] For how long, or indeed whether at all, the two forts worked in tandem is difficult to say. However, Caister was certainly in operation somewhat earlier than Burgh Castle.

The construction and layout

Like Brancaster, this fort appears to have been constructed in the early 3rd century, perhaps during the reign of Caracalla, between AD 211 and 217. It was square, with rounded corners, and covered 3.5ha (Fig 178). It was surrounded by two external ditches. Construction made use of local building materials:[12] flint nodules came from outcrops some 50km to the west, while cobbles came from the north-east coast.

Just one corner turret has been identified. The defensive wall, the construction of which interspersed tile bonding courses with masonry, probably stood 4 or 5m tall. Excavation uncovered a rectangular guard chamber on the west side of the south gate.[13] Two internal buildings were excavated. Building 1 initially had a domestic function, which was later changed to an industrial one connected with slaughtering animals and butchery. It had a simple rectangular plan, and was subdivided into seven rooms, one of which was heated by a hypocaust. Building 2 had *opus signinum* floors and a range of flint and timber-framed rooms which were decorated with wall plaster; another hypocaust was present there. A quantity of ladies' shale bracelets was also found, although it is unclear whether these relate to activities carried out there or to the occupants.

Gurney has suggested that if this site (like Brancaster) dates from the early 3rd century, before Saxon raiding became a significant problem, it may initially have had another function.[14] He argues that its role was more related to the safeguarding of coastal trade and merchant shipping. The fort declined in the later 4th century, with occupation finally ceasing sometime after AD 370.

There was probably a period of overlap with Burgh Castle, during which, as mentioned above, the two forts may have operated in tandem. However, Caister was eventually replaced altogether by Burgh Castle.

Extra-mural settlement

A *vicus* is known to the west of the fort. Although the evidence is very limited, coins, brooches and some pottery have been recovered from this area over the years.

Military finds from the site

We do not have any indication of specific units that served at Caister, but a range of military equipment has been recovered, including strap bindings and fittings, iron spearheads and arrowheads, an artillery bolt head and a shield boss. There is also part of a reinforcement strip from a helmet.

Industrial and economic activity

A range of activities here are well attested by evidence from excavations. A large volume of animal bones were recovered. Most were cattle bones, with lesser amounts of sheep, goat and pig. These remains indicate that butchery was being carried out on site. It has also been suggested that rooms within Building 1, which had waterproof *opus signinum* plaster, may have served as tannery *tanks*, in which raw animal hides were converted into leather.[15]

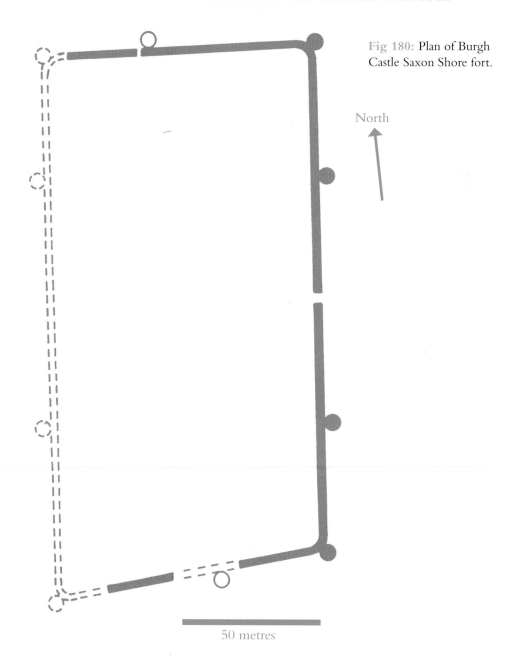

Fig 180: Plan of Burgh Castle Saxon Shore fort.

North

50 metres

A range of needles, spindles, loom weights and spindle-whorls attest to the working of textiles. There is also evidence for both ferrous and non-ferrous metalworking, mostly in the form of smithing slag. Numerous items, both finished and partly worked, indicate that antler and bone working were undertaken at Caister. The presence of uncut pieces of shale from Dorset suggest that this material was also being worked at the site.

Burgh Castle

The name *Gariannonum*, which is mentioned in the *Notitia Dignitatum*, has long been attributed to Burgh Castle. However, this name could now equally be seen as that of its 'sister' fort at Caister-on-Sea. A third possibility for the name has now arisen at Reedham, which is considered below.

This spectacular fort stands on high ground, at a most picturesque setting, some 30m above fenland and the River Yare. The preservation is remarkable. Much of the north, east and south walls still stand to a relatively uniform height of around 4.6m above the original ground level (Fig 179). Today the fort stands some distance from the present coastline but in the Roman period it was located at the first landing point on the south side of the estuary, commanding a safe anchorage and a substantial stretch of water, whose outflow to the sea lay through the area now occupied by Great Yarmouth.

Fig 181: Close-up of the wall at Burgh Castle, showing the squared flint and tile construction.

The construction and layout

As with Caister-on-Sea, local building materials were used:[16] flint came from further west and cobbles from north-east Norfolk. The walls originally formed a trapezoidal shape, enclosing an area of 2.2ha (Fig 180). The west wall, which ran parallel to the standing eastern wall, has fallen and traces of masonry have been located in the marshlands below; debris from the wall was visible on the surface of the marsh in the 1960s. The walls are built of a rubble core faced with split flints and are about 3.2m wide at their base, tapering to about 1.5m at the top (Fig 181). These dimensions are so uniform that they seem unlikely to have been the effect of erosion and are, rather, probably the result of a number of stepped offsets on the interior side. Vertical cracks can be seen in the walls on all sides of the fort, implying that distinct sections were constructed separately, by different teams of labourers, and were subsequently joined, which may also have been the case with the bastions.

Fig 182: An external
bastion at Burgh Castle.

Externally, the walls are protected by solid projecting towers, or
bastions, which are horseshoe-shaped in plan, the lower 2.2m of which
are not bonded to the walls (Fig 182). The missing north-west bastion
was observed in the side of an adjacent dyke by a farmer in the 1960s.
All the towers have a circular hole in their tops, 0.6m in diameter
and of similar depth. It had been thought that artillery, in the form
of *ballistae*, or giant crossbows, occupied these towers, but it is now
thought more likely that the holes represent the fittings for a timber
superstructure forming a protective walkway with roofed chambers
above the bastions.

Between 1958 and 1961 Charles Green examined two main areas
within the fort.[17] Traces of mortar floors were located, possibly belonging
to timber-framed Roman buildings with wattle and daub walls. Adjacent
to the fort, enigmatic traces of oak piles and stonework were located
during the last century. Finds of anchors have also been reported in the
locality.[18] These may all be related to a Roman quay, indicating that large
vessels were using the Great Estuary and anchoring in deep water at this
point, although no boats have yet been located in the marshes.

The garrison

In 1960 Green recovered pieces of an elaborate cavalryman's helmet
similar to others found at Concesti in Romania and Deurne in Holland.
(Fig 183)[19] It originally comprised four iron segments which formed a
dome shape. A central crest of iron ran along the top from front to back,
while rivets provided a decorative appearance to the surface. It belonged
to an auxiliary horseman who was part of a troop of Stablesian cavalry

and was used during the 4th century. This shows that the fort was a cavalry station as well as a naval base.

Finds from the site

Two major metal-detector surveys were undertaken in the early 1990s, prior to the site being taken into the care of the Norfolk Archaeological Trust (Fig 184). Before these surveys, the coin total from excavation stood at 240 site finds. The second survey alone produced nearly 1000 Roman coins, an assemblage which is invaluable in evaluating the chronology of the site (Fig 185). Coins recovered from both excavation and metal-detector surveys suggest very little activity there before the 4th century: coin loss started late and only appreciably in the AD 320s, with peaks in the mid-Constantinian years – the 330s and 340s – and again in the Valentinianic period, between 364 and 378.

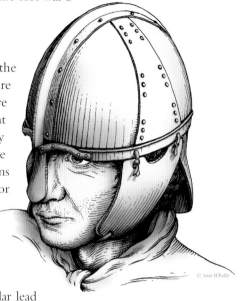

Fig 183: Reconstruction of the Burgh Castle Helmet (by Sue White).

Another significant find from the site is a small circular lead seal depicting a stag and the letters PBS,[20] an abbreviation of the title *Provinciae Britannia Superioris*. Burgh Castle was within the Roman administrative area of 'Upper Britain', which was established around AD 200. The seal would have arrived attached to an important official document.

Extra-mural settlement

In 1994, excavation by the Norfolk Archaeological Unit in the chuchyard extension to the east of the fort revealed a complex sequence of 3rd- and 4th-century fields or enclosures cut into the subsoil. As described in Chapter 13, these features, together with rectilinear cropmarks east

Fig 184: The finds identification shed at the second Burgh Castle metal-detector survey.

of the Church Loke, irregular cropmarks further south and general recorded surface finds show that there was up to 40ha of Roman occupation around the fort.

The bone assemblage

The collection of animal bones during the excavation appears to have been selective, being biased towards larger bones and thus making comparisons with other sites difficult. However, butchery can be inferred.[21] The nature of cuts on bones also indicate that there had been bone working, as well as antler working, at the site.

ECONOMIC ACITIVITY AT THE NORFOLK SHORE FORTS

Some similarities are evident between the three Norfolk Shore forts. To begin with, all were involved in economic activity and trade: evidence from these sites shows trading contacts across southern Britain and right across the Roman Empire.

Moreover, judging by the large numbers of animal bones found at all sites, butchery was commonly undertaken at the forts. In all cases, cattle were most common, with sheep and pigs also represented. Similar observations can be made for the Shore sites of Portchester (Hampshire), Richborough (Kent) and Bradwell (Essex).[22] It has been noted that at the Norfolk sites there is a bias towards non–meat-bearing bones, which suggests that the prime joints may have been going elsewhere. This might have been part of a large-scale processing operation in which tanning and the preparation of hides were carried out alongside meat production, and which possibly involved onward transhipment to the army.

The presence of spinning and weaving materials was also observed inside all the forts, and the presence of women participating in these activities can thus be inferred. This industry, too, may have been geared towards servicing a military market.

The pottery assemblages from the Norfolk sites all contain ceramic material from Britain more widely: fine wares and mortaria from the Nene Valley, pottery from Oxfordshire and Much Hadham, Essex, and small amounts of Black Burnished pottery from Dorset.

There is also, as noted above, material evidence from the Norfolk forts which demonstrates widespread contacts with the broader Roman world.[23] Samian ware pottery from central and eastern Gaul entered Brancaster and Caister in their initial phases. Argonne Ware and ceramique a l'eponge from Gaul and Mayen wares from Germany were

Fig 185: Very rare coin struck by the Emperor Carausius (AD 287–93) from Burgh Castle. Inscribed CARAVSIVS ET FRATRES SVI, combining the busts of Diocletian and Maximianus, and declaring PAX AVGGG on the reverse. Diameter 24mm.

found at Caister, together with amphorae from Gaul, southern Spain and North Africa. Other items of long-distance trade include quern fragments from the Eifel region of Germany.

SIGNAL STATIONS

There are three or possibly four smaller coastal sites between Wells and Cromer, on the north Norfolk coast, which may be associated with the Saxon Shore system. Although none of these sites has yet been fully investigated archaeologically, they are all in raised positions with clear views of the surrounding land and sea, and appear to have served as signal stations; they would have had structures on top and probably supported beacons and semaphore stations.

Warborough Hill, Stiffkey

At Warborough Hill, just east of Wells, is a mound which is clearly the edge of an artificial platform (Fig 186). It is capped with layers of mortared flint and Roman pottery sherds and tile have been recovered from above and below the mortar. Much of the original platform has been robbed away. In 1934 Rainbird Clarke partially excavated at this site and recovered a cremation of Iron Age date. He also noted 4th-century pottery, together with Roman building materials, in the vicinity. Subsequently, a trial section across the west edge of the hill revealed further evidence of a late Roman construction, in the form of disintegrating masonry, flint, brick and stone bound by coarse lime-rich mortar.

Gramborough Hill, Salthouse

At Gramborough Hill is an isolated mound located on the beach between Salthouse and Weybourne, between the sea and marshland (Fig 187). This construction bears a close similarity to the Stiffkey site. It is square in plan, each side measuring approximately 100m in length, and has a flat top. A ditch, which has recently been destroyed by sea action, was recorded on the seaward side.

Finds from the site include Roman greyware pottery, animal bones, oyster shells and iron nails.[24] A small number of Iron Age and Roman coins and a single Roman brooch have also been found. Burnt clay containing wattle impressions, together with fragments of Roman roof tile, attests to the former present of a substantial building either on or beside the mound.

Muckleburgh Hill, Kelling

Slightly further inland, at Muckleburgh Hill, Kelling, is a much higher natural dome-shaped hill. A Roman site has been identified on its top and it has been speculated that this was a signal station. However, its

proximity to Gramborough Hill and its immensely greater height make it improbable that both sites were part of the same signalling system. This is, therefore, a less strong candidate than Gramborough Hill but it does provide an excellent line of sight right through to Cromer.

Fig 186: Warborough Hill, Stiffkey.

Other sites

Another outstanding natural feature, between Muckleburgh Hill and Cromer and just east of Sheringham, is known as Beeston Hump. No Roman site has been identified here, but this would have been too good a natural location to be ignored by the Romans. It is midway between Kelling and Cromer and shows a resemblance to Muckleburgh Hill. It may well have housed another signal station.

Remains of another station have been seen during the 1990s at California, on the east coast, three miles north of Great Yarmouth, where the cliffs are crumbling away at an alarming rate. Masonry associated with Roman pottery could be seen on the highest point, which has since tumbled onto the beach below and been removed.

Beyond Norfolk to the south, the presence of signal stations have been postulated at Corton and Dunwich in Suffolk. At Corton, cliff falls in 1814 revealed a square timber structure. This was too large for a well, leading to speculation that it was a signal station. However, there

Fig 187: Gramborough Hill, Salthouse.

was no other associated evidence, and no dating evidence at all. The configuration of the coastline at Dunwich has led to the suggestion that such a site was also present here. In Roman times this formed a strategic promontory mid-way between Burgh Castle and Walton Castle, allowing views across long stretches of coastline, as well as shelter for ships in the creeks. However, this idea remains speculation.

REEDHAM

Reedham is situated due west of Burgh Castle. In Roman times it was at the southern end of a tongue of land where the Rivers Yare, Chet and Waveney joined the Great Estuary. The location is now made conspicuous by the siting of the 11th- or 12th-century parish church of St John the Baptist, which stands on a bluff on the bank of the River Yare, overlooking the confluence of the three rivers (Figs 188-189). Today the church commands breathtaking views across marshland; this would once have been a imposing position overlooking the Great Estuary.

In the 19th century the foundations of a circular Roman building were reported to have been discovered immediately south of, and adjacent to, the church; these were interpreted as those of a Roman *pharos* or lighthouse. However, the fields to the south of the church occupy much lower ground and would have been covered by water when the estuary waters were at their height. The presence of a Roman lighthouse in such a location must be questioned. If a *pharos* was located at Reedham it must have stood on higher ground and its signalling would have been visible from Burgh Castle. However, those who constructed the church here made extensive use of Roman building materials, suggesting that there was indeed significant construction in the vicinity. More recent discoveries of building materials nearby suggest that Roman buildings were widespread across the area covered by today's village. This would probably have comprised a settlement centred around a quay or port.

In the church large quantities of Roman tile can be seen, laid in alternate herringbone and horizontal courses in the north wall of the nave. (Fig 188) The tower walls are formed of alternate panels of grey sandstone and knapped and squared flints. (Fig 189) Investigation by Edwin Rose has shown that the grey stone is of the same type as that identified as having been used in the fort at Brancaster.[25] These building materials appear to have come from an exceptionally large Roman building. As the only other recorded use of the same type of stone in the region is, as mentioned, at the Saxon Shore fort of Brancaster, it is suggested that the structure which provided the church's building materials at Reedham had been associated with that system. Recent studies of the surviving building materials have suggested the construction of a military building, perhaps on the scale of a substantial auxiliary fort,[26] in the second quarter of the 3rd century, a date range which suggests a broad contemporaneity for its construction with that of the Brancaster fort.

The most attractive interpretation of the remains at Reedham is that this was a third fort situated on the Great Estuary, strategically positioned at the entrance to the Rivers Yare, Chet and Waveney. It would have been constructed after Caister and before Burgh Castle. The presence of a third Saxon Shore fort in the east would serve to reinforce the immense importance to the Roman authorities and traders of maritime and riverine access, trade and communications at the entrance to the Great Estuary. Such an interpretation for the remains at Reedham also adds yet another candidate for the name *Garrianonum* (see above).

THE NORTH COAST

There is a very long stretch of coastline in the north, to the east of Brancaster, that has no late Roman fortification. If the purely defensive interpretation of the Shore forts is adhered to, this lack of sites does pose a problem. This led Tony Gregory to suggest, based on a strategic and military distribution of the sites, that another fort may have existed in the region of Cromer or Mundesley.[27] However, the presence of a fort here is pure speculation.

Fig 188: Church of St John the Baptist, Reedham, showing re-used Roman building materials.

Fig 189: Church of St John the Baptist, Reedham, showing the grey sandstone blocks.

A THREAT FROM THE SEA?

Although the generally accepted explanation of the Saxon Shore has been essentially a military one, other theories have been put forward over the years. In 1961 Donald White proposed that that Saxon raiding in the 3rd century was insufficient to warrant such massive coastal defences.[28] He considered that the sites must have been constructed for purposes other than just defence against the Saxons.

In recent years a number of scholars have continued to cast doubt on the conventional interpretation of the role of the Saxon Shore forts.[29] More emphasis is now being placed on their economic function, an interpretation which fits comfortably with the evidence coming forward from Norfolk. A major factor in this reinterpretation has been the concern voiced by some scholars over the reality of the barbarian threat to Britain during the 3rd and early 4th centuries.

The first written reports of Saxon raiding are associated with the usurper Carausius' seizure of power in Britain in AD 287. However, neither of the two historians Aurelius Victor and Eutropius mentions Britain in this context. In fact, Belgica and Armorica were the regions under attack. Re-examination of the writings of Ammianus Marcellinus suggests that trouble from the Picts, Scots, Attacotti and Saxons, which he described as taking place in AD 362–4, really related to Gaul and not to Britain.[30] With regard to the barbarian conspiracy of AD 367–8, it has been argued that only the coasts of Gaul were threatened by Saxons at that time.[31] In relation to other historical texts – the contemporary panegyrics – it has now been argued that it was the German and Gallic, rather than the British, coasts that were being threatened in the 3rd and 4th centuries.[32]

The first real evidence of Saxon raiding of Britain does not come until the 5th century, from a passage in the Gallic Chronicle of AD 452 relating to the British rebellion of AD 409. Wood suggests that the Saxon Shore was so-named in hindsight, at a time when the Saxons were a serious issue, and that it was not known as the Saxon Shore in the 3rd and 4th centuries.[33]

Today it is becoming clearer that the threat posed by coastal raiding may have been over-stated. It can be argued that a major *raison d'être* for the Saxon Shore forts could have been one more associated with trade, rather than purely with coastal defence.

THE FUNCTION OF THE SAXON SHORE FORTS IN NORFOLK

It is probable, therefore, that Norfolk's Saxon Shore forts were more than purely military installations. They clearly also played an important role in relation to economic and trading activities, including the safeguarding of the transport of perishable commodities to a variety of destinations in and out of the region, perhaps serving as transhipment centres or fortified ports. The movement of traded commodities over long distances elsewhere in the Roman Empire is known to have involved chains of such sites, where cargoes were transferred from cart to river barge and from barge to sea-going vessel. Such centres were situated all over the Empire and include the port of Ostia, near Rome, and Colijnsplaat and Domburg on the Scheldt estuary in the Netherlands.

Access to the sea, and therefore to bulk transport at relatively low cost, offered significant economic advantages.[34] Coastal towns and cities were able to dispose of their own local produce and receive other products by sea in a way that inland sites could not. In this context, the Saxon Shore sites may be considered to have overseen bulk trade along the major routes in late Roman Norfolk – particularly that in grain, given the development of Norfolk as the 'breadbasket' of the east. Such trade may have been a major reason for the construction of these fortified sites (Fig 190).

One of the major trade routes in the Roman period was between the Rhine mouth, the east coast and south-east England. The Shore forts of the east can be seen to have been strategically placed in relation to the important estuaries, from which trade would have been a principal

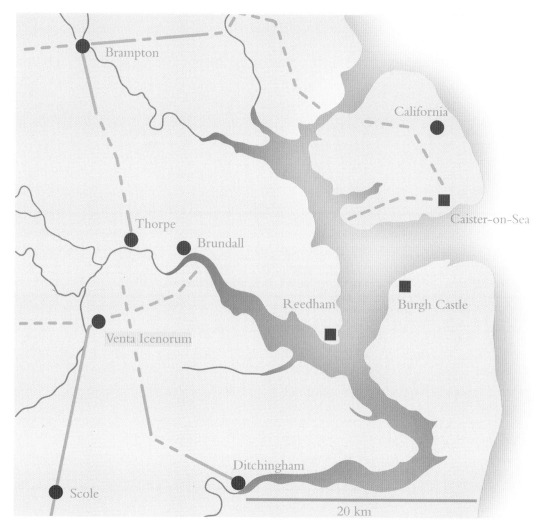

Fig 190: The Great
Estuary and the eastern
river system, showing the
original Roman coastline.

activity. Studies of traded commodities show that glass vessels were
extensively transported along the River Rhine.[35] There is also clear
epigraphic evidence for trade with the Rhineland (Fig 191).[36]

Each of the Norfolk forts may have served its local region in facilitating
trade. Brancaster, for example, is situated close to the Fenland, with its
imperial and villa estates. Bulk commodities from those estates could
have been collected and transferred to barges at Brancaster fort, and
then on to seagoing vessels in Brancaster Bay.

TRADE, MERCHANTS AND THE ROLE OF THE INLAND SITES

The importance of trade in Roman Norfolk was reviewed in the
previous chapter. The *civitas capital* at *Venta Icenorum* was at the hub of
the local trading network for Roman Norfolk: produce from the local

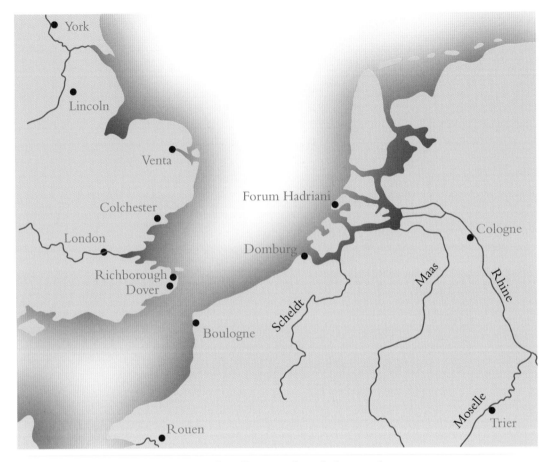

Fig 191: Eastern Roman Britain and the Rhineland.

countryside and from the network of small towns flowed there to be sold, redistributed and processed into manufactured goods. *Venta* was at the route centre for regional traffic and roads, connecting it with sites as far away as those in the agricultural area of the Fenland.

Goods from right across the administrative district of the Iceni were brought into this trading focus. These goods would have been transferred from wheeled transport to barges. Caister-on-Sea, Burgh Castle and possibly Reedham then serviced produce sent downstream, such as grain and woollen produce from the surrounding countryside. It may be no coincidence that the massive flint walls at *Venta Icenorum* were constructed at around the same time as those of the coastal forts. Some degree of common purpose and relationship between these sites is suggested by this development.

In order to recreate how the inland and coastal sites worked together, it might be helpful to construct an imaginary trading scenario. The Roman trading system involved forward planning, and there was a developed network of merchants, of all nationalities, in all trading centres and ports throughout the Roman Empire. We may envisage a local shopkeeper at *Venta* needing to place an order for several barrels of olives. He would initially need to meet a locally based representative of a foreign merchant, who would undertake to obtain and deliver the barrels by an agreed date. Following the communication of the order, the initial delivery of the olives would be made to Britain by ship – probably to either Burgh Castle or Reedham. There they would have been off-loaded by the local representative, who would arrange for the barrels to be ferried by barge along the Rivers Yare and Tas to *Venta*, where they would be off-loaded onto dry land. They would finally be delivered to the local shopkeeper on the agreed date, who would then sell them on to local consumers.

So, it is perhaps more fitting to see the Saxon Shore forts in the context of the trading life of Roman Norfolk, possibly with a role similar to that of medieval walled towns. One of the key reasons for the proliferation of walled towns in the earlier middle ages was the number of people seeking protection for their trading activities.[37] Those engaged in trade actively sought the protection of fortresses and settled within the shelter of the walls. Could this have been a parallel situation for what was happening in the walled sites of late Roman Norfolk?

The importance of the region's trade is one reason for the extraordinarily high level of late Roman wealth evidenced by archaeology in this area. Numerous discoveries of gold and silver have been made in recent decades, which will be considered below.

TREASURE FROM THE GROUND

In 1993 two metal detectorists undertook a survey at Deopham, near Wymondham in south Norfolk, to investigate an area where occasional Roman finds had appeared to define the outer limits of a low-order settlement. First one, then two, sparkling gold coins were revealed. When yet another signal revealed a third gold coin, the finders immediately contacted staff at Norfolk Museums Service to notify them of their exciting discovery and to obtain assistance in excavating what was clearly a hoard of undetermined size. Archaeologists quickly went out to the site and were able to undertake an excavation of the area, upon which a whole spread of gold coins was revealed (Fig 192).

After a full investigation, a total of 27 late Roman gold *solidi* were found, all in beautiful and uncirculated condition (Fig 193), together with three silver *siliquae*.[38] All the coins were dated to between AD 375 and 395, and had been struck at mints in Trier (Germany), Sirmium (Pannonia, on the Danube) and Milan (Italy). Despite their exceptional condition, no traces of a container were found, although two groups of the coins were arranged face-to-face in the soil, suggesting that they had originally been stacked together in a roll or tube, in the way that

coins are delivered from the Royal Mint today. They had probably been held together within a cloth wrap, which did not survive.

Fig 192: The discovery of the Deopham hoard in 1993.

This spectacular discovery of late Roman treasure is far from being a unique find from the soils of northern East Anglia. A period of instability during the final decades of Roman Britain is reflected by a large number of very rich late Roman coin and metalwork hoards which have been discovered in Norfolk and in locations close to the county's boundaries.

THE WEALTH OF ROMAN EAST ANGLIA

Remarkable discoveries of treasure have been discovered across northern East Anglia over a 60-year period beginning in 1942, when a hoard of late Roman silver objects was found on the fen-edge at Mildenhall (Suffolk).[39] The story of the discovery, which was made at the height of the Second World War, has since been immortalised in a short story by Roald Dahl.[40] The 34 items of mostly 4th-century silver tableware are stunning examples of late Roman craftsmanship: the Great Dish contains decorative friezes in a mainly Classical style and of the very highest quality. This important group served to change the national view of the status of Roman Britain and those who lived here. It was proof that this was not a backwater nor an impoverished part of the great Roman Empire.

Three decades later, in 1974, another great silver hoard was discovered in East Anglia, at Water Newton, near Peterborough (Cambridgeshire).

This find consisted of a hoard of early Christian treasure[41] made up of a single gold and 27 silver items, including 9 vessels and 19 plaques; it was accompanied by 30 gold coins from the middle years of the 4th century. The vessels consisted of a great dish, goblets, spoons, ladles and bowls.

In November 1992 an even more spectacular find was made at Hoxne, in north Suffolk.[42] Now known as the Hoxne Treasure, this is the largest hoard of Roman gold and silver ever found on British soil. The bizarre story of its accidental discovery has been recounted by Richard Hobbs.[43] Records made during its excavation show how the hoard had originally been packed inside a treasure chest. Stacks of spoons and bracelets were accompanied by necklaces and finger rings, as well as elaborate silver pepperpots, one in the shape of a Roman woman, wearing clothing and hairstyle of the period. Another unusual item was a complete gold body chain, as worn by a woman from a very wealthy family.

A staggering number of 14,500 coins, of which 563 were gold, 13,900 silver and 24 bronze, had finally been packed into the chest in cloth bags. These coins have a slightly wider date range than those from Deopham, from c AD 358 to the reign of Constantine III (AD 407–11). The whole Hoxne treasure was buried after AD 407, at the time of the Roman withdrawal from Britain, when the governor Constantine III, who was proclaimed emperor by the legions of Britain, chose to cross to Gaul and challenge the authority of the Emperor Honorius. There was no trace of occupation in the immediate vicinity of the findspot, although the small town of Scole lay just two miles distant.

Norfolk itself yielded yet another spectacular find in 1979. A deposit known as the Thetford Treasure was discovered by metal detector during the construction of an industrial warehouse on the outskirts of the modern town.[44] Like the Hoxne hoard, it was originally held within a box, although this was smaller and made from shale. There were 22 gold finger rings and 17 other items of gold jewellery, together with silver strainers, spoons, beads and gems (Fig 194). The spoons can be divided into the 'duck-handled' form and the 'long-handled' type, and appear to make up a distinct group from a single workshop. Both the gold and the silver items can be dated on typological grounds to the second half of the 4th century. The hoard was probably buried in the AD 380s or early 390s.

Other Roman hoards have been discovered in the soils of south and south-west Norfolk. Hoards of bronze vessels have been discovered at locations at Hockwold and Weeting, both on the fen-edge. Pewter hoards of 4th-century date are also known from the Norfolk fen-edge.[45] Although less spectacular, such deposits reinforce a developing picture of people hoarding metalwork in south and west Norfolk and adjacent areas during the late Roman period. In addition, all but two of the

Fig 193: Gold solidi from the Deopham hoard. Diameters approx. 22mm.

Fig 194: Buckle from the Thetford Treasure. Height 59mm. (this replica is displayed in Thetford Museum) (photo by Peter Silk).

25 known 4th-century coin hoards from Norfolk were buried in the southern half of the county. Most of them were located in places near the Waveney valley, the eastern river system (especially the River Yare) and the fen-edge.[46]

So why were so many hoards being buried in this restricted area, around what is now the border of Norfolk and around the fen-edge, in the final years of Roman Britain? They represent accumulations of wealth and fine objects, and include items of exceptionally high-quality workmanship. These decades were troubled times of great uncertainty; the Roman army was being withdrawn from Britain to defend the central Empire on mainland Europe and, as Roman administration was breaking down, people were burying their wealth in the ground for safe-keeping. The owners of the hoards listed here never managed to return to recover them. We can only guess at what happened to these wealthy individuals. It appears that they chose to deposit their wealth at places of long-standing significance, along the Waveney and Little Ouse valley, the fen-edge and also the area around Caistor St Edmund, in the vicinity of the headwaters of the Great Estuary.

A significant question is raised by these discoveries, however. Did all of this wealth derive from the people living in northern East Anglia? Other forms of archaeological evidence do not suggest that Roman Norfolk was exceptionally rich compared with other parts of Roman Britain. Is it possible that people were coming to the area from further afield in order to deposit their wealth? If so, these places must have had a significance that was recognised way beyond the region itself.

THE FINAL YEARS OF ROMAN NORFOLK

Consideration of the Saxon Shore sites and late Roman treasure have drawn us into the final few years of Roman administration. There are many factors which probably contributed to the end of Roman Britain.[47] Archaeology shows that long-distance trade links were fragmenting during the later 4th century and that economic prosperity was breaking down. The 6th-century historian Gildas also mentions a deadly plague at this time, although the validity of the reference has been questioned. In any event, the authority of the Roman Emperor had declined by the end of the 4th century, as the barbarian tribes of Goths, Huns and Vandals poured across Europe from east to west. Garrisons from outlying provinces were recalled to Italy to fight a rearguard action against the aggressors.

Coin finds allow us to date the decline of Roman Norfolk.[48] The quantity of Roman coins found in the county drops dramatically after the death of the Emperor Valentinian I, in AD 378, with a slightly earlier decline at sites in north Norfolk. During the final years of Roman rule, the Roman generals Magnus Maximus (in AD 383) and Constantine III (in AD 407) gathered armies and crossed from Britain to the continent in attempts to win the Imperial throne. Their armies never returned to Britain, being absorbed into what was left of the Roman armies in Gaul and Italy. Roman administration and civil order in Britain steadily broke down. The end finally came in AD 410, when the Emperor Honorius withdrew the last remnants of the army. It is to this year that we ascribe the end of Roman Britain.

By the closing decades of the 4th century, Saxon raiding was having an impact on the east coast. As Roman authority waned and Saxon incursions gathered pace, individual communities began to take it upon themselves to provide their own defence. Anglo-Saxon cemeteries began to appear in the county from the early 5th century, as evidenced in the landscape around *Venta Icenorum*, where three separate cemeteries have been identified in the immediate vicinity of the Roman town.[49]

By AD 450 the Saxons were settling in appreciable numbers and the locals were no longer able to resist. These new settlers began to turn what had been Roman Norfolk into Anglo-Saxon Norfolk.

BOUDICA'S LAND – A POSTSCRIPT

So, the final threat to Roman Norfolk once again came from the direction of the sea. During those increasingly unsettled late Roman years the native population again put trust in their deeply established relationship with the landscape, which had developed over many thousands of years, and consigned their wealth to the soils of East Anglia. In this way, the culture of Boudica's descendents has lived on.

Tracing the story of prehistoric and Roman Norfolk has witnessed the development of a vibrant and robust society who showed qualities of strength and endurance over time. The process of Romanisation had been a relatively short-lived veneer upon this local culture, which was able to survive in many ways through the Roman occupation and manifested itself on occasions, especially at times of stress, through the deposition of material in the ground, which is now being found by archaeologists.

The story of Norfolk has also been one of struggle: against a harsh and changing environment; against invaders moving into the area from across the North Sea; against the elements and the sea itself. Characters throughout Norfolk's history have become associated with toughness, an independence of spirit, and political and religious dissent.

The historical figure of Boudica has long been associated with these traits. She can be placed at the forefront of a line of local personalities who were prepared to stand up and confront conformity or unfairness in a way that would lead either to eventual justice or to glorious defeat. A lasting place in history was assured in either event.

THE STUDY CONTINUES

The proliferation of finds and the pace of new discoveries continues to make Norfolk an exciting place to be an archaeologist. The area has been shown to have been anything but a backwater. Most of the discoveries mentioned in the pages above are recent ones and the picture is developing all the time.

This study has made use of new information which has come in the form of artefact finds and fieldwork projects. During my working life in Norfolk I have been fortunate to see and identify many of these finds at first hand, as well as to visit discoveries as they are happening in the field. The sense of excitement from making such contact with our ancestors is something that we can all experience as we learn more about our past and come closer to understanding the people who walked this land before us.

This work has been pulled together in what is, inevitably, a personal interpretation, which is centred on a number of important discoveries relating to all of the main archaeological periods. However, there continue to be many thousands of less spectacular finds each year which, collectively, are just as important in terms of their contribution to the overall emerging picture.

In the future, new electronic ways of ordering and interpreting the proliferating banks of raw data that are still being compiled will facilitate deeper study. This will be complemented by new scientific analyses looking at bloodlines and the ancestry of modern populations and movements of people through DNA studies. It is certain that the pace of our understanding will accelerate and continue to be refined over the coming years.

Finally, it must be emphasised that this understanding of the county's past stems directly from the people of Norfolk. It is their contribution that has made such work possible and it is to them that all such studies should be dedicated.

References

Chapter 1. Norfolk: the land of Boudica

1. T Pocock, 1995 *Norfolk*, Pimlico, London.
2. B Sykes, 2006 *Blood of the isles*, Bantam Press, London; S Oppenheimer, 2006 *The origins of the British*, Constable, London; R McKie, 2006 *Face of Britain*, Simon & Schuster, London.

Chapter 2. The Norfolk landscape

1. G P Larwood and B M Funnell, 1961 The geology of Norfolk, *Transactions of the Norfolk and Norwich Naturalists' Society* 19(6), 267–375; C P Chatwin, 1961 *East Anglia and adjoining areas*, British Regional Geology (4th edn).
2. C A H Hodge, R G O Burton, W M Corbett, R Evans and R S Seale, 1984 *Soils and their use in eastern England*, Soil Survey of England and Wales Bulletin 13, Harpenden.
3. J M Parmenter, 2001 The development of the wetland vegetation of the Broadland region, unpub PhD thesis, Centre of East Anglian Studies, Univ East Anglia.
4. B J Coles, 1998 Doggerland: a speculative survey, *Proc Prehist Soc* 64, 45–81.
5. www.mammuthus.org.
6. R Pestell and D Stannard, 1995 *Eccles-Juxta-Mare, a lost village discovered*, Wortley, North Walsham.
7. T Williamson, 1993 *The origins of Norfolk*, Manchester University Press; D Dymond, 1990 *The Norfolk landscape*, St Edmundsbury Press, Bury St Edmunds.
8. T Williamson and K Skipper, 1994 *The clayland landscapes of central East Anglia: history and conservation*, Centre of East Anglian Studies, University of East Anglia.
9. J N Jennings, 1952 *The origin of the Broads* John Murray, London; M George, 1992 *The land use, ecology and conservation of Broadland*, Packard Publishing, Chichester; B Moss, 2001 *The Broads*, Harper Collins, London.
10. D W Yalden, 2003 Mammals in Britain – a historical perspective, *British Wildlife* 14(4), 243–51.

Chapter 3. The age of ice

1. S G Lewis et al, 2004 Age and palaeoenvironmental setting of the pleistocene vertebrate fauna at Norton Subcourse, Norfolk, in *The Quarternary mammals of southern and eastern England field guide* (ed D C Schreve), Quarternary Research Association, Doveridge.

2.   A J Stuart, 2000 The West Runton Freshwater Bed, in *The Quarternary of Norfolk & Suffolk field guide* (eds S G Lewis, C A Whiteman and R C Preece), Quarternary Research Association, London.

3.   A J Stuart, 1997 *The West Runton Elephant: discovery and excavation*, Norfolk Museums Service, Norwich.

4.   M Pitts and M Roberts, 1998 *Fairweather Eden*, Arrow, London.

5.   Dr Peter Robins, pers. comm.

6.   R Hobbs, 2003 *Treasure: finding our past*, British Museum Press, London, 99–100.

7.   From the transcript of an interview with Mike Chambers at Norwich Castle Department of Archaeology 2005, by Jonathan Draper of Norfolk Record Office and Ruth Burwood of Norfolk Museums & Archaeology Service.

8.   J Wymer and P Robins, 2006 Happisburgh and Pakefield, the first Britons, *Curr Archaeol* 201, 458–67.

9.   S A Parfitt et al, 2005 The earliest record of human activity in northern Europe, *Nature* 438, 1008–12; J Wymer and P Robins, *op. cit.* in note 8.

10.   J Wymer, 1982 *The Palaeolithic age*, Croom Helm, London, chapter 4.

11.   A J Stuart, 1991 The Ice Age in Norfolk, *The Quarterly, The Journal of the Norfolk Archaeological and Historical Research Group* 2, 3–9; A J Stuart, 1989 *The Ice Age in East Anglia*, Norfolk Museums Service Information Sheet, Norwich.

12.   A J Stuart, 1988 *Life in the Ice Age*, Shire, Princes Risborough.

13.   J J Wymer, 1996 'Norfolk and the history of Palaeolithic archaeology in Britain', in *A Festival of Norfolk Archaeology* (eds S Margeson, B Ayers and S Heywood), Norfolk and Norwich Archaeological Society, Hunstanton, 3–10; R C Preece and S A Parfitt, 2000 'The Cromer Forest Bed Formation: New Thoughts on an Old Problem', in *The Quarternary of Norfolk & Suffolk Field Guide* (eds S G Lewis, C A Whiteman and R C Preece), Quarternary Research Association, London.

14.   S Oppenheimer, 2006 *The origins of the British*, Constable, London, 129–30.

15.   Information supplied by Tony Stuart and Tony Irwin, Natural History Department at Norwich Castle Museum.

16.   C Stringer and C Gamble, 1993 *In search of the Neanderthals*, Thames and Hudson, London.

17.   C Stringer, 2006 *Homo Britannicus*, Allen Lane, London.

18.   A J Lawson, 1978 A hand-axe from Little Cressingham, *E Anglian Archaeol* 8, 1–8.

19.   J Lord, 2002 A flint knapper's foreword to Lynford, *Lithics* 23, 60–70.

20.   W A Boismier, 2003 A middle Palaeolithic site at Lynford Quarry, Mundford, Norfolk: interim statement, *Proc Prehist Soc* 69, 315–24.

21.   Study undertaken and information provided by Russell Coope.

22.   P Robins and J Wymer, 2006 Late Upper Palaeolithic (long blade) industries in Norfolk, *Norfolk Archaeol* 45(1), 86–95.

23.   News headline used by the *Eastern Daily Press*.

Chapter 4. The age of wood

1.   M C Burkitt, 1932 A Maglemose harpoon dredged up recently from the North Sea, *Man* 138, 118; J G D Clark, 1932 *The Mesolithic age in Britain*, Cambridge University Press, Cambridge; H Muir Evans, 1932 'The Maglemose harpoon', *Proc Prehist Soc East Anglia* 7, 131–2.

2.   B J Coles, 1998 Doggerland: a speculative survey, *Proc Prehist Soc* 64, 45–81.

3.   J N Jennings, 1955 Further pollen data from the Norfolk Broads. Data for the study of post-glacial history. XIV, *New Phytologist* 54(2), 199–207.

4.   J M Parmenter, 2001 The Development of the Wetland Vegetation of the Broadland Region, unpub PhD thesis, Centre of East Anglian Studies, Univ East Anglia.

5.   R Jacobi, 1984 The Mesolithic of northern East Anglia and contemporary territories, in *Aspects of East Anglian pre-history* (ed C Barringer), Geo Books, Norwich, 43–76.

6.   Jacobi, The Mesolithic.

7.   J J Wymer and P Robins, 1994 A long blade flint industry beneath boreal peat at Titchwell, Norfolk, *Norfolk Archaeol* 42, 13–37; J J Wymer, 1988 Flandrian coastal stratigraphy at Titchwell, Norfolk, in *Fenland Research* 5 (eds T Lane and P P Hayes), Fenland Project, Lincolnshire, 27–31.

8.   Jacobi, The Mesolithic.

9.   A Lawson, 1978 The investigation of a Mesolithic and later site at Banham, *E Anglian Archaeol* 8, 9–18.

10.   J J Wymer and P A Robins, 1995 A Mesolithic site at Great Melton, *Norfolk Archaeol* 42, 125–47.

11.   F Healy, 1988 *The Anglo-Saxon cemetery at Spong Hill, North Elmham, part VI: occupation during the seventh to second millennia BC*, E Anglian Archaeol 39.

12.   R R Clarke, 1960 *East Anglia*, London; C Wells, 1961 Un crane humain de Strumpshaw, Norfolk, Angleterre, *L'anthropologie* 65, 271–6.

Chapter 5. The first farmers

1.   F Healy, 1984 Farming and field monuments: the Neolithic in Norfolk, in *Aspects of East Anglian pre-history* (ed C Barringer), Geo Books, Norwich, 77–140.

2.   S Oppenheimer, 2006 *The origins of the British*, Constable, London, chapter 5.

3.   B Holmes, 2004 Manna or millstone, *New Scientist* 2465, 29–31.

4.   E Owen and M Frost, 1999 *The Dover Bronze Age Boat Gallery Guide*, The Dover Bronze Age Boat Trust.

5.   G Beckett, 1999 Man, the landscape and plants…an historical perspective, in *A Flora of Norfolk* (G Beckett, A Bull and R Stevenson), Jarrold, Thetford, 16–24.

6.   J M Parmenter, 2001 The development of the wetland vegetation of the Broadland region, unpub PhD thesis, Centre of East Anglian Studies, Univ East Anglia.

7.   D Hall and J Coles, 1994 *Fenland Survey. An essay in landscape and persistence*, Engl Heritage Archaeol Rep 1, London.

8.   Healy, Farming.

9.   Healy, Farming.

10.   G J Wainwright, 1973 Prehistoric and Romano-British settlements at Eaton Heath, Norwich, *Archaeol J* 130, 1–43.

11.   G J Wainwright, 1972 The excavation of a Neolithic settlement on Broome Heath, Ditchingham, Norfolk, England, *Proc Prehist Soc* 38, 1–97.

12.   F Healy, 1988 *The Anglo-Saxon cemetery at Spong Hill, North Elmham, part VI: occupation during the seventh to second millennia BC*, E Anglian Archaeol 39.

13.   I Smith, 1965 *Windmill Hill and Avebury: excavations by Alexander Keiller 1925–1939*, Oxford University Press, Oxford, 19.

14.   C Renfrew, 1973 *Before civilization*, London.

Chapter 6. Henge land

1.   I A Kinnes, 1979 *Round barrows and ring ditches in the British Neolithic*, British Museum Occas Pap 7, London; S Limbrey and J G Evans, 1978 *The effect of Man on the landscape: the lowland zone*, Counc Brit Archaeol Res Rep 23, London; A W R Whittle, 1978 Resources and population in the British Neolithic, *Antiquity* 52, 34–42.

2. J G D Clarke, 1936 The timber monument at Arminghall and its affinities, *Proc Prehist Soc* 2, 1–51.

3. W F M Beex and J W M Peterson, 2003 The Arminghall henge in space and time: how virtual reality contributes to research on its orientation, www.archaeologie-wien.at/caa2003/papers/34.htm.

4. T Ashwin, 2006 A possible henge monument at Costessey, *Norfolk Archaeol* 45(1), 95–7.

5. G J Wainwright, 1972 The excavation of a Neolithic settlement on Broome Heath, Ditchingham, Norfolk, England, *Proc Prehist Soc* 38, 1–97.

6. T Ashwin, 1996 Neolithic and Bronze Age Norfolk, *Proc Prehist Soc* 62, 41–62.

7. F Healy, 1984 Farming and field monuments: the Neolithic in Norfolk, in *Aspects of East Anglian pre-history* (ed C Barringer), Geo Books, Norwich, 77–140.

8. T Barton, 1852 Antiquities discovered at Little Cressingham, Norfolk, *Norfolk Archaeol* 3, 1–2; A Lawson, 1984 The Bronze Age in East Anglia with particular reference to Norfolk, in *Aspects of East Anglian pre-history* (ed C Barringer), Geo Books, Norwich, 153.

9. Healy, Farming.

10. F Healy, 1988 *The Anglo-Saxon cemetery at Spong Hill, North Elmham, part VI: occupation during the seventh to second millennia BC*, E Anglian Archaeol 39.

11. R Bradley, P Chowne, R M J Cleal, F Healy and I Kinnes, 1993 *Excavations on Redgate Hill, Hunstanton, Norfolk, and at Tattershall Thorpe, Lincolnshire*, E Anglian Archaeol 57.

12. B Green, 1993 *Grime's Graves, Norfolk*, English Heritage, London.

13. R J Mercer, 1981 *Grimes Graves, Norfolk: excavations 1971–72*, Fascicule 1, Dept. of the Environment Report 11, London; R Burleigh, A Hewson, N Meeks, G de G Sieveking and I H Longworth, 1979 British Museum natural radiocarbon measurements X, *Radiocarbon* 21(1), 41–7.

14. Healy, Farming.

15. Healy, Farming.

16. H M Bamford, 1982 *Beaker domestic sites in the fen edge and East Anglia*, E Anglian Archaeol

17. Healy, Farming.

18. M Champion, 2000 *Seahenge, a contemporary chronicle*, Barnwell, Aylsham.

19. Research undertaken by Alan West.

20. C Watson, 2005 *Seahenge: an archaeological conumdrum*, English Heritage, Swindon.

21. F Pryor, 2001 *Seahenge: new discoveries in prehistoric Britain*, Harper Collins, London.

22. F Pryor, *Seahenge*.

Chapter 7. An empty land

1. This observation was pointed out by Alan West.

2. A Lawson, 1984 The Bronze Age in East Anglia with particular reference to Norfolk, in *Aspects of East Anglian pre-history* (ed C Barringer), Geo Books, Norwich, 141–77; I am also grateful to Alan West for discussion on this issue.

3. R J Mercer, 1981 *Grimes Graves, Norfolk: excavations 1971–72*, Fascicule 1, Dept. of the Environment Report 11, London.

4. R Bradley, 1990 *The passage of arms*, Cambridge University Press, Cambridge.

5. T Champion, 1999 The later Bronze Age, in *The archaeology of Britain: an introduction from the Upper Palaeolithic to the Industrial Revolution* (eds J Hunter and I Ralston), Routledge, London, 95–112.

6. T Ashwin, 1996 Neolithic and Bronze Age Norfolk, *Proc Prehist Soc* 62, 41–62.

7. A J Lawson, E A Martin and D Priddy, 1981 *The barrows of East Anglia*, E Anglian Archaeol 12.

8.   Ashwin, Neolithic and Bronze Age Norfolk.

9.   Lawson, The Bronze Age in East Anglia.

10.   M J Rowlands, 1976 *The production and distribution of metalwork in the Middle Bronze Age in southern Britain*, BAR Brit Ser 31, Oxford; C Fox, 1923 *The archaeology of the Cambridge region*, Cambridge University Press, Cambridge.

11.   Rowlands, *Metalwork*.

12.   S Oppenheimer, 2006 *The origins of the British*, Constable, London, 238.

13.   C Burgess, 2001 *The age of Stonehenge*, Phoenix Press, London.

14.   Lawson, The Bronze Age in East Anglia.

15.   Information provided by Alan West.

16.   T H McK Clough and C Green, 1978 The first Late Bronze Age founder's hoard from Gorleston, Great Yarmouth, Norfolk, *Norfolk Archaeol* 37(1), 1–18.

17.   Norfolk Museums Service, 1977 *Bronze Age metalwork in Norwich Castle Museum*, Gallpen Press, Norwich (2nd edn).

18.   Alan West, pers. comm.

19.   R Hobbs, 2003 *Treasure: finding our past*, British Museum Press, London, 102–7; C Rudd, 2001 Is 'ring money' really money? *Chris Rudd List* 58, 2–3.

20.   Hobbs, *Treasure*.

Chapter 8. The rise of chiefdoms

1.   T Williamson, 1987 Early co-axial field systems on the East Anglian boulder clays, *Proc Prehist Soc*, 53, 419–31.

2.   A Davison, 1990 *The evolution of settlement in three parishes in south-east Norfolk*, E Anglian Archaeol 49.

3.   G Lloyd-Morgan, 1995 Appearance, life and leisure, in *The Celtic World* (ed M J Green), Routledge, London, 95–120.

4.   J P Gardiner, 1993 The flint assemblage, in Excavation of an Iron Age pit group at London Road, Thetford (J A Davies), *Norfolk Archaeol* 41, 456–8.

5.   P Robins, 1996 Worked flint, in Excavation of an Iron Age site at Silfield, Wymondham, Norfolk 1992–3 (T Ashwin), *Norfolk Archaeol* 42, 266–70.

6.   R R Clarke and H Apling, 1935 An Iron Age tumulus on Warborough Hill, Stiffkey, Norfolk, *Norfolk Archaeol* 25, 408–28.

7.   H Apling, 1932 A Hallstatt settlement at West Harling, Norfolk, *Proc Prehist Soc* 7(1), 111–22.

8.   H Martingell, 1988 The flint industry, in *Archaeology and environment in south Essex* (T J Wilkinson), E Anglian Archaeol 42, 70–3.

9.   A Rogerson, 1999 Arable and pasture in two Norfolk parishes: Barton Bendish and Fransham in the Iron Age, in *Land of the Iceni: the Iron Age in northern East Anglia* (eds J Davies and T Williamson), Centre of East Anglian Studies, Norwich, 125–31.

10.   P Shand, 1984 Cauldron Field, Feltwell. Excavations of an Early Iron Age settlement on the fen edge, 1962, unpubl document, Norfolk HER.

11.   J G D Clark and C I Fell, 1953 The early Iron Age site at Micklemoor Hill, West Harling, Norfolk, *Proc Prehist Soc* 19(1), 1–40.

12.   R Bradley, P Chowne, R M J Cleal, F Healy and I Kinnes, 1993 *Excavations on Redgate Hill, Hunstanton, Norfolk, and at Tattershall Thorpe, Lincolnshire*, E Anglian Archaeol 57.

13.   J A Davies, 1993 Excavation of an Iron Age pit group at London Road, Thetford, *Norfolk Archaeol* 41, 441–61.

14.   T Ashwin, 1996 Excavation of an Iron Age site at Silfield, Wymondham, Norfolk 1992–3, *Norfolk Archaeol* 42, 241–82.

15. T Ashwin and S Bates, 2000 *Excavations on the Norwich southern bypass, 1989–91. Part I: excavations at Bixley, Caistor St Edmund, Trowse, Cringleford and Little Melton*, E Anglian Archaeol 91.

16. David Whitmore, Norfolk Archaeological Unit, pers. comm.

17. R R Clarke and C F C Hawkes, 1955 An iron anthropoid sword from Shouldham, Norfolk, with related continental and British weapons, *Proc Prehist Soc* 21, 198–227.

18. J A Davies, 1992 Excavations at Ford Place 1985–86, in *The Iron Age forts of Norfolk* (J A Davies, T Gregory, A J Lawson, R Rickett and A Rogerson), E Anglian Archaeol 54; R R Clark and H Apling, An Iron Age tumulus.

19. R R Clark and H Apling, An Iron Age tumulus.

20. T Ashwin and S Bates, *Excavations on the Norwich southern bypass*.

21. I M Stead, 1979 *The Arras Culture*, Yorkshire Philosophical Society, York.

22. A P Fitzpatrick, 1996 *Westhampnett, West Sussex, Volume 2: the Iron Age, Romano-British and Anglo-Saxon cemeteries*, Wessex Archaeology Report 13, Salisbury.

23. F M Pryor, C French, D Crowther, D Gurney, G Simpson and M Taylor, 1985 *The Fenland Project No. 1. Archaeology and environment in the lower Welland valley*, E Anglian Archaeol 27.

24. F Pryor, 2001 *Seahenge: new discoveries in prehistoric Britain*, Harper Collins, London, 287–91.

25. Michael de Bootman, pers. comm.

26. R Bradley, 2000 *An archaeology of natural places*, Routledge, London.

27. P Wade-Martins, 1974 The linear earthworks of west Norfolk, *Norfolk Archaeol* 36, 23–38; C Fox, 1923 *The archaeology of the Cambridge region*, Cambridge University Press, Cambridge.

28. J A Davies, 1996 Where eagles dare: the Iron Age of Norfolk, *Proc Prehist Soc* 62, 63–92.

29. D Gurney, 1993 Excavations and surveys in Norfolk 1992, *Norfolk Archaeol* 41, 523–4.

30. B Cunliffe, 1990 Before hillforts, *Oxford J Archaeol* 9, 323–36.

31. Fox, *Cambridge*; Davies, Where eagles dare.

32. J A Davies, T Gregory, A J Lawson, R Rickett and A Rogerson, 1992 *The Iron Age forts of Norfolk*, E Anglian Archaeol 54.

33. K Penn, 2006 Excavation and survey at the Iron Age fort at Bloodgate Hill, South Creake, 2003, *Norfolk Archaeol* 45(1), 1–27.

34. R R Clarke, 1954 The early Iron Age treasure from Snettisham, Norfolk, *Proc Prehist Soc* 20, 27–86; R R Clarke, 1952 Notes on recent archaeological discoveries in Norfolk (1943–8), *Norfolk Archaeol* 30, 156–9.

35. I M Stead, 1995 Die Schatzfunde von Snettisham, *Heiligtumer Und Opferkulte Der Kelten*, Theiss, Stuttgart, 100–11.

36. R Hobbs, 2003 *Treasure: finding our past*, British Museum Press, London, 141–2.

37. R Megaw and V Megaw, 1989 *Celtic art from its beginnings to the Book of Kells*, Thames and Hudson, Toledo.

38. M Dennis, 2005 Silver in Late Iron Age and early Roman East Anglia, unpubl DPhil thesis, The Queen's College, Oxford.

39. Davies, Where eagles dare.

40. M Dennis and N Faulkner, 2005 *The Sedgeford hoard*, Tempus, Stroud.

41. J W Brailsford, 1971 The Sedgeford torc, in *Prehistoric and Roman studies* (G De G Sieveking), Trustees of the British Museum, Oxford, 16–19.

Chapter 9. The age of Boudica

1. A Fraser, 1993 *The warrior queens*, Mandarin, Reading.

2. Caesar, *The Gallic War*.

3. Tacitus, *Annals*.

4. J A Davies, 2000 The metal finds, in Excavations at Quidney Farm, Saham Toney, Norfolk 1995 (S Bates), *Britannia* 31, 226–30.

5.   J Foster, 1977 *Bronze boar figurines in Iron Age and Roman Britain*, BAR Brit Ser 39, Oxford.

6.   Foster, *Bronze boar figurines*.

7.   J Moreau, R Boudet and U Schaaff, 1990 Un sanglier-enseigne Gaulois a Soulac-sur-Mer, Dep. Gironde, *Archaologisches Korrespondenzblatt* 20, 439–42.

8.   T Gregory, 1991 *Excavations in Thetford, 1980–1982, Fison Way*, E Anglian Archaeol 53.

9.   T Gregory, 1977 The enclosure at Ashill, in *E Anglian Archaeol* 5 (ed P Wade-Martins), 9–30.

10.   G Davies, M Dennis and R Thirkettle, 2004 A hoard of Iron Age coins discovered at Sedgeford, 2003, *Norfolk Archaeol* 44, 538–40.

11.   M Dennis, 2005 Silver in Late Iron Age and early Roman East Anglia, unpubl DPhil thesis, The Queen's College, Oxford, chapter 4.

12.   Information from Amanda Chadburn.

13.   Information supplied by Mr John Talbot.

14.   Information supplied by Mr John Talbot.

15.   Dennis, Silver, chapter 3.

16.   A Chadburn, 2006 The currency of kings, *Brit Archaeol* March–April, 27–9.

17.   Information supplied by Mr John Talbot.

18.   J A Davies and A Gregory, 1991 Coinage from a civitas: A survey of the Roman coins found in Norfolk and their contribution to the archaeology of the *Civitas Icenorum*', *Britannia* 22, 97.

19.   J A Davies, 2001 *Venta Icenorum, Caistor St Edmund Roman town*, Norfolk Archaeological Trust, Norwich.

20.   D Hall and J Coles, 1994 *Fenland Survey. An essay in landscape and persistence*, Engl Heritage Archaeol Rep 1, London.

21.   A Davison, 1990 *The evolution of settlement in three parishes in south-east Norfolk*, E Anglian Archaeol 49.

22.   Dennis, Silver.

23.   N Smedley and E Owles, 1958 Archaeology in Suffolk, 1958, *Proc Suffolk Inst Archaeol* 38(1), 90–6.

24.   R Rickett, 1995 *Spong Hill, North Elmham part VII: the Iron Age, Roman and early Saxon settlement*, E Anglian Archaeol 73, chapter 13.

25.   G J Wainwright, 1973 Prehistoric and Romano-British settlements at Eaton Heath, Norwich, *Archaeol J* 130, 1–43.

26.   Strabo, *Geography*.

27.   Dennis, Silver.

28.   T Ashwin, 1994 *Report on archaeological evaluation, Cherry Tree Holiday Park, Burgh Castle*, unpub Norfolk Archaeological Unit Evaluation Report 112.

29.   B Cunliffe, 1987 *Hengistbury Head Dorset*, University Committee for Archaeology Monograph 13, Oxford.

30.   C Rudd, 2006 The Belgae and Regni, in *Celtic coinage: new discoveries, new discussion* (P de Jersey), BAR Int Ser 1532, 147.

31.   P Macdonald, 1996 Llyn Cerrig Bach. An Iron Age votive assemblage, in *Art, Ritual and Death in Prehistory* (ed S Aldhouse-Green), Cardiff, 32–3.

32.   R Jackson, 2005 Roman bound captives: symbols of slavery? in *Image, craft and the classical world. Essays in honour of Donald Bailey and Catherine Johns* (ed N Crummy), Monogr. Instrumentum 29, Montagnac, 143–56.

33.   M Aldhouse-Green, 2004 Chaining and shaming: images of defeat, from Llyn Cerrig Bach to Sarmitzegetusa, *Oxford J Archaeol* 23(3), 319–40.

34.   S Worrell, 2005 Finds reported under the Portable Antiquities Scheme: Lincolnshire, *Britannia* 36, 455–6.

35.   T Gregory, 1991 *Excavations in Thetford, 1980–1982, Fison Way* E Anglian Archaeol 53.

36.   R Bradley, 2005 *Ritual and domestic life in prehistoric Europe*, Routledge, Abingdon.

Chapter 10. The Roman invasion and the end of Iron Age Norfolk

1.   Caesar, *The Gallic War*.

2.   Tacitus, *Annals*.

3.   P R Sealey, 1997 *The Boudican revolt against Rome*, Shire, Haverfordwest.

4.   I am grateful to Paul Sealey for this information.

5.   C Johns, 1986 The Roman silver cups from Hockwold, Norfolk, *Archaeologia* 108, 1–13; J M C Toynbee, 1964 *Art in Britain under the Romans*, Clarendon Press, Oxford, 301–3.

6.   J A Davies, 1999 Patterns, power and political progress, in *Land of the Iceni: the Iron Age in northern East Anglia* (eds J Davies and T Williamson), Centre of East Anglian Studies, Norwich, 14–43; J Orna-Ornstein, 1997 Early hoards of denarii from Britain, in *Coin Hoards from Roman Britain Volume X* (eds R Bland and J Orna-Ornstein), British Museum Press, London, 23–9.

7.   G Webster, 1999 *Boudica: the British revolt against Rome AD 60*, Routledge, London.

8.   Dio Cassius, *Epitome of books lxi and lxii of his Roman history* (trans E Cary), Loeb Classical Library, London (1968 reprint).

9.   J Davies and B Robinson, 2009 *Boudica: her life, times and legacy*, Poppyland, Norwich.

Chapter 11. The establishment of Roman Norfolk

1.   P Murphy, 2005 Coastal change and human response, in *An historical atlas of Norfolk* (eds T Ashwin and A Davison), Phillimore, Chichester (3rd edition), 6–7.

2.   J M Lambert, J N Jennings, C T Smith, C Green and J N Hutchinson, 1960 *The making of the Broads*, The Royal Geographical Society, London.

3.   B Moss, 2001 *The Broads*, Harper Collins, London.

4.   B P L Coles and B M Funnell, 1981 Holocene palaeoenvironments of Broadland, England, *Special Publications of the International Association of Sedimentologists* 5, 123–31.

5.   A A C Hedges, M Boon and F Meeres, 2001 *Yarmouth is an antient town*, Blackall Books, Great Yarmouth (revised edn).

6.   R F Kenyon, 1992 The copying of bronze coins of Claudius I in Roman Britain, unpubl PhD thesis, Univ London.

7.   Data supplied by Dr Robert Kenyon.

8.   R A Brown, 1986 The Iron Age and Romano-British settlement at Woodcock Hall, Saham Toney, Norfolk, *Britannia* 17, 1–58.

9.   T Gregory, 1977 The enclosure at Ashill, in *East Anglian Archaeology* 5 (ed P Wade-Martins), 9–30.

10.   B Robinson and T Gregory, 2003 *Celtic fire and Roman rule*, Poppyland, North Walsham (revised edn), 47.

11.   J A Davies, 2001 *Venta Icenorum, Caistor St Edmund Roman town*, Norfolk Archaeological Trust, Norwich.

12.   R Kenyon, 1996 A countermarked *as* of Claudius I from Caistor St Edmund, *Norfolk Archaeol* 42(3), 376–9.

13.   Notes supplied by Dr Paul Holder.

14.   R W Bagshawe, 1979 *Roman roads*, Shire Archaeology, Aylesbury.

15.   R J Silvester, 1988 Fieldwork in the Norfolk Fens 1987–88, in *Fenland Research* 5 (eds T Lane and P P Hayes), Fenland Project, Lincolnshire, 50–4; M Leah, 1992 The Fenland Management Project, Norfolk, in *Fenland Research* 7 (ed C Evans), University of Cambridge, 49–59.

16. J Webster, 1995 Translation and subjection: *interpretatio* and the Celtic gods, in *Different Iron Ages: studies on the Iron Age in temperate Europe* (J D Hill and C G Cumberpatch), BAR Int Ser 602, Oxford 175–83.

17. Information supplied by Dr Adrian Marsden.

18. R S O Tomlin, 2004 A bilingual Roman charm for health and victory, *Zeitschrift fur Papyrologie und Epigraphik* 149, 259–66.

19. R G Collingwood and R P Wright, 1992 *The Roman inscriptions of Britain, volume II*, Alan Sutton, Stroud, 57.

20. I am indebted to Adrian Marsden, who undertook the identification and translation.

21. J A Davies and A Gregory, 1991 Coinage from a civitas: A survey of the Roman coins found in Norfolk and their contribution to the archaeology of the *Civitas Icenorum, Britannia* 22, 65–101.

22. J Ornstein and R Kenyon, 1997 North Suffolk: 110 plated denarii to AD 51, in *Coin hoards from Roman Britain X* (R Bland and J Orna-Ornstein), British Museum Press, London, 37–46.

23. J A Davies, 1992 West Acre, Norfolk: 20 radiates to AD 284, in *The Chalfont Hoard and other Roman coin hoards* (R Bland), British Museum Press, London, 206–7.

24. A Marsden, 2003 Bars, blanks and barbarous radiates, in *Treasure Hunting* November, 38–40; additional information also compiled by Dr Adrian Marsden; A Marsden, forthcoming *Irregular coinage in Roman Britain: collected papers*, Heritage Publications.

25. S S Frere, 2000 A *limitatio* of Icenian territory? *Britannia* 31, 350–5.

Chapter 12. The towns

1. J A Davies, 2001 *Venta Icenorum, Caistor St Edmund Roman town*, Norfolk Archaeological Trust, Norwich.

2. S S Frere, 1971 The forum and baths at Caistor by Norwich, *Britannia* 2, 1–26.

3. Frere, Caistor by Norwich.

4. D Gurney, 1986 A Romano-Celtic temple site at Caistor St Edmund, in *Excavations at Thornham, Warham, Wighton and Caistor, Norfolk* (T Gregory and D Gurney), E Anglian Archaeol 30, 37–58.

5. Information supplied by William Bowden.

6. A K Knowles, 1977 Brampton, Norfolk: interim report, *Britannia* 8, 209–22; C Green, 1977 Excavation in the Roman kiln field at Brampton, 1973–4, in *E Anglian Archaeol* 5 (ed P Wade-Martins), 9–30.

7. H Wallis, forthcoming *Romano-British and Saxon occupation at Billingford, central Norfolk*, E Anglian Archaeol.

8. T Ashwin and A Tester (eds), forthcoming A Roman settlement in the Waveney valley: excavations at Scole, 1993–4, *E Anglian Archaeol*; A Rogerson, 1977 Excavations at Scole, 1973, in *E Anglian Archaeol* 5 (ed P Wade-Martins), 97–224.

9. J A Davies, 1999 Patterns, power and political progress, in *Land of the Iceni: the Iron Age in northern East Anglia* (eds J Davies and T Williamson), Centre of East Anglian Studies, Norwich, 14–43.

10. L G Kett, 1959 A Romano-Celtic temple at Crownthorpe, Norfolk, unpublished typescript, Norfolk HER.

11. I am indebted to James Albone for providing interpretation of aerial photographs of this area.

12. D Gurney, 1995 Small towns and villages of Roman Norfolk. The evidence of surface and metal-detector finds, in *Roman small towns in eastern England and beyond* (ed A E Brown), Oxbow Monogr 52, Oxford, 53–67.

13. A Lawson, 1976 Excavations at Whey Curd Farm, Wighton, *E Anglian Archaeol* 2, 65–99.

14.   J Bagnall Smith, 1999 Votive objects and objects of votive significance from Great Walsingham, Norfolk, *Britannia* 30, 21–56.

15.   J Davies, 1997 Old Buckenham, Norfolk: 14 denarii to AD 45, in *Coin Hoards from Roman Britain X* (R Bland and J Orna-Ornstein), British Museum Press, London, 35–6.

16.   J Orna-Ornstein, 1997 Early hoards of denarii from Britain, in *Coin Hoards from Roman Britain X* (R Bland and J Orna-Ornstein), British Museum Press, London, 23–9.

17.   M de Bootman, 1984 A preliminary report on a Romano-British kiln excavated at Pentney, 1981 (Kiln C), *NARG News* 39, 19–22.

18.   D Gurney, 1986 *Settlement, religion and industry on the fen-edge: three Romano-British sites in Norfolk*, E Anglian Archaeol 31.

19.   Gurney, *Settlement, religion and industry*.

20.   P Wade-Martins, 1980 *Fieldwork and excavation on village sites in Launditch Hundred, Norfolk*, E Anglian Archaeol 10, 29–31.

21.   D Gurney, A salt-production site at Denver; excavations by Charles Green, 1960, in Small towns and villages of Roman Norfolk (D Gurney), 93–148.

22.   S Frere, 1941 A Claudian site at Needham, Norfolk, *Antiq J* 21, 40–55.

23.   J Davies, A Meadows and J Williams, 1997 Needham, Norfolk, in *Coin Hoards from Roman Britain X* (R Bland and J Orna-Ornstein), British Museum Press, London, 47–8.

24.   J A Davies, 1993 The study of Roman coins from towns, in *Roman towns: the Wheeler inheritance* (ed S Greep), Counc Brit Archaeol Res Rep 93, York, 123–33.

Chapter 13. Beyond the towns

1.   T Gregory, 1982 Romano-British settlement in west Norfolk and on the Norfolk fen edge, in *The Romano-British countryside: studies in rural settlement and economy* (ed D Miles), BAR Brit Ser 103, Oxford, 351–76.

2.   D Atkinson, 1929 The Roman villa at Gayton Thorpe, *Norfolk Archaeol* 23, 166–209.

3.   M de Bootman, 1998 Re-evaluation of the Romano-British villa at Gayton Thorpe, Norfolk, *Norfolk Archaeol* 43(1), 133–42.

4.   A Lyons, 2004 *Archaeological investigations at Strickland Avenue and Station Road, Snettisham, 1991, 1994, 1998 and 2000*, E Anglian Archaeol Occas Pap 18.

5.   J Hinchliffe with C Sparey Green, 1985 *Excavations at Brancaster 1974 and 1977*, E Anglian Archaeol 23.

6.   R P J Jackson and T W Potter, 1996 *Excavations at Stonea, Cambridgeshire*, British Museum Press, London.

7.   J A Davies and A Gregory, 1991 Coinage from a civitas: A survey of the Roman coins found in Norfolk and their contribution to the archaeology of the *Civitas Icenorum*, *Britannia* 22, 65–101.

8.   D Gurney, 1986 *Settlement, religion and industry on the fen-edge; three Romano-British sites in Norfolk*, E Anglian Archaeol 31.

9.   D Gurney and K Penn, 2004 Excavations and surveys in Norfolk 2003, *Norfolk Archaeol* 44(3), 587.

10.   D Gurney and T Ashwin, 1995 Excavations and surveys in Norfolk 1994, *Norfolk Archaeol* 42(2), 232.

11.   B Robinson and T Gregory, 1987 *Celtic fire and Roman rule*, Poppyland, North Walsham (1st edn), 64.

12.   R Rickett, 1995 *Spong Hill, North Elmham Part VII: The Iron Age, Roman and Early Saxon Settlement*, E Anglian Archaeol 73, chapter 13.

13.   Information supplied by Andy Shelley, formerly of the Norfolk Archaeological Unit.

14.   B Cunliffe, 2005 *Iron Age communities in Britain*, Routledge, London (4th edition).

15.   A Bell, D Gurney and H Healey, 1999 *Lincolnshire salterns: excavations at Helpringham, Holbeach St Johns and Bicker Haven*, E Anglian Archaeol 89.

16.   M Leah, 1992 The Fenland Management Project, Norfolk, in *Fenland Research* 7 (ed C Evans), University of Cambridge, 49–59.

17.   D Gurney, 1986 *Settlement, religion and industry on the fen-edge; three Romano-British sites in Norfolk*, E Anglian Archaeol 31, 93–146.

18.   R F Tylecote and E Owles, 1960 A second century iron smelting site at Ashwicken, Norfolk, *Norfolk Archaeol* 32, 142–62.

19.   I am grateful to Barrie Sharrock for supplying this information.

20.   V G Swan, 1984 *The pottery kilns of Roman Britain*, HMSO, London; also information from Alice Lyons.

21.   D R Howlett, 1960 A Romano-British pottery kiln at Upper Sheringham, Norfolk, *Norfolk Archaeol* 32, 211–19.

22.   A K Knowles, 1977 Brampton, Norfolk: interim report, *Britannia* 8, 209–22.

23.   M de Bootman, 1984 A preliminary report on a Romano-British kiln excavated at Pentney, 1981 (kiln C), *NARG News* 39, 19–22.

24.   R J Silvester, 1988 *The Fenland Project, no. 3: Norfolk survey, marshland and the Nar valley*, E Anglian Archaeol 45.

25.   D Gurney, 1990 A Romano-British pottery kiln at Blackborough End, Middleton, *Norfolk Archaeol* 41(1), 83–92.

26.   J Bayley, D F Mackreth and H Wallis, 2001 Evidence for Romano-British brooch production at Old Buckenham, Norfolk, *Britannia* 32, 93–118.

27.   C Johns, 1997 *The Snettisham jeweller's hoard*, British Museum Press, London.

28.   The sherd was identified by Harriet Foster.

29.   J Price, 2000 Late Roman glass vessels in Britain, from AD 350 to 410 and beyond, in *Glass in Britain and Ireland AD 350–1100* (ed J Price), British Museum Occas Pap 127, London, 1–32.

30.   J Price and S Cottam, 1998 *Romano-British glass vessels: a handbook*, Practical Handbook in Archaeology 14, Council for British Archaeology, London.

31.   I am very grateful to Harriet Foster for supplying me with this information.

Chapter 14. Late Roman Norfolk

1.   A K Knowles, 1977 Brampton, Norfolk: interim report, *Britannia* 8, 209–22.

2.   S Johnson, 1976 *The Roman forts of the Saxon Shore*, Paul Elek, London.

3.   Johnson, *Roman forts*; D E Johnson (ed), 1977 *The Saxon Shore*, Counc Brit Archaeol Res Rep 18, London; V A Maxfield (ed), 1989 *The Saxon Shore: a handbook*, University of Exeter.

4.   H Spelman, 1698 Icenia, in *Reliquiae Spelmannianae: the posthumous works of Sir Henry Spelman Kt*, Oxford, 135–62.

5.   J Hinchliffe with C Sparey Green, 1985 *Excavations at Brancaster 1974 and 1977*, E Anglian Archaeol 23.

6.   J R L Allen, E J Rose and M G Fulford, 2003 Re-use of Roman stone in the Reedham area of east Norfolk: intimations of a possible 'lost' Roman fort, *Britannia* 34, 129–41.

7.   D Gurney, 2002 *Outposts of the Roman Empire: a guide to Norfolk's Roman forts at Burgh Castle, Caister-on-Sea and Brancaster*, Norfolk Archaeological Trust, Norwich.

8.   J C Mann, 1989 The historical development of the Saxon Shore, in *The Saxon Shore* (V A Maxfield), 1–11.

9.   Hinchliffe, *Excavations at Brancaster*, 176.

10. G Jones, 1985 The animal bones from the 1974 excavations, in *Excavations at Brancaster* (J Hinchliffe), 129–74.

11. M J Darling and D Gurney, 1993 *Caister-on-Sea: excavations by Charles Green 1951–55*, E Anglian Archaeol 60.

12. J R L Allen and M G Fulford, 1999 Fort building and military supply along Britain's eastern Channel and North Sea coasts: the later second and third centuries, *Britannia* 30, 163–84.

13. Gurney, *Outposts of the Roman Empire*.

14. Gurney, *Outposts of the Roman Empire*.

15. A Pearson, 2002 *The Roman shore forts*, Tempus, Stroud, chapter 7.

16. Allen and Fulford, Fort building and military supply.

17. S Johnson, 1983 *Burgh Castle: excavations by Charles Green 1958–61*, E Anglian Archaeol 20.

18. C Green and J N Hutchinson, 1960 Archaeological evidence, in *The making of the Broads* (J M Lambert, J N Jennings, C T Smith, C Green and J N Hutchinson), The Royal Geographical Society, London, 113–44.

19. S Johnson, 1980 A late Roman helmet from Burgh Castle, *Britannia* 11, 303–12.

20. D Gurney, 1995 A Roman provincial lead seal from Burgh Castle, *Norfolk Archaeol* 42, 217–18.

21. A Grant, The animal bones, in *Burgh Castle* (S Johnson), 108–11.

22. B Cunliffe, 1975 *Excavations at Portchester Castle, volume 1: Roman*, Report of the Research Committee of the Society of Antiquaries of London 32, Dorking; B W Cunliffe (ed), 1968 *Fifth Report on the Excavations of the Roman Fort at Richborough, Kent*, Soc Antiq Res Rep 23, London; Pearson, *The Roman shore forts*.

23. Hinchliffe, *Excavations at Brancaster*; Johnson, *Burgh Castle*; Darling and Gurney, *Caister-on-Sea*.

24. A Vines, The Romano-British site at Salthouse, Norfolk, unpubl typescript, Norfolk HER.

25. E J Rose, 1994 The church of Saint John the Baptist, Reedham, Norfolk: the re-use of Roman materials in a secondary context, *J Brit Archaeol Ass* 147, 1–8.

26. J R L Allen, E J Rose and M G Fulford, 2003 Re-use of Roman stone in the Reedham area of east Norfolk: intimations of a possible 'lost' Roman fort, *Britannia* 34, 129–41.

27. B Robinson and T Gregory, 2003 *Celtic fire and Roman rule*, Poppyland, North Walsham (revised edn).

28. D A White, 1961 *Litus Saxonicum: the British Saxon Shore in scholarship and history*, University of Wisconsin, New York.

29. I Wood, 1987 The fall of the Western Empire and the end of Roman Britain, *Britannia* 18, 251–62; G Milne, 1990 Maritime traffic between the Rhine and Roman Britain: a preliminary note, in *Maritime Celts, Frisians and Saxons* (ed S McGrail), Counc Brit Archaeol Res Rep 71, 82–5; J Cotterill, 1993 Saxon raiding and the role of the late Roman coastal forts of Britain, *Britannia* 24, 227–41; see also Pearson, *The Roman shore forts*, 136–8.

30. R Tomlin, 1979 The date of the 'Barbarian Conspiracy', *Britannia* 5, 303–9.

31. P Bartholomew, 1984 Fourth-century Saxons, *Britannia* 15, 169–85.

32. Wood, The fall of the Western Empire.

33. Wood, The fall of the Western Empire.

34. M Fulford, 1987 Economic interdependence among urban communities of the Roman Mediterranean, *World Archaeol* 19, 58–75.

35. J Price, 1978 Trade in Glass, in *Roman shipping and trade: Britain and the Rhine Provinces* (J du Plat Taylor and H Cleere), Counc Brit Archaeol Res Rep 24, 70–8; D P S Peacock, 1978 The Rhine and the problem of Gaulish wine in Roman Britain, in *Roman shipping and trade* (J du Plat Taylor and H Cleere), 49–51.

36. M Hassall, 1978 Britain and the Rhine Provinces: epigraphic evidence for Roman trade, in *Roman shipping and trade* (J du Plat Taylor and H Cleere), 41–8.

37. H Pirenne, 1925 *Medieval cities: their origins and the revival of trade*, Princeton.

38. J Davies, 1997 Deopham, Norfolk: 26 solidi and 4 siliquae to AD 402, in *Coin Hoards from Roman Britain X* (R Bland and J Orna-Ornstein), British Museum Press, London, 468–9.

39. K S Painter, 1977 *The Mildenhall Treasure: Roman silver from East Anglia*, British Museum Press, London; R Hobbs, 2003 *Treasure: finding our past*, British Museum Press, London.

40. R Dahl, 1999 *The Mildenhall Treasure*, Jonathan Cape, London.

41. K S Painter, 1977 *The Water Newton early Christian silver*, British Museum Press, London.

42. R Bland and C Johns, 1993 *The Hoxne Treasure*, British Museum Press, London.

43. Hobbs, *Treasure*.

44. C Johns and T Potter, 1983 *The Thetford Treasure*, British Museum Press, London.

45. D Gurney, 1986 *Settlement, religion and industry on the fen-edge; three Romano-British sites in Norfolk*, E Anglian Archaeol 31, 149–53.

46. J A Davies and T Gregory, 1991 Coinage from a civitas: a survey of the Roman coins found in Norfolk and their contribution to the archaeology of the *Civitas Icenorum*, *Britannia* 22, 65–101.

47. A S Esmonde Cleary, 1989 *The ending of Roman Britain*, Batsford, London.

48. Davies and Gregory, Coinage from a civitas.

49. J A Davies, 2001 *Venta Icenorum, Caistor St Edmund Roman town*, Norfolk Archaeological Trust, Norwich.

Index